CATHERINE HOSKYNS

VERSO
London • New York

First published by Verso 1996

Verso
UK: 6 Meard Street, London W1V 3HR
USA: 180 Varick Street, New York NY 10014–4606

Verso is the imprint of New Left Books

ISBN 1–85984–953–9
ISBN 1–85984–078–7 (pbk)

British Library Cataloguing in Publication Data
A catalogue record for this book is available from the British Library

Library of Congress Cataloging-in-Publication Data
A catalog record for this book is available from the Library of Congress

Typeset by Keystroke, Jacaranda Lodge, Wolverhampton.
Printed and bound in Great Britain by Biddles Ltd, Guildford and King's Lynn.

Contents

Acknowledgements

Research upon which this book is based has been in progress for more than ten years. During this time the emphasis has changed considerably and I owe a great deal to people who have helped me along the way and pointed me in new directions. The work has been bounded by two collective projects in which I participated: the production by Rights of Women Europe of the guide *Women's Rights and the EEC*, in 1983, and the publication of the report *Confronting the Fortress: Black and Migrant Women in the European Community*, in 1993. I want to pay tribute here to the importance of those collective experiences. I have also benefited from membership of the European Forum of Left Feminists, an organisation which has stuck admirably to its principles through difficult times.

I could not have produced this book without support from the Nuffield Foundation which awarded me a travel grant in 1983 and a Research Fellowship in 1993–94. I am deeply appreciative of their supportive and straightforward procedures.

Throughout this project, I have met with and interviewed people in a number of different countries. Many of these people have helped me with intellectual discussion, with tracking down documents and have generally made my stays abroad more pleasant. For help in some or all of these respects, I should particularly like to thank the following: Rosheen Callender, Marie-Thérèse Cuvelliez, Pauline Conroy, Christine Delphy, Chris Docksey, Eva Eberhardt, Rebecca Franceskides, Gabriele Freidank, Barbara Helfferich, Jean Jacqmain, Chandra Jayamanne, Liesbeth Klaver, John Lambert, Jaqueline Nonon, Truus Ophuysen, Ilona Ostner, Jyostna Patel, Ina Sjerps, Marie-Françoise Stewart and Joke Swiebel. Thanks also to Mme. Huego and M. Stoltz at the archives of the Council of Ministers in Brussels. Some European Union and national officials did not want to be named: I should like to make a collective thank you here.

As for my British friends, relations and contacts, I owe a particular debt to: Caitriona Carter, Cynthia Cockburn, Emma Franks, Avis

Furness, Jeanne Gregory, Anthony Hoskyns, Katharine Hoskyns, Siân Miles, Martha Osamor, Annie Phizacklea, Erika Szyszczak, Ruth Raymond, Anna Ward and Umran Beler.

At Coventry University, I should like to thank Dorothy Parkin, Marina Orsini-Jones and Ann Stanyer for sharing their expertise with me, Alex Kazamias for replacing me with charm and efficiency on a variety of occasions, and Helen McMenamin for unstinting administrative support. Arthur Owens, Geoff Stratford and Dave Teague in the Library have been patient with my many requests.

Anne Phillips has been a supportive editor and her comments and criticisms have always been constructive and to the point. Thanks also to Ruth Petrie and Liz Rawlings and to Robin Blackburn and Jane Hindle at Verso for taking me through the final stages.

At home a number of people have provided stimulating companionship and have helped to introduce me to new areas of feminist and legal research. I should like to thank Pauline Anderson, Sonya Andermahr, Maureen MacDonald, Helen Taylor, and particularly Linda Luckhaus in this respect. Sol Picciotto has given me both emotional and intellectual support, has generously shared his ideas and has read all the chapters as I produced them. Thanks also to Anna, our daughter, for love and welcome distractions.

I am grateful to Weidenfeld and Nicolson and Prentice Hall/ Harvester Wheatsheaf for permission to reproduce respectively Figure 2.1 on p. 27 and Figure 2.3 on p. 32.

Many people have helped with this book: the opinions expressed in it, and any errors, are mine alone.

Catherine Hoskyns
September 1995

List of Abbreviations

AP	Action Programme
CEC	Commission of the European Communities
CREW	Centre for Research on European Women
COREPER	Committee of Permanent Representatives
DG	Directorate General
DGB	*Deutscher Gewerkschaftsbund*
EC	European Community
ECJ	European Court of Justice
ECSC	European Coal and Steel Community
EMU	Economic and Monetary Union
ENOW	European Network of Women
EOC	Equal Opportunities Commission (UK)
EPD	Equal Pay Directive
EP	European Parliament
ESC	Economic and Social Committee
ESF	European Social Fund
ETD	Equal Treatment Directive
ETUC	European Trade Union Confederation
EU	European Union
FGTB	*Fédération Générale du Travail de Belgique*
ILO	International Labour Organisation
IGC	Intergovernmental Conference
OECD	Organisation for Economic Co-operation and Development
OJ	*Official Journal of the European Communities*
SAP	Social Action Programme
SEA	Single European Act
SED	Self-Employed Directive
SSD	Social Security Directive
TEU	Treaty on European Union
WOE	Women's Organization for Equality

Introduction

In November 1994, Anita Gradin, the newly designated European Commissioner for Sweden, expressed dismay at the overwhelming number of 'grey-suited men' in the upper echelons of the European Commission. This forthright opinion put the spotlight on a situation previously regarded by the vast majority of visitors and commentators as 'normal', and thus unworthy of comment. My intention in writing this book has been to do something similar: to subject the operations of the European Union[1] to a feminist scrutiny, and in so doing to open up hitherto ignored spaces and ask new questions. Such a project, I believe, not only says something about gender politics but adds necessary components to the general interpretation of EU activities and effects.

I hope in this way both to add to the growing body of feminist work which is now focusing on international issues and to support the extension of the discipline of international relations to a broader range of phenomena and approaches. Bringing together material and perspectives from women's studies and European studies, even if at times awkward, reveals the extent to which in the past gender blindness has had a constitutive effect on issues and debates. In calling the book *Integrating Gender* I have attempted to unite terminology from European studies and women's studies, and thus to symbolise the connection.

The analysis in this book is based on a detailed piece of contemporary history which has involved tracking the development of the EU policy on women's rights from its origins in Article 119 of the Treaty of Rome on equal pay, through to its current spread of policy initiatives, legislative provisions and funding programmes. The women's policy is the most developed of the EU's social policy programmes, and the only one where legislative measures have been activated by a mobilised political constituency for more than two decades. Following these developments in detail gives some idea of the density of EU political practices and of the complex interactions which take place between governments, institutions and policy networks.

I have reconstructed this history mainly by the collection and analysis of documents and secondary sources, and by interviews with a cross-section of those involved. For events in the fifties and early sixties, I have been able to supplement published sources with material from the archives of the Council of Ministers in Brussels. My detailed account ends in December 1992, with the Treaty on European Union signed, and the single market about to come into force. Significant developments after that point are referred to in chapter 10 and elsewhere, where they illuminate what has gone before or appear to set a clear marker for the future. Though my narrative continues after the point when Greece, Spain and Portugal joined the EU, I have not for practical reasons been able to deal substantially with the situation of or the input from women in those countries.

While doing this research, I have maintained an involvement with women's politics across Europe, and with recent developments in both feminist theory and the analysis of the European Union. This has included participation in some of the activities and initiatives which I discuss in the book. In these instances, I have indicated where my knowledge derives from personal experience, what my position was, and what additional sources have been used.

Though my starting point as an activist has been feminist politics and the combating of discrimination based on gender, I have become increasingly aware that 'women are not only women' and that other types of disadvantage are equally in need of remedy. This has become an issue within the women's movement as the denting of patriarchy has allowed more complex women's identities to emerge. How to represent these shifting identities, within or beyond the general designation of women, at the level of the EU and elsewhere, seems to me to be one of the major issues for women's politics in the nineties.

The threads

There are three main threads to my analysis. They concern first, the substantive content of the EU women's policy and its implications and effects; second, the impact of different kinds of organisation and mobilisation among women on EU policy making; and third, the structural development of the EU itself. These three threads are woven together in the narrative, but each one prompts separate questions and relates to different intellectual debates and discourse.

The EU experience has much to contribute to feminist and other debates about the relative merits of equal treatment and special treatment for women, and how this apparent polarisation can be transcended. In this context, I have been particularly concerned to see where the boundaries to the EU women's policy were and are being set, and by whom, and what has happened to pressure for the policy to 'spill over' beyond the employment relation, into areas such as caring, unpaid work and sexual politics more generally. The equality standard for men and women is one of the few principles established in EU law which applies directly to social relations. Despite its importance, the absence of other social standards and programmes at EU level has severely limited its impact and the kinds of women who can benefit from it.

The second thread concerns women's activism and organisation, and how these relate to policy development. Here I have looked particularly at the interface between women inside and outside the European institutions and at the characteristics and actions of what I have called the 'women's European policy network'. I have also sought to explain the lack of congruence between women's activism at the European level and the actions of the European labour movement more generally. Looking at the European level helps to disentangle trends, and I have attempted to identify where and on what issues groups of women perceive a common interest and how these perceptions have changed over time. I have tried to assess the shifting combination of factors which brought the EU women's policy into being and has so far ensured its continuation.

The final thread concerns the development of the EU itself. A case study of this length enables various analytical frameworks to be tested out, and throws light on the relation between the economic, the social and the political in the EU context. One of the purposes of the study has been to evaluate the role of the European Court of Justice and the significance of European law, in this particular field. As my knowledge of the social and political context has increased, I have come to situate the law differently and to challenge a reading which would see autonomous legal action as the lead element in the EU women's policy.

In all of this, the eighties emerge as a crucial decade. During this time European political leaders, caught up in a fragmenting world, sought to make further advances in economic integration, while as far as possible corralling popular loyalty and social provision within the national frame. The women's policy to some extent escaped from these restraints and thus provides a small but significant example of what a more developed European social and political polity might look like. The way it has developed raises central issues about representation, democracy and disadvantage.

Integrating gender

Integrating Gender is used, partly at least, in an ironic sense in the title of this book. Integration is the word commonly used to describe the drawing together of the member states of the EU. It is also a word viewed with suspicion by immigrant communities and others as implying assimilation to dominant cultures and society. Gender refers not only to biology but also to the social and cultural construction of what it is to be female and male. Paradoxically, as this book shows, the integration of states (and of markets) has the effect of destabilising existing patterns of social integration, including those relating to gender. This opens up space for challenge and re-formulation, with unpredictable outcomes at EU as well as member state level. My title is intended to convey a sense of this engagement.

Notes

1 The name 'European Union' was adopted by the Treaty on European Union (TEU) in December 1991 to cover not only the central activities of the European Community but also the areas of intergovernmental cooperation in justice and home affairs and in foreign and security policy. For convenience, this term has been used since November 1993 when the TEU came into force as the umbrella term to refer to all 'European' initiatives and institutions. I have used the term European Union in this book, therefore, in any context which involves either the present day or the whole span of EU development up to and including the present day, as in the subtitle. I have retained the term European Community for references or accounts of events which clearly took place before November 1993, when the name change came into effect.

1

Themes and Issues

This chapter aims to set out some of the debates and issues which have most influenced me in writing the book. These range from those which concern women's organisation and position in politics to those which deal with the particular processes surrounding and producing the European Union. At first sight there appears to be little connection between the personalised and broadly social concerns of grassroots women's politics and the diplomatic and interstate bargaining over markets and economic regulation, which characterises the EU system. This assumption is reinforced by the theory and practice of international relations which still tends to disregard the interaction of the international with national politics, and gives the latter the revealingly denigratory label of 'domestic'.

However, once one can see that far from being separate women's organisation *is* one of the processes 'surrounding and producing' the EU, the picture becomes very different, and a surprising number of links are revealed. For example, current debates in feminism about legal discourse or the issues involved in democratic representation, have direct relevance to the practices and problems of the EU. In this sense issues of gender are already 'integrated', although this is not normally recognised in either discourse or practice. Similarly, debates in the women's movement about what constitutes unity, and how to represent diversity, relate quite closely to the present contestation at EU level over what the European collectivity consists of, and whether it is possible to develop an 'ever closer union' while allowing for local, regional and national differences. These linkages are demonstrated and reinforced by the existence of the EU women's policy and the growth of women's politics around it.

In this chapter, and bearing in mind these connections, I shall examine issues concerning: unity and diversity among women, the role that gender plays in policy making, feminist interpretations of the law, current theories about transnationalism and policy networks, and aspects of European integration theory. First, however, I need to explain some terminology.

At various points in the book, I have used the term 'women's politics' as a shorthand to describe the areas of political action and activity which particularly concern (or target) women or groups of women, or where issues have been forced onto the agenda by women. I do not intend in this way to essentialise this area of politics, but merely to describe it succinctly. I use the term while recognising that women have substantial interests in other, indeed *all* other, areas of policy and politics, and that men may sometimes be involved in these activities. In a similar way, I have used the term 'the women's policy' to describe all the policies developed in the EU specifically in respect of women, although this would not be the term normally used. An 'equal opportunities' or 'equal treatment' policy, or even a policy on 'women's rights', does not, it seems to me, adequately convey the ramifications and unintended outcomes of such a policy development.

The term 'women's movement' is used in the book in a broad sense, to include all of those who are working or have worked for an improvement in the status of women. Any analysis of the negotiation and implementation of public policy on these issues shows that a wide variety of groups and individuals become involved, and that links need to be fostered between those inside and outside the formal system, if progress is to be made. In these circumstances, it makes little sense to define the term 'women's movement' in a way that would exclude some of the key participants.

The term 'feminist' is used in a somewhat narrower sense to refer to those who acknowledge (though often in very different ways) the deep roots of women's oppression, and seek to eradicate it through some transformation of society. But in general these distinctions are not (and cannot be) rigorously applied: the way people identify themselves is usually the safest guide.

Unity and Diversity Among Women

One of the key issues to emerge in this book is the relationship between the unity of women and diversity among women and how this affects organisation. Questions involving common and divergent interests and how to organise have caused conflict at times among feminists in all of the countries looked at. Generally, the result has been to diversify and to fragment. Thus across Europe in the late seventies there were very few umbrella organisations of (or even including) feminist groups. As a result, consultation and 'mainstreaming' on women's issues, if it took place at all, was for the most part left to the more traditional and structured women's organisations, or to official bodies.

More recently, the situation has begun to change, with feminist groups drawing nearer to the mainstream and traditional groups becoming somewhat more radical. This poses the question of what kinds of organisations are appropriate and in what circumstances women can represent other women. Dealing with the EU exacerbates the issues. The gaps to be bridged are enormous, divergencies abound and resources are inadequate.

The debate about organisation hinges on perceptions of what it is that women have in common and how differences can be accommodated. Since this is a crucial theme in the book (and underlies many of the developments it describes) it seems useful to trace briefly some relevant developments in theory and practice.

The basis for unity

During the early days of second wave feminism in Britain, differences of ideology, strategy and class among women were talked about extensively – and the women who were active were certainly aware of the generally narrow class base of the movement.[1] Nevertheless, this was not enough to curb action or induce apathy. Quite the reverse. The driving force was so strong that women felt compelled to continue with protest and activity in the belief that the actions being taken were, and in the end would be seen to be, in the interests of the majority of women. This general pattern seems to have been common across Europe, and is discussed in more detail in chapter 2.

Out of this energy some surprising alliances were made, with considerable repercussions in the public sphere. This was particularly true in America, where for a brief but powerful moment in the early seventies, middle-class and professional women in the National Organisation for Women (NOW) and much younger, radical women joined together to target the political establishment.[2] The American experience was an important influence in Western Europe, despite major differences in political culture.

In most countries, including America, this moment of unity did not last long, although underlying bonds of sisterhood remained, and effective campaigning continued on single issues. The divisions (for example, in France and Britain) seemed at first to be largely ideological and resulted in the collapse of any attempts to form broad-based alliances or organisations. The result of these kinds of conflicts was to encourage decentralisation and the spread of women's activity through small self-help groups and organisations.

It gradually became clear, however, that some of the conflicts were based on very substantial differences of identity and interest which went beyond ideology or theories of organisation. In Britain this was first demonstrated by lesbian women, whose powerful images expressed both solidarity with other women and separation from them.[3] By the eighties, black and ethnic minority women, particularly in the Netherlands and Britain, were challenging the hegemony of white women in the feminist movement, and reconstructing their separate histories and experiences.[4]

These examples show strong separate identities among groups of women being given expression, while expectations about unity between women still persist. The existence of these separate identities does not suggest that there is no common interest among women, but it does suggest that some way of recognising cross-cutting identities needs to be found before commonality can take effect. The issue of class among and between women, in the sense of differential access to resources and status, underlies many of these debates about difference, although this is not always made explicit.

Difference and diversity

Drawing on these experiences, the American author Elisabeth Spelman, in a sustained critique of feminist scholarship and practice, showed how 'innocent concepts and methodological strategies' ended up lodging middle-class white women at the centre of feminist enquiry. She advocated a self aware and pluralist approach.[5] This practice-oriented view dovetailed neatly into more lyrical and postmodern expressions of difference and diversity. So Gyatri Spivak, talking of the work of Hélène Cixous, pointed up the need 'to split open and fill all generalised, unified struggles with plurality'.[6]

The emphasis on plurality and difference, particularly in its post-modern forms, has been questioned by those who maintain that such approaches risk losing the clear sense of oppression on account of gender, which is seen as feminism's main achievement, and lead to a concentration on identity which can be both individualistic and apolitical.[7] However, it is noticeable that, while using postmodern ideas to break down previous rigidities in analysis, many feminist writers have continued to keep a political project in mind. As Jane Flax points out, if all becomes fragmented and uncertain then 'power alone will determine the outcome of competing truth claims'.[8] Thus women have an interest in rejecting the more nihilistic aspects of postmodern theory, while using its insights to help piece together a base for common action.

I would suggest that unity among women rests on two conditions. First, the particular relation to reproduction and the bodily forms that go with that; and second, the experience of living within a patriarchal world and feeling its effects.[9] Other characteristics which many women share, like taking on caring work and being confined to low pay jobs, derive directly or indirectly from these conditions. Beyond this commonality, women experience and shape their lives in vastly different ways. Culture, ethnicity, access to resources, skills and temperament all mean that women feel these unifying factors differently, and negotiate them in varied contexts and with different means at their disposal. The task for organisation is both to take up special issues and continue to reveal the common ground.

Where does the EU stand in all of this? For most of the period covered in this book, EU discourse constructed 'women' as a unified and homogeneous category. It is symptomatic of the distortions this produces that, until very recently, what 'women' actually meant in terms of EU policy was 'white women in paid employment'. The totalising discourse concealed the exclusion of women at home, black and migrant women, and other marginalised women. Diversity is an important concept in the EU, but it refers mainly to national difference. Considerable care is taken to balance activities in relation to the interests and cultures of the different member states.

EU institutions encourage some degree of lobbying and the representation of interest groups which are involved in or affected by EU policies. However, as is demonstrated later in this chapter, this is biased towards elite groups and organisations with resources. Thus the existence of the women's policy establishes a framework which promotes networking and contacts among women and groups of women, but only at a certain level. Some very specific examples of women organising to influence or gain advantages from the EU are discussed in later chapters. These suggest that the harnessing of women's energies in the nineties, and the maximising of the common interest at EU level, require loose but connected forms of organisation which, while being involved with the EU system, also act to challenge its priorities and assumptions.

Gender and Policy Making

Much of this book is concerned with public policy making on women's issues – that is public policy which directly targets, for whatever motive, the situation of women. It is concerned at the level of the EU with all stages of the policy process: initiation, negotiation, implementation and outcomes. Issues relating to gender arise at every point and in many varying forms. Such study inevitably raises questions about the way women are represented in the political process as a whole.

Detailed work from a feminist perspective on policy making has been slow to develop, mainly it would seem because it involves areas of activity which much of the feminist movement has sought to avoid and which are seen by many women as de-energising and as leading to co-option. What work there is comes predominantly from the US where this kind of policy making in the post-war period has a longer history. More recently, however, when 'entering the mainstream' and embarking on what the Dutch call 'the long march through the institutions', has become for much of the women's movement both more necessary and more acceptable, interest has focused on similar issues in the context of Western Europe.[10]

Virtually all public policy making on women's issues takes place within structures that are male-dominated, in the sense that they reflect male life-patterns, are largely controlled by men, and support a process which presents different but essentially male views of problems and solutions. Gelb and Palley use Schattschneider's term 'mobilisation of bias' to show how the organisation of 'values, beliefs, rituals and institutional procedures' can work to exclude or filter both women and women's issues.[11] In these policy-making structures the absence of women is obviously significant; the presence of women, however, does not necessarily imply change. Institutions and processes are much more than 'conglomeration(s) of individual biological men' and much more has to change than just the bodies in control.[12] Joyce Outshoorn has shown that the Dutch state administration has chosen to focus on 'more women in higher employment' (an issue it feels it can accommodate) at the expense of more radical, feminist demands for expanded childcare and a reduction in working-time.[13]

Nevertheless, the role that women play inside the administration and representative politics in promoting women's issues can be significant. In this context, although the categories can never be clear-cut (especially when applied to individual women), I have found it useful to distinguish between 'system women', who in the main identify with prevailing norms, 'lone women', who can exert considerable influence as a result of personal conviction and commitment, and 'supported women' who are part of networks both inside and outside the formal system. The role of departments and agencies set up to promote women's issues is also relevant here, and some analysis now exists of the array of such bodies across Europe, for example, the French Ministry of Women's Rights (now demoted to a *service*), the Dutch Department for the Co-ordination of Emancipation Policy, and the UK Equal Opportunities Commission.[14] In all of these examples of lobbying and pressure, it is important to identify what specific interests and which particular groups of women are being promoted by these means.

Representation

The policy-making process in the majority of EU member states has proved slow to respond to demands for greater gender equality, for some of the reasons discussed above. This is well illustrated by the figures given in Appendix 4 for the representation of women in EU national parliaments. The result has been a new focus in the nineties on the issue of women's representation on public bodies, in political parties and in the legislature. These demands take two main forms. The first requires the setting of targets and quotas, usually on a step-by-step basis, to create something in the institutions nearer to a 'critical mass of women'. The most compelling version of this is the demand for 'parity democracy', that is full equality for men and women in all decision-making bodies of the state, particularly elected assemblies.[15] The second demand is for greater support in the political process for disadvantaged and under-represented groups, in order to assist self-organisation and make participation easier. This demand can either be made for women only or for a range of different social groups.[16]

Any of these demands, if implemented, would make a striking difference to the way the political process operates and might well contribute to a much needed rethinking of what democracy actually means. Frigga Haug sees the demand for quotas for women as particularly subversive since it challenges both the 'ethos of achievement' and the mechanisms used to keep women in isolation.[17] The parity democracy demand is significant in that it appears to be sparking off both an intellectual debate and some mobilisation among women, particularly in France. It has the advantage as an objective that it can appeal to both traditional and feminist women, and as a slogan that it conveys a simple and easily understood message. Its problematic aspect is that it prioritises the sex/gender division above all other differences among and between people and seeks to impose a rigidity on the process of representation which might inhibit other equally necessary reforms.[18] Appendix 3 shows that a significant number of EU member states are beginning to adopt measures giving women some kind of preferential treatment in the process of representation. In a new twist to the European women's policy, the European Court in October 1995 ruled that such positive action, if it created discrimination against men in the process of selection, was contrary to EU equality law.[19]

The demand for 'bottom-up assistance' has received less publicity and less support. It corresponds to and seeks to meet some of the issues around diversity raised in the previous section. Some countries, notably the Netherlands, already give help to organisations representing disadvantaged groups, or taking up special issues, for example on the environment. This help is specifically designed to encourage participation at local, national and international levels by groups which might otherwise be excluded.[20] Measures creating women's sections in political parties or trade unions can have a similar effect, although as British evidence makes clear such policies can be hotly contested, even by women themselves.[21]

Anne Phillips, in a judicious summing up of both the debate on representation and experience so far, argues that there can be no going back now on what she calls 'the politics of presence', but that thought needs to be given to the other measures which may be needed to put the emphasis on what representatives do, as well as who they are, and to encourage transformatory politics rather than confrontation. She cites a wealth of evidence from the US, with regard to the representation of the black community, about the dangers of moving ahead on electoral reform alone.[22] Cynthia Cockburn, in a thoughtful study of women's representation in European trade union movements, recommends a dual strategy of quotas and special measures.[23]

It is clear from this that some part of women's politics is increasingly focusing on the public sphere and that an attempt is growing to unite women around certain goals in this respect. The greater awareness of women, together with the frustrations experienced in operating within patriarchal decision-making structures, have played an important part in this. One crucial question is whether this is a movement which engages mainly educated and professional women, or whether it sets objectives which resonate also with the needs of women in less privileged situations.

The points raised above have been drawn from analysis and experience predominantly at the national level. They are equally relevant, however, to EU processes, and will be used as a framework for discussing the gender aspects of these as this book proceeds. 'Lone' women have played an important role in pushing forward the EU's women's policy, and 'supported' women are beginning to have more influence, particularly in the European Parliament. Appendix 5, giving figures for 1994, shows how few women there still are in the top ranks of the European Commission.

The issue of the political representation of women is already being raised in the EU context and an emphasis on decision making has been noticeable since the mid eighties in the women's policy. The tendency in this has been to see women as a homogeneous entity rather than consider how their different interests can best be represented. The creation of a new category of 'European citizen' in the Treaty on European Union, although currently without much substance, opens up space for both debate and action on these issues at EU level.

Feminism and the Law

The EU is above all a legal structure and economic integration through law is the central principle upon which it is based. In order to carry this through effectively, it has been accepted that EU law should not only be binding on member states but also have direct effect and overrule inconsistent national law. The main mechanism for this has been the European Court of Justice (ECJ) which has considerable powers to compel member states to adopt the necessary implementing legislation, and to see that as far as possible rules are interpreted in the same way by the different national courts and have a comparable effect. In order to achieve this, national courts can refer cases which involve the application of European law to the ECJ for an authoritative opinion.

The EU women's policy fits within this context. The policy centres on legal instruments and has been initiated partly in the interests of fair competition and partly as a social measure. It is based centrally on the concept of equality (equal treatment) between men and women. The strength of the EU legal system from the point of view of women lies in the binding nature of the rules which are set, and in the possibilities which arise from the interaction of different systems of law; its weakness lies in the fact that the rules are hard to apply and disappointingly limited when matched to the substantive needs of particular groups of women.

In recent years there has been a great deal of debate within feminism about the nature of law and the particular ways in which legal rules and procedures affect the situation of women. This has evolved from a concentration on locating and contesting forms of discrimination towards a deeper level of research which looks at the way law operates and at the 'ideas and social structures' it conceals.[24] Part of the reason for this new direction is a growing disillusion with the effects of legal change on women; and the feeling that although the rules may change, the structures remain obdurately the same.[25] All of this has raised questions about whether or to what extent women's campaigns should be based on demands for legal reform.

Feminist analysis has highlighted the dual nature of law: that on the one hand it reinforces patriarchal relations and on the other holds out the possibility of rights (or justice) for individuals. Inevitably, the one reduces the content of the other. In the mid eighties, Catherine MacKinnon demonstrated this very clearly in analysing law for women which was based either on the concept of equality or on the need for special rights. In each case, she pointed out, the male life pattern was regarded as the norm to which women must either aspire, or be compensated for not attaining.[26] Nicola Lacey's critique of UK anti-discrimination legislation in the same period showed how these conceptual flaws (and the practical problems flowing from them) were preventing the laws from having a decisive impact on the situation of women.[27] Carol Smart made a very similar argument with regard to law and legal procedures dealing with rape, pornography and sexual abuse. The law dealt with the problems from a perspective grounded in the male position, women's accounts were largely disregarded, and women gained little from the legal process.[28]

This emphasis on the female legal subject has led more recently to attempts to deconstruct existing legal norms and to reformulate them taking account of women's varied activities, lifestyles and needs. This produces significant results when applied to equality law. Carol Bacchi, for example, has questioned the apparent opposition between law for women which is based on equal treatment with men and that based on special treatment. If, she argues, the concept of equality is applied in ways which take account of difference (she calls this 'same difference') then the effect is not to reinforce MacKinnon's 'male life pattern' or 'male norm' but to modify it. The aim of such adjustments would be to alter the standard or norm to which people are equated, to take account of the (different) female situation.[29] Titia Loenen expands this by insisting that this 'equality standard' must take account of the caring burden which falls mainly on women.[30]

From these concerns, a body of feminist legal writing has developed which challenges not only the impact of the law but also the discourse it uses, the assumptions on which it is based, and the context within which it operates. This makes clear that far from applying neutral rules to gendered subjects the law itself is actually part of the gendering process.[31] Such an analysis encourages scepticism about the use of law, and lays a firmer base for challenges to it.

Feminist approaches to law are used in the following chapters to provide a framework for assessing how European law is affecting the situation of women, and the role of the European Court. In particular, new views about what might be expected from equality law provide a useful standard against which ECJ judgments can be tested. By 1993, over sixty cases on equal treatment had been referred to the ECJ from the national courts, and these provide a wealth of material from which to extract the particular constructions of 'woman' developing in European law. These constructions, as demonstrated in chapter 8, show the judges still trying to preserve firm boundaries in equal treatment law between the public and the private, despite the fact that it is now abundantly clear that such distinctions constitute a prime source of women's disadvantage.

Transnationalism and Policy Networks

One of the purposes of this book is to examine examples of, and possibilities for, transnational politics among women within the EU arena, and to see what such an examination can contribute to the current debate about the nature and importance of policy networks. The term 'transnational' is used here to refer to non-state political activity which transcends the national orientation of groups and individuals, and on that basis creates new channels for communication and new forms of organisation and action. This can cover activities geared to profit, to the sharing of technical information and to the pursuit of values.[32] The expansion of transnationalism among unofficial groups has led to talk in recent years about the growth of 'global civil society'.[33]

Since the mid eighties much academic analysis has focused on interest group articulation and policy networks at both the national and transnational level. As the term implies, the aim of a policy network is to influence, develop or control policy. Policy networks are on the whole informal and horizontal in structure, creating non-hierarchical links among relatively autonomous groups and individuals.[34]

The EU is an important focus for this kind of activity, representing as it does a strongly developed institutional form of coordination among states. One way of analysing the EU is to see it as representing a number of overlapping policy regimes or policy communities focused upon and coordinated through a common institutional framework. This kind of a system clearly lends itself to the creation of policy networks which are set up to influence outcomes in particular areas.[35]

The EU system itself embodies a certain element of corporatism, in that channels exist for regular consultation with employers and trade unions, the 'social partners' as they are called in EU jargon. There has been a continuing assumption in the European Commission that certain matters, particularly industrial relations, are best dealt with within such a framework. However, these patterns of policy making, currently represented by the so-called 'social dialogue', have not so far functioned well or produced significant results. Arguably, the policy network framework, in which employers and trade unions participate, but on a more fluid and fragmented basis, affords at the moment a better picture of how power and influence are exerted within the system.[36]

The EU institutions, particularly the European Commission, assist in the development of such networking. The Commission in Brussels is ringed with agencies, consultants and advisory groups and a great deal of its work is now farmed out to such bodies. The policy network strategy is one way of keeping track of all this activity for those both inside and outside the decision-making arena. Such developments are overwhelmingly bureaucratic and secret, and though members of the European Parliament may sometimes be involved, to a large extent these networks escape from either public scrutiny or democratic accountability.[37]

The idea of networking, with its emphasis on informal, horizontal contact, in essence fits in well with the patterns of organisation which came out of the women's movement in the early seventies. Indeed, one could argue that the information-based, spontaneous contacts which developed then among women helped to pioneer the idea of networking at least among social groups and organisations. Second-wave feminism also practised its own form of transnationalism, mainly through informal contacts, word of mouth, and the rapid distribution of texts from one country to another. Since then, many of the activities which women have developed, around theoretical research, single-issue campaigns, and practical actions, have had the effect of creating fluid, flexible, and sometimes enduring transnational links. The Greenham Common women's peace camp in the UK in the early eighties generated its own direct and virtually costless form of transnationalism: it is estimated that in its heyday more than 200,000 women visited the camp, a high proportion from overseas.[38]

Gradually, however, a more sustained expression of women's international networking has emerged from these and other influences. Margaret Keck and Kathryn Sikkink, in their study of transnational issue networks, see issues to do with women as one of the three fastest expanding areas of transnational social movement activity.[39] Much of the development here has come from activities sparked off by the UN Decade for Women, which has directed considerable funding into the preparation and holding of four global conferences on women's issues, the most recent of which is being held in Beijing as this book goes to press. Arvonne Fraser shows that the informal NGO forums which accompanied these official conferences played a significant role in establishing contacts and information exchanges among a broad range of women's organisations, and on a wide variety of topics.[40] One result of women's increasing involvement at international level is the attention now being paid in the UN and elsewhere to a range of issues concerning violence against women. This international activity sets an important frame for women's involvement with the EU.

Women outside the EU's formal structures can influence its proceedings in two different ways. Women's activism in the sixties and seventies had an important effect on the EC because of the way it influenced the context within which policies were generated. This happened for the most part without any direct intention to target the EC, or indeed any other institution. Subsequently networking which directly targets the EU has developed. This is limited because of the narrow range of issues to do with women over which the EU has competence, because of lack of resources, and because of residual doubts which many women have over what the EU represents in terms of politics and priorities.

Despite these limitations, I would argue that a women's European policy network does now exist. This is a diverse and fluid entity with many different elements in it, not all of them in touch with each other. What is unusual about this network is that it has the capacity, by no means always realised, to stretch down into the grassroots politics of the member states and up into the EU decision-making process. It also influences and responds to a well-established programme of EU law and policy. This combination makes it exceptional, if not unique.

Theorising the EU

The dominant discourses and debates in an academic field have a crucial influence on how events are interpreted and what issues are given prominence. In the case of the EU, this process plays a large, if indirect, part in shaping popular reactions and perceptions.

While researching and writing this study, I followed closely the theories and explanations about the nature of European integration being developed within the disciplines of international relations and political science. For most of the time these were marked by a division between neo-functionalist and neo-realist analyses which used apparently different approaches to and assumptions about European developments. As my work progressed, I found that not only were these theories unhelpful when applied to my material, but also that the way they attempted to order the European arena marginalised issues and approaches which appeared to me important. As I finished the book, alternative views and analyses were beginning to appear.[41]

Since these theoretical approaches have played an important role in constructing European politics (and the women's policy within it) it seems useful to trace their outlines here. In this example, as elsewhere, material and theoretical developments dovetail in interesting ways.

Explaining the process

The starting point for the process which has produced the EU as we know it today was the formation in 1952 of the European Coal and Steel Community (ECSC). The ECSC was set up on the basis of a proposal from Jean Monnet, then Director of French Economic Planning, and its aim was to put the crucial coal, iron and steel industries of France and Germany under common management.[42] The ECSC was to be run by a strong central 'European' High Authority which Monnet hoped would develop working practices which would bind elites and interest groups together and reveal and consolidate a common purpose. Little public involvement or democratic institutional base was envisaged in these arrangements.[43]

This may have been the only type of proposal that stood a chance of acceptance in the fifties, and it did succeed in providing a framework for economic integration which had been lacking before. Nevertheless, the fact that the initial steps towards European integration were technical, economic and elitist, rather than political and public, has proved to be of lasting significance. At the time, it was by no means clear what style of politics would develop from this 'functional' base.[44]

The ECSC experiment (Monnet became its first president) was subjected very quickly to intense examination by an American political scientist, Ernst Haas. Haas examined the reactions of all those involved in the ECSC project and assessed what types of change were taking place in attitudes and actions. From this extensive empirical work he suggested that Monnet's structures, inserted into a pluralist society with many diverse elements, and dealing with sectors crucial to the economies of the member states, would in the end lead to a political union between the countries concerned.[45]

This, Haas suggested, would take place as a result of a 'spillover' of integration from one sector to another, and because those involved would start to switch their focus and their loyalties to the central institutions. This would happen, not because of a 'vision', but by the consolidation and development of common interests. This process required a permissive public opinion but not direct popular involvement. Thus began the 'neo-functionalist' school of European integration theorists – which has had considerable influence since then on how European developments have been explained and interpreted.[46]

Haas later retracted his predictions about political union, but the assumption remained that given the right circumstances, bureaucratic cooperation in economic and technical matters could bring about profound political change, discreetly and without any widespread political mobilisation or ideological debate. Haas was challenged very quickly by those who thought he underestimated the resilience of the nation state, and its complexities. Stanley Hoffmann was one of the first to argue in this way, spawning a long line of followers termed 'neo-realists', because of the centrality they continued to give to the 'high politics' role of the state.[47]

A recent study, in this general tradition, is that of Alan Milward in his evocatively titled book, *The European Rescue of the Nation State.* Milward uses detailed socio/economic material to argue his case that the arrangements initiated by Monnet were always part of the national plan of governments, and were shaped, not to promote integration or a supranational Europe, but to supply a firm economic base for the revival of the nation state in Western Europe. As a result politics, 'vision' and the shaping of culture were firmly kept in national hands.[48]

Avoiding ideology

The theories of neo-functionalism and neo-realism are normally seen as in conflict, pitting supranational institutions and processes against national entities and governments. At best, the European process is explained as combining insights from both. This supposed dichotomy in fact conceals how much these theories and explanations have in common. Both prioritise the economic and the technical in the integration process, neo-functionalism because this is seen as the starting point, and neo-realism because anything beyond these aspects is seen as the prerogative of the nation state. Both explanations also preclude, or at least do not engage with, debate in ideological or political terms about the objectives and implications of European integration. The effect of this has been to marginalise more political analyses.[49]

In the sixties, the French president, General de Gaulle, acted to restrain the pace of European developments and any effective move to supranationalism. The result was a continuing if uneven expansion of economic integration, with only very limited democratic control. Theorising followed this trend by putting the emphasis on horizontal networking and policy coordination (as discussed in the last section) which did not require further supranational development.[50] Crucially, this new emphasis disguised or failed to point out the extent to which these developments (in the absence of more formal structures) favoured those actors with resources and transnational know-how. Once again elite conduct in the economic sphere was being given priority.

What was noticeable was the lack of a political debate about what 'Europe' stood for, and an analysis of what political systems were being built on the original functional structure. Picking up on this lack of definition, Rosi Braidotti wrote that women should explode 'the empty rhetoric' of the European Community and concentrate on 'the analysis of the conditions that may lead to the creation of a shared cultural and political space'.[51] This space, however, has been effectively closed off. Distinct national cultures, as Milward has pointed out, were deliberately created and reinforced in post-war Europe.[52] Since the aim of these was to buttress the nation state, they have for the most part been geared to celebrating the separate (national) past, rather than the joint (European) future.

The return of the political

International relations theorists were taken aback by the developments which led in the mid eighties to the decision to create the single market by 1992 and to the adoption of the Single European Act. Was this *another* European 'rescue' of the nation state – a response to Europe's growing lack of competitiveness in comparison with Japan and the USA? Or was it a sign of the correctness of Haas's original predictions, proving neo-functionalists right after all? Both arguments were made and controversy revived.[53]

International events are not as easily packaged as this. The negotiation of the Treaty on European Union in 1991, and the responses to it, suggested that other factors were at work, and explanations which prioritised elite decision making in the economic field began to look increasingly thin. At the same time, the 'permissive public opinion' which both neo-functionalism and neo-realism assumed seemed to be on the wane. However, as people have begun to mobilise on European issues, it has become clear how weak the political channels are. Worries about what 'Europe' is, and what is being done, can only it seems be expressed in national terms and through antagonism to the European project and its bureaucratic agents. Very little has prepared the populations of the EU for political debate and action at the European level.

Nevertheless, politics and popular attitudes have now moved centre stage, and with this a more open debate about what (and who) the EU is for. For the first time also, political alternatives are being presented. In these circumstances, a somewhat different analytical framework is required and there are signs that this is emerging.

In a recent study, Wolfgang Streeck examines the balance of forces between labour, business, governments and institutions in the EU. He states that neo-functionalist and neo-realist perspectives, while important, are not enough. What is needed is to look at the 'entire political-institutional complex . . . and the integrated internal market economy that is embedded in it.' He goes on to give a skilful analysis of the way in which the EU institutional structure and ethos has shaped the roles of labour, business and people. The result has been to give business at the European level the freedom 'not to be redistributive'. European citizens, he predicts, will now seek to protect national democracy and identity.[54]

The importance of Streeck's approach is that he points out that the EU is an artificially constructed arena within which power struggles take place. In particular, he shows how the institutional structure, established by Monnet's pragmatism and rigidified by the nation states, has had the effect of preventing a political 'balance' emerging at the EU level.

Streeck's analytical framework is confirmed, though from a different perspective, by John Lambert's recent book *Solidarity and Survival: a Vision for Europe*.[55] Lambert, with long experience both of Brussels politics and European protest movements, also treats the EU as a complex political arena, and is concerned with ideas and 'alternative' visions as well as class forces. He shows very clearly how alternative views about what might happen in Europe (over agriculture or energy policy, for example) are frozen by the stranglehold of the big lobbies. The considerable potential for transnational civil society in Europe which, he maintains, could enormously enrich policy and debate, is constantly frustrated while the European Parliament acts as a 'mere figleaf for democracy'.

I have found these emerging perspectives more helpful than the earlier ones in situating the women's policy and helping to explain its particular shape and effects. In this context one can see that the narrow focus of the neo-functionalist/neo-realist debate had the effect of sidelining other agendas and masking the way in which a certain type of politics was growing up around the European structures. The failure to pay attention to informal politics and keep democratic values to the fore had the effect, by default at least, of endorsing such developments.

The writings of Milward on the one hand, and Streeck and Lambert on the other, begin to create a more appropriate framework. By using this and the other approaches discussed in this chapter to describe and explain the women's policy, I hope to contribute to a more open debate about how the EU has developed and the nature of its current operations.

Notes

1 This account is drawn from material in Michelene Wandor, *Once a Feminist – Stories of a Generation*, Virago, London, 1990; and from my own experiences in the women's movement in Coventry and London in the early seventies.

2 Jo Freeman, *The Politics of Women's Liberation*, David McKay, New York, 1975, chapters 6 and 7; see also Alice Echols, *Daring to be Bad: Radical Feminism in America 1967–75*, University of Minnesota Press, Minneapolis, 1989.

3 For an account of this uneasy relationship, see Wendy Clarke, 'The Dyke, The Feminist and The Devil', *Feminist Review*, no. 11, summer 1982, pp. 30–39. I am grateful to Sonya Andermahr for directing me to this and other material on the subject.

4 See 'Many Voices One Chant – Black Feminist Perspectives', *Feminist Review*, no. 17, autumn 1984; and Philomena Essed, 'Black Women in White Women's Organizations: Ethnic Differentiation and Problems of Racism in the Netherlands', *New Feminist Research*, vol. 18, no. 4, 1989, pp. 10–15.

5 Elizabeth V. Spelman, *Inessential Women – Problems of Exclusion in Feminist Thought*, The Women's Press, London, 1990 (American edition, Beacon Books, Boston, 1988).

6 Gayatri Chakravorty Spivak, 'French Feminism Revisited: Ethics and Politics', in J. Butler and J.W. Scott, eds, *Feminists Theorize the Political*, Routledge, New York, 1992, p. 70.

7 Mary Louise Adams, 'There's No Place Like Home: on the Place of Identity in Feminist Politics', *Feminist Review*, no. 31, spring 1989, pp. 22–33. For the debate on this issue see Diana Fuss, *Essentially Speaking – Feminism, Nature and Difference*, Routledge, London, 1989.

8 Jane Flax, 'Postmodernism and Gender Relations in Feminist Theory', *Signs: Journal of Women in Culture and Society*, vol. 12, no. 4, 1987, p. 625.

9 Teresa de Lauretis argues that the (shifting) 'essence' of woman is living in a 'female-sexed body', and what that implies, and 'living in the world as female'. 'Upping the Anti [sic] in Feminist Theory' in M. Hirsch and E.F. Keller, eds, *Conflicts in Feminism*, Routledge, London, 1990, p. 257.

10 See, for example, Mary Katzenstein and Carol Mueller, eds, *The Women's Movements of the United States and Western Europe – Consciousness, Political Opportunity and Public Policy*, Temple University Press, Philadelphia, 1987. This research suggested that in the eighties, although the women's movement was commonly seen as being in decline, awareness among women was actually on the increase in most European countries.

11 Joyce Gelb, Marian Lief Palley, *Women and Public Policies*, Princeton University Press, Princeton, 1987, ch. 1.

12 Carol Smart, *The Ties That Bind – Law, Marriage and the Reproduction of Patriarchal Relations*, Routledge & Kegan Paul, London, 1984.

13 Joyce Outshoorn, 'Is This What We Wanted? Affirmative Action as Issue Perversion', in E. Meehan and S. Sevenhuijson, eds, *Equality Politics and Gender,* Sage, London, 1991, p. 115.

14 For up-to-date case studies of these and other similar bodies see Dorothy McBride Stetson and Amy G. Mazur, eds, *Comparative State Feminism*, Sage, Newbury Park, 1995.

15 The term seems first to have been used in the course of a seminar organised by the Council of Europe in 1989. Since that time papers setting out the proposal have been drafted by Elizabeth Guibert-Sledziewski and by Eliane Vogel-Polsky.

16 For a full discussion of what these kinds of proposals imply and the debates around them see Iris Marion Young, *Justice and the Politics of Difference*, Princeton University Press, Princeton, 1990.

17 Frigga Haug, 'The Quota Demand and Feminist Politics', *New Left Review*, no. 209, 1995, pp. 136–45.

18 The French feminist journal *Nouvelles Questions Féministes* opened a debate on parity democracy in its issues of November 1994 and May 1995; see also Joyce Outshoorn, 'Parity Democracy: a critical look at a "new" strategy', paper for *European Consortium for Political Research*, Leiden, April 1993.

19 *Kalanke* v. *Freie Hansestadt Bremen*, ECJ Case C-450/93. For further discussion of the issues in this case see chapter 10 this volume.

20 Information from Truus Ophuysen, international officer for the Women's Exchange Programme International in the Netherlands. Part of her job is to assist women's groups with international lobbying.

21 The current controversy in Britain about the Labour Party's decision to have women-only shortlists in a certain number of winnable seats at the next election, is a good example of this.

22 Anne Phillips, 'Political inclusion and political presence. Or, why should it matter who our representatives are?', paper for *European Consortium for Political Research*, Leiden, April 1993.

23 Cynthia Cockburn, *Women and the European Social Dialogue – Strategies for Gender Democracy*, CEC, v/5465/95.

24 Riki Holtmaat, 'The Power of Legal Concepts: the Development of a Feminist Theory of Law', *International Journal of the Sociology of Law*, no. 17. 1989, pp. 481–502.

25 Linda Luckhaus, 'Changing Rules, Enduring Structures – Equal Treatment and Social Security', *Modern Law Review*, vol. 53, no. 5, 1990, pp. 655–68.

26 Catharine A. MacKinnon, *Feminism Unmodified – Discourses on Life and Law*, Harvard University Press, Cambridge, Massachusetts, 1987, pp. 32–45.

27 Nicola Lacey, 'Legislation Against Sex Discrimination – Questions from a Feminist Perspective', *Journal of Law and Society*, vol. 14, no. 4, 1987, pp. 411–21.

28 Carol Smart, *Feminism and the Power of Law*, Routledge, London, 1989.

29 Carol Bacchi, 'Do Women Need Equal Treatment or Different Treatment?', paper for International Political Science Association Congress, Buenos Aires, 1991. For the evidence from which these arguments are drawn, see Bacchi, *Same Difference – Feminism and Sexual Difference*, Allen & Unwin, Sydney, 1990.

30 Titia Loenen, 'Different Perspectives in Different Legal Studies: A Contextual Approach to Feminist Jurisprudence in Europe and the USA', paper for Conference on Feminist Approaches to Law and Cultural Diversity, European University Institute, Florence, November 1993.

31 Carol Smart, 'The Woman in Legal Discourse', *Social and Legal Studies*, vol. 1, no. 1, 1992, pp. 29–44.

32 Margaret Keck and Kathryn Sikkink, 'Transnational Issue Networks in International Politics', unpublished conference paper, April 1994.

33 Ronnie D. Lipshutz, 'Reconstructing World Politics: the Emergence of Global Civil Society', *Millennium: Journal of International Studies*, vol. 21, no. 3, 1992, pp. 389–420.

34 Bernd Marin, Renate Mayntz, eds, *Policy Networks – Empirical Evidence and Theoretical Considerations*, Westview Press, Boulder, Colorado, 1991. For a critique of policy network analysis from a feminist perspective see, Liz Sperling and Charlotte Bretherton, 'Women's Networks and the European Union – Towards an Inclusive Approach?', *Journal of Common Market Studies*, forthcoming 1996.

35 Sol Picciotto, 'The Control of Transnational Capital and the Democratisation of the International State', *Journal of Law and Society*, vol. 15, no. 1, 1988.

36 For a general discussion the role of the social partners in the EU system see Paul Teague, *The European Community: the Social Dimension*, Kogan Page, London, 1989, ch. 5.

37 For an up-to-date analysis of these arrangements see Justin Greenwood, Jurgen R Grote and Karsten Ronit, eds, *Organized Interests and the European Community*, Sage, London, 1992.

38 Estimates from women involved in Greenham over a number of years.

39 Keck and Sikkink, 'Transnational Issue Networks', p. 2.

40 Arvonne S. Fraser, *The UN Decade for Women – Documents and Dialogue*, Westview, Boulder, Colorado, 1987. The three earlier conferences were held in Mexico in 1975, in Copenhagen in 1980, and in Nairobi in 1985.

41 I am mainly talking here about the Anglo-American strand in this debate. I regret that so far I have not been able to follow how the issue of European integration is treated outside academic work in English.

42 Belgium, the Netherlands, Luxembourg and Italy (but not Britain) eventually joined as well.

43 Jean Monnet, *Memoirs*, Collins, London, 1978, chs 12 and 13.

44 For an exposition of these issues see Kevin Featherstone, 'Jean Monnet and the 'Democratic Deficit' in the EU', *Journal of Common Market Studies*, vol. 32, no. 2, 1994, pp. 149–70.

45 Ernst B. Haas, *The Uniting of Europe; Political, Social and Economic Forces 1950–1957*, Stanford University Press, Stanford, 1958.

46 For an account of how the theories of neo-functionalism have developed see Jeppe Tranholm-Mikkelsen, 'Neo-functionalism: Obstinate or Obsolete? A Reappraisal in the Light of the New Dynamism of the EC', *Millennium – Journal of International Studies*, vol. 20, no. 1, 1991, pp. 1–22.

47 Stanley Hoffmann, 'Obstinate or Obsolete: the fate of the nation state and the case of Western Europe', *Daedalus*, vol. 95, 1966, pp. 862–915.

48 Alan S. Milward, *The European Rescue of the Nation State*, Routledge, London, 1992, ch. 1.

49 For example, those of the Belgian marxist, Ernest Mandel, or the Italian MEP, Altiero Spinelli, a member of the Italian Communist party and an advocate of European federalism.

50 See, for example, Donald J. Puchala, 'Of Blind Men, Elephants and International Integration', *Journal of Common Market Studies*, vol. 10, 1972, pp. 267–84.

51 Rosi Braidotti, 'The Exile, the Nomad and the Migrant – Reflections on International

Feminism', *Women's Studies International Forum*, vol. 15, no. 1, 1992, p. 8. Braidotti is an Italian feminist and philosopher. She spent many years in Paris before taking up a chair in Women's Studies at the University of Utrecht.
52 Milward, *The European Rescue*, p. 14.
53 Andrew Moravcsik, 'Negotiating the Single European Act: National Interests and Conventional Statecraft', *International Organisation*, vol. 45, no. 1, 1991, pp. 19–56; and Tranholm-Mikkelsen, 'Neo-functionalism'.
54 Wolfgang Streeck, 'From Market-Making to State-Building? Reflections on the Political Economy of European Social Policy', in S. Leibfried and P. Pierson, eds, *European Social Policy: Between Fragmentation and Integration*, The Brookings Institution, Washington DC, 1995.
55 John Lambert, *Solidarity and Survival – a Vision for Europe*, Avebury, Aldershot, 1994.

2

European Feminism in the Seventies

There are a number of possible starting points for a history of the women's policy of the European Union. Here I want to begin by examining the origins and development of second-wave feminism in Western Europe in the late sixties/early seventies, and the circumstances which produced it. Without that explosion of feminism, it is unlikely that we would now be concerned with the origins of Article 119 or its subsequent development.

Second-wave feminism represented 'women's politics' at its most compelling, and created a situation where, across a wide range of countries, actions deriving from women's deep feelings and experiences impacted upon the political world. Two aspects of this are crucial: first, the material conditions which lay behind these phenomena and second, the nature of the consciousness and forms of organisation which emerged. Examining these during this period provides a benchmark against which subsequent developments can be measured.

Revealing Material Conditions

In assessing the material conditions of women over a particular period it is useful to distinguish between contemporaneous views and levels of analysis, and those which benefit from the longer timescale of hindsight and the reinterpretation of data. Here I present the contemporaneous perspective, partly because it gives a flavour of the times, and partly because the women who were active in creating it in many cases at a later stage became involved with policy at the EC level. In this particular example, the way the material evidence was taken up and by whom, and how it became known, had an important influence on the policy process. More recent analysis is used to illuminate this material and fill in the gaps.

By the sixties a gender breakdown in aggregate national statistics was becoming established in most countries. Not much was made of this and detailed national analyses were rare. Significantly, it was the international organisations active in the area which first began to make comparisons and look at long-term trends. The Organisation for Economic Co-operation and Development (OECD) and the Council of Europe were well in advance of the EC in this, perhaps because they were freer to speculate and, at least in the case of the OECD, more influenced by developments in the US. Some of the best contemporary material comes from Viola Klein's study of women workers for the OECD, the Kok Report for the Council of Europe on the status of women, and the report of the OECD's 1968 trade union seminar on women's employment.[1]

The compilation of this data and its analysis began to create a small group of professional women from a variety of countries who established an expertise on different aspects of the situation of women. Françoise Picq shows how influential such women were in France in the sixties.[2] These were 'lone' women par excellence, who fell clearly within the parameters of what Elisabeth Wilson has called the 'reasonable feminism' of the fifties and sixties.[3] These women were not seeking to challenge the economic and political system as such, and were often conventional in approach and tactics; they were, however, deeply committed to investigating and improving the status of women.

One of the most influential of these was the French sociologist, Evelyne Sullerot. Her major work *Histoire et sociologie du travail féminin*, broke new ground, and in it she strongly criticised the lack of attention given to the work women do (both paid and unpaid) and the inadequacies of the available statistical data.[4] Sullerot was a shrewd observer and analyst, who cared passionately about the situation of women, and who, as a result of her work for the international oganisations referred to above, began to develop a European perspective. She is of particular interest for this study because it was to her that civil servants in the European Commission turned when they wanted facts and information on which to base a policy for women.

Demography

A good starting point for looking at the situation of women during this period (and for comparing what was known then with what we understand now) is Sullerot's 1970 study, *Women, Society and Change*.[5] It focused on two aspects of women's changing circumstances: demography and participation in the labour market. On demography, Sullerot emphasised the expanding lifespan of women in the West, the striking decrease in the ratio of pregnancies to surviving children, the tendency of women to have children at a younger age, and the extent to which women outlive men. The result was a shrinking of the maternity years, a progressive dissolving of the link between sexuality and reproduction, and, as is shown in Figure 2.1, a radical change in the periodisation of women's lives.

Sullerot concluded:

> 'This is a truly revolutionary change; in the past woman has always been defined by reference to her maternal role, yet at present the years devoted to maternity hardly add up to a seventh of her life-span. From now on the longest phase in her life will be that which follows the completion of her family.'[6]

This evocative but somewhat impressionistic analysis was borne out by subsequent statistics produced for the EC. Table 2.1 shows the life expectancy of women increasing substantially between 1950 and 1970 in all of the ten actual and prospective EC member states, and going up again steeply in the seventies. Figure 2.2 shows the average number of children per woman dropping sharply over the same period, except in Greece and Ireland. During this time, on average, numbers of marriages were declining and the divorce rate increasing.[7] Overall there is remarkable homogeneity in these trends, intensifying after the hinge point of 1970.

Figure 2.1 Periodisation of Women's Lives, 1900 and 1970

Period devoted to maternity in the average life of a woman in 1900

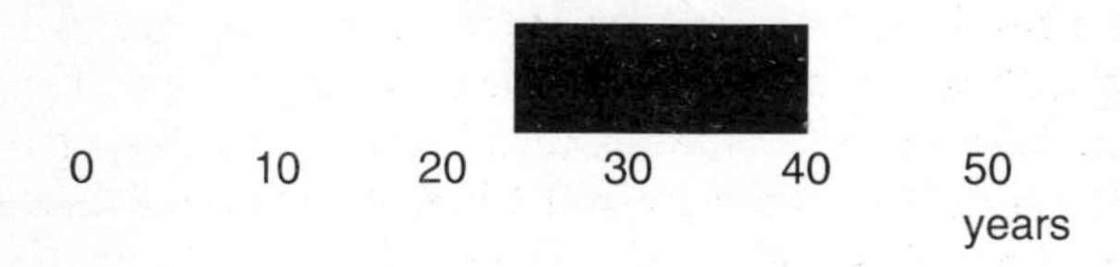

Period devoted to maternity in the average life of a woman in 1970

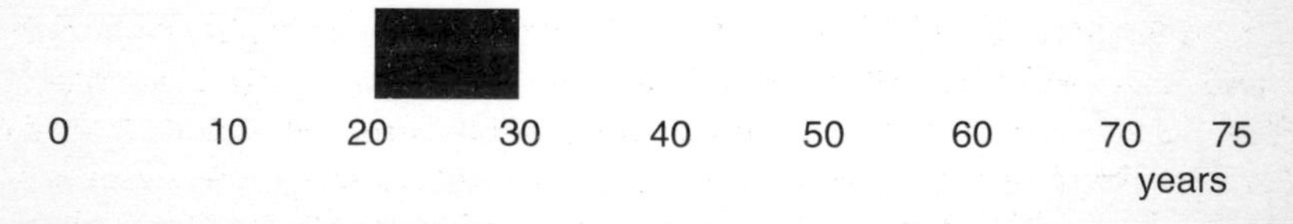

Source: Sullerot, *Women, Society and Change*, Weidenfeld, 1971, p. 75

Table 2.1 Life Expectancy of Women

	West Germany	*France*	*Italy*	*Netherlands*	*Belgium*	*Luxembourg*	*United Kingdom*	*Ireland*	*Denmark*	*EUR 9*	*Greece*	*EUR 10*
				Life expectancy of women: at birth								
1950	68.5	68.5	67.2	72.9	66.8	65.7	71.2	67.1	:	68.3	66.7	68.2
1960	72.4	73.6	72.3	75.3	73.0	71.9	73.7	71.9	74.4	73.7	:	73.6
1970	73.8	75.9	:	76.5	:	:	75.0	73.5	75.9	75.1	73.4	75.1
1974/79	76.4	78.4	75.9	79.2	75.1	75.1	76.2	:	77.2	:	:	:
						aged 60 years						
1950	17.5	18.4	17.5	18.6	17.5	16.9	17.9	16.8	:	17.8	18.0	17.8
1960	18.5	19.5	19.3	19.7	18.7	18.3	18.9	18.1	19.3	19.0	:	19.0
1970	19.1	20.8	:	20.5	:	:	19.8	18.7	20.6	19.9	19.3	19.9
1974/79	20.6	22.4	20.3	22.5	19.7	19.8	20.5	:	21.5	:	:	:

Source: Eurostat *Social Indicators for the EC*, 1984, p. 63

Figure 2.2 Average Number of Children per Woman, 1960 and 1979

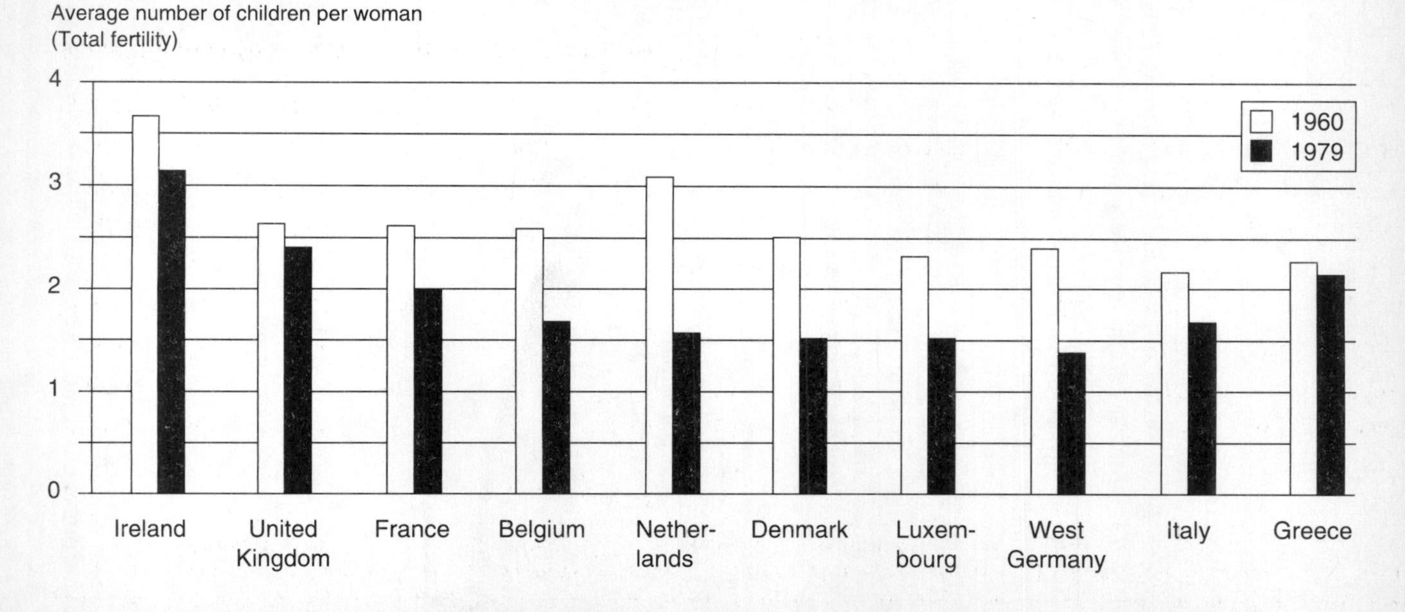

Source: Eurostat, *Social Indicators for the EC*, 1984, p. 56

The labour market

On women's participation in the labour market, Sullerot documented the gradual if uneven increase in the numbers of women in paid employment, showing that by the late sixties women on average formed one third of the total labour force in Western European countries. Differences between one country and another were accounted for by the sharp decline in agricultural employment and by particular cultural and social factors. She showed that women were increasingly working until later in life, more continuously, and when married; and that the average 'working curve' for women was coming closer to that of men.

In what is the most developed and original section of the book (it draws heavily on her earlier work) Sullerot showed how the expansion of the labour market in services and public sector employment was creating jobs which women felt they could do. At the same time, this development trapped women into a limited range of occupations and encouraged job segregation. She also attempted to measure the earnings gap between men and women, cited gross breaches of the equal pay principle, and gave striking examples of the biased way in which jobs were valued. This strong emphasis on barriers to women's participation in the labour market was picked up by both the OECD and the EC when shaping policies on women's employment in the next decade.

Both immediate and more long term analyses confirmed these findings. OECD figures in Table 2.2 show the generally upward trend in women's labour market participation continuing into the seventies. The figures given in Appendices 6.1 and 6.3, which span the post-war period, show that the growth both in married women's employment and in the development of the service sector had their roots in the sixties. The importance of Sullerot and other women like her was that they grasped these facts in advance of more traditional analysts, either because of their own experience or because they were attuned to what women were actually doing.

Sullerot believed, in the late sixties, that society was on the brink of a profound transformation.[8] She saw women as dissatisfied, and a dissonance existing between the reality of their lives and the ideology and attitudes which surrounded them. The main report to the OECD trade union seminar in 1968 found similarly that there was an 'uneasy feeling' among women because of the contradictions they faced.[9]

Political representation

These views were endorsed in a more political sense by the Kok Report for the Council of Europe. The Report pointed out that women made up half of the population and one third of the labour force and were

Table 2.2 Women as a Percentage of Civilian Employment in Seventeen Countries

Country	*Year*	*%*	*Year*	*%*	*Difference*
Australia	1964	28.2	1975	34.2	6.0
Austria	1968	38.4	1975	38.4	–
Belgium	1963	31.1	1975	34.4	3.3
Canada	1963	28.4	1976	36.9	8.5
			1977	37.0	8.6
Denmark	1965	34.8	1975	41.6	6.8
Finland	1964	44.0	1975	46.8	2.8
France	1968	35.2	1975	37.2	2.0
Germany	1963	36.9	1975	37.7	0.8
Greece	1961	32.3	1971	27.5	–5.1
Italy	1964	28.2	1975	28.1	–0.1
Ireland	1966	26.6	1975	27.4	0.8
Japan	1964	39.8	1975	37.4	–2.4
New Zealand	1964	26.1	1975	30.4	4.3
Norway	1963	29.6	1975	37.4	7.8
Sweden	1964	36.7	1975	42.3	5.6
United Kingdom	1964	34.3	1975	38.8	4.5
United States	1963	34.1	1975	39.6	5.5

Source: OECD, *Labour Force Statistics 1963–74*

increasingly moving out of the family. And yet they met a political environment hostile or indifferent to their needs and in which they were seriously under-represented. Women in Western societies, the report concluded, constitute 'the largest area of unorganised persons'.[10]

Figure 2.3 illustrates this in graphic form. With the exception of Sweden and Finland, no country in Western Europe in 1965 had more than 10 per cent of women representatives in the Lower House. Britain and France (and the USA) had less than 5 per cent. Significantly, only in the Scandinavian countries was the greater public presence of women in the seventies translated relatively quickly into increased political representation.[11]

Despite this situation, neither Kok nor Sullerot saw women as moving into a revolutionary mode – women's lives and interests, they believed, were too intertwined with society as a whole and with the dominant male. However, they did predict rapid change, and the need for adjustments in the social, economic and political spheres.

Of all of these issues, it was the position of women in the labour market that was picked up first by the OECD and then by the EC. In the early seventies it was noted that certain important gaps in the labour supply had been met by women workers, but doubts were expressed about the 'attachment' of women in general to the world of paid work.

Figure 2.3 Political Representation of Women, 1960–81

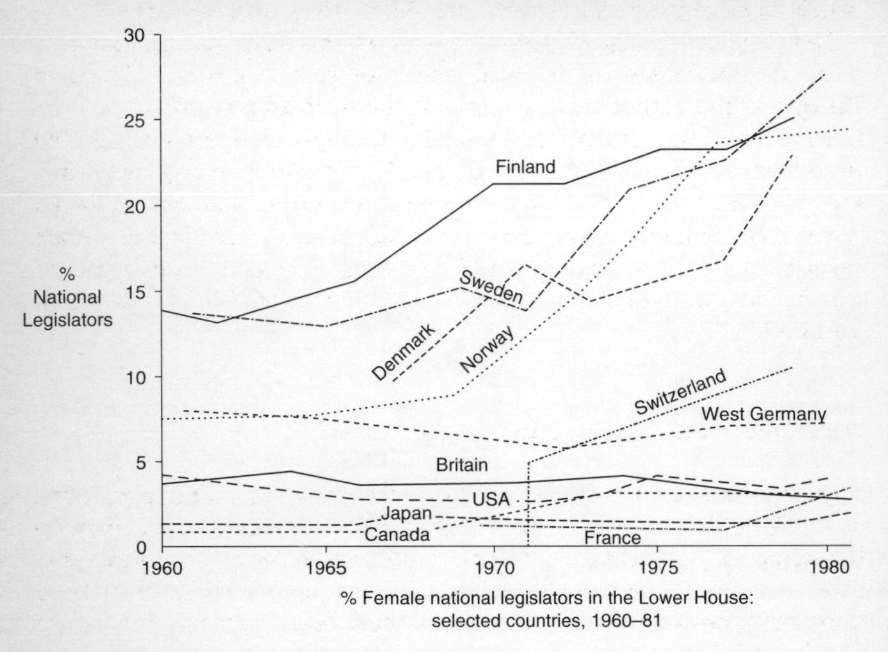

Source: Norris, *Politics and Sexual Equality*, Wheatsheaf, 1987, p. 119

The recession of the seventies made clear the attachment – and also the advantages of these workers to employers because of their low cost and greater flexibility. Cautious consideration was then given to the need to 'integrate' women into the economy. At the same time, the particular characteristics of women workers, as discussed above, were given more serious and sustained analysis as women themselves became politically active. Policy at the level of international organisations represented on the whole a progressive view and one which sought to balance economic and social needs and to identify trends. The sequence of OECD reports on women's employment over this period indicated a gradual broadening of concern and a more sophisticated level of analysis.[12]

All of the material discussed above is fairly dry. Perceptive as Sullerot is, her work seems to lack a vibrant voice. On the whole, lone women dealt with derived experience and directed their conclusions primarily at the established authorities. Their work was also characterised by what Acklesberg and Diamond have called the flight from the body, in that issues to do with sexuality, reproduction and the physical self are notably absent.[13] Also lacking in most of this work, and in official statistics, is any clear sense of the specific characteristics of different groups of women. Using this data alone one would be hard put to predict which kinds of women would be most likely to generate change.

Nevertheless, this work does begin to set the scene for, and identify some of the causes of, the emergence of second-wave feminism in Europe in the seventies. In particular, the mismatch between assumptions and reality, women's increasing labour market experience, and the obsolescence of many aspects of family structure emerge as prime factors. These texts also prefigure the conclusion that Pippa Norris reached much later, that it was the sense of relative deprivation among certain categories of women (and by this stage she could specify them) which laid the basis for the explosion of feminism in the years that followed.[14]

Awareness and Organisation

These then were some of the underlying factors. But material conditions of this kind do not always produce political results and even if they do the nature of those results is by no means certain. So I want to examine what it was in the particular circumstances of the late sixties that made different types of collective action among women possible, creating a visible and widespread movement – subsequently labelled as second-wave feminism – across so many countries. The origins and shape of the movement are important as they help to explain the diverse emphases, assumptions and goals carried forward into the seventies and eighties. This section looks at the issues in general; the next at how these strands came together in one particular country – Italy.

The forms of feminism

The sixties were a time of change and fluidity – in many ways the product of post-war expansion and conflicting expectations. In these circumstances many women were able to see their situations in new ways and make analogies with and draw techniques from other areas of social protest. New forms of communication and types of networks were available, and critiques were developing which helped to uncover the core areas of women's disadvantage.

Second-wave feminism in some form or another emerged during this period in all of the six original member states of the EC, and in each of the three due to join in 1973: Britain, Denmark and Ireland. It was thus a widespread phenomenon across the Community. The countries concerned were all pluralist democracies with mixed economies, but within that framework, economic, political and social conditions varied considerably. The spread of feminism in these circumstances showed the force of the pressure for change, and the ability in the right climate for ideas to be carried 'across the boundaries of socio-economic conditions and across national frontiers'.[15]

The late sixties and early seventies were periods of intense activity among social movements in both the United States and Western Europe. These movements represented new and emerging interests and most of their activities took place outside formal politics. Though they might incorporate pressure group activity, their main emphasis was on self-awareness, mobilisation and the transformation of society. Within such movements individuals found their personal problems lessened or resolved by their involvement in collective action.[16]

Such characteristics help to explain many of the salient features of feminism in this period. Of particular interest to this study are the kinds of analysis developed and gaols sought, the forms of organisation and their relation to mainstream politics, and the extent to which movements in one country were linked to or influenced by developments in others.

The feminist movement at this point, whether looked at as a whole or separately in each country, was made up of a kaleidoscope of activities, experiences and responses, and at the level neither of organisation nor of ideas was it ever possible to impose a straitjacket or create uniformity. Nevertheless, out of this began to emerge certain sets of ideas and types of action. Sometimes these were conflicting; in the long run they often proved complementary.

Many attempts have been made to identify and explore these different tendencies, and it is interesting that similar developments occurred in widely differing societies.[17] Early accounts of feminism point up and define the distinctions between:

liberal feminism: mainly concerned with equality in the public sphere and using fairly traditional means to exert pressure

radical feminism: supremely innovative both in focusing analysis on sexuality and the family and in creating new and flexible forms of organisation

cultural feminism: the most separatist of the tendencies, demanding space for women's activities and a revaluing of women's culture

socialist feminism: important at the level of theory and in attempting to keep links between the insights and concerns of feminism and those of the left.

However, although these distinctions have some relevance (and identifications along these lines were often the cause of rivalry and disputes), later and more detailed accounts have found them too rigid and determining. In particular, as interest in tackling mainstream politics has revived, more sympathetic and complex evaluations are being made of what tended to be dismissed as liberal feminism. The tendency now is to view the phenomenon of second-wave feminism as a whole, and to see it as consisting of fluid and eddying currents, influencing and responsive to a wide variety of circumstances.[18]

Commonalities and differences

One of the most important characteristics of second-wave feminism was its ability to shock. Women picked symbolic issues and came out in public in a quite new style. This led to some very public events across Europe: for example, the disruption of the Miss World competition in London in 1970 when Bob Hope was forced off the stage; the abrasive cross-questioning of Irish politicians on television by enraged feminists; and the demonstration by French feminists at the Arc de Triomphe in Paris on 26 August 1970 for the wife of the unknown soldier. The French women carried slogans reading '*Il y a plus inconnu encore que le soldat: sa femme*' ('There is someone more unknown than the soldier: his wife') and '*un homme sur deux est une femme*' ('One "man" in two is a woman').[19]

What lay behind all this, and why it had such impact, was the lateral thinking involved, and the sharp switch in perspective which taking a women-centred view entailed. The essence of this is well illustrated by a play put on by a radical feminist collective near Bologna in 1975. The play was called *Nonostante Gramsci* ('Despite Gramsci') and was based on detailed research concerning the three Russian/Italian sisters who supported Gramsci in different ways during his life. The collective's aim was 'to rewrite history, inscribing in it the missing voices of women, and therefore to examine the relationships between the private and the public, love and revolution.' The play contended that the public elevation of Gramsci as a Marxist theorist and activist had led to a distortion of his life and its meaning, and had relegated the women to oblivion.[20]

Lateral thinking of this kind involved the prioritising and celebrating for its own sake of the private, the domestic and the sexual, the aspects of life which were normally hidden away and denied public recognition and importance. Frigga Haug wrote rather wryly that in the German feminist movement suddenly sexuality seemed to have become the central terrain of women's oppression, 'certainly not the economy'.[21] Sheila Rowbotham and Michèle le Doeuff, in their parallel accounts of the early days of the British and French women's movements, showed surprisingly similar reactions to this switch in perspective. Both felt an escape from the 'rigour' and 'discipline' and the 'single correctness' imposed on women. Both revelled in, but were slightly wary of, the 'huge creativity' released and the possibility 'to play a full part in life'.[22]

The core organisations of second-wave feminism were small consciousness-raising groups. In them women were able to share experiences, deal with personal problems and expand and consolidate a new world view. How and to what extent these spread out into action varied a great deal from one group to another and from one country to another. Petra De Vries described how in the Netherlands this new energy flowed into four very different types of action: feminist adult education, cultural and social activities, therapies of all kinds to deal with violence, and finally an attempt to influence from this new position, trade unions and the parties of the left.[23]

Frigga Haug's list is almost the same – without the last item. The German autonomous women's movement was more separatist, with strong elements determined to keep away from formal institutions and establish a women's culture and a women's space. In general, however, the incentive to engage with mainstream politics at this stage was not great. Feminism was more about the definition of politics than about demands. Where demands were made – mainly over the legalisation of abortion and reproductive rights – pressure was exerted through demonstrations and campaigns, rather than lobbying.

Out of this ebullience came a huge amount of writing – magazines, newsletters, fiction, journals, pieces of history – drawing on all the diverse viewpoints of feminism. What started out as short papers and articles gradually began to develop into more sustained analysis. As Sheila Rowbotham pointed out, at a certain point experience needed theory, as a challenge to men's hold over ideas, and to help others to follow.[24] Teresa de Lauretis has argued that second-wave feminism made it possible to move beyond the relatively crude discussion of sex differences to the much more complex analysis of how gender and power relations are produced.[25]

All of this radically altered women's perceptions, and perceptions of women, and even if direct interventions were not made, something of the essence infiltrated the policy-making process. One has only to look at accounts of policy making on women's issues in the sixties to realise the extent of change. Although enormous difficulties still remain in achieving objectives, the stance and the discourse of current policy making reflect at least to some extent these altered perceptions.[26]

Gradually in the late seventies the movements began to fragment and lose their public presence. In these circumstances, there were considerable differences as to how much structure was left and how much capacity for common action. On the whole, smaller countries like Ireland and the Netherlands retained some elements of broad front politics among women; whereas in the bigger countries, Britain in particular, attempts at national organisation were abandoned in favour of single issue organisations and a further dispersal of activity. Though to some this was a sign of the demise of the women's movement, in reality it was taking a different shape.

There is evidence in these early days of considerable interchange between one country and another. Many of the movements in Europe were sparked off or encouraged by texts sent or visitors coming from America. However, feminist interchange between the US and Europe was by no means all one way. Juliet Mitchell's *Women – the Longest Revolution*, first published in 1966 in Britain, was widely read in the US, and it has been argued that Betty Frieden's classic text, *The Feminine Mystique*, is in fact a 'boiled down and deradicalised version' (unacknowledged) of Simone de Beauvoir's *The Second Sex*, first published in 1949.[27] In addition to this, in the early seventies, there was considerable criss-crossing of the continent by feminists, travelling to seminars, conferences and events. Feminist archives in a number of capital cities bear witness to this.

In each of the countries of Western Europe, these common features of feminism came out of and were inserted into particular national cultures and were redefined in relation to specific problems and traditions. This meant that as well as the similarities there were also considerable differences. In order to illustrate this process, I want to look, by way of an example, at Italian feminism; at how it emerged out of the struggles on the left at the end of the sixties, and the course it took in the following years. A similar account could be given of early feminism in any of the EU member states.[28]

The Example of Italy

The late sixties in Italy was a time of extreme crisis. Protests and occupations by students and workers were widespread, fuelled by the failure of the state to adjust to new wealth, or develop services in response to people's needs and expectations.[29] As in other countries, small groups of radical feminists emerged out of these conflicts. But the traditions they came from and the political contexts in which they operated were very different.

In Italy liberal feminism (what the Italians call the 'emancipationist tradition') was comparatively weak and found its main expression in the policies of the Italian Communist Party (PCI), then the main opposition party in Italy and the largest Communist party in Western Europe. The PCI's declared policy was to press for equal rights for women in the public sphere and to encourage women into paid employment. This did not involve any questioning of male control in the family or in sexual relations.[30] On the other side from the PCI was the ruling Christian Democrat Party (DC) which, drawing its support from the Catholic Church and from fear of Communism, used its immense influence to try to keep women in more passive and traditional roles. One of the main demands of Italian feminists in the early seventies was for 'unedited versions' of women's experiences, that is versions unmediated by either of these two opposing monoliths.[31]

An early challenge to this orthodoxy was made by the DeMau group (Demystification of Authority), a mixed collective active in Milan in the mid to late sixties. In their writings they opposed the emancipationist tradition because it sought to integrate women into a social system dominated by men, stated that women's needs could not be met by a set of 'demands', and urged a much deeper analysis of the actual experience of women.[32] These ideas were taken up and acted upon by the radical groups coming out of the student movement, which in turn were influenced by developments in the US. Small self-awareness (*auto-coscienza*) groups were formed to develop a stronger sense of women's identity, and to challenge male assumptions in intellectual analysis, in definitions of sexuality and in the organisation of the family. Carla Lonzi's *'Sputiamo su Hegel'* ('Let's Spit on Hegel') gives a sense of the times.[33]

In 1970, in another strand of development, a member of the Italian Radical Party (PR) came back from the US with texts and documents about women's liberation. The Radical Party was a small party, which had been active in the campaign for divorce reform and which was based to some extent on the American civil rights tradition. Women close to the PR then set up the *Movimento de Liberazione della Donna* (MLD) which demanded among other things greater sexual autonomy for women and the legalisation of abortion. Spanning the gap between conventional politics and the more autonomous groups, it envisaged a policy which involved 'law-making as well as law-breaking'. On this basis a campaign for abortion reform was begun.[34]

By 1972 most of the radical groups, after some initial hesitations, had become fully involved in this campaign, using the issue of abortion to show how completely women's sexuality and reproductive capacity were controlled by male norms. The development of alternative health clinics, the widespread dissemination of information, and the eventual decision of the PCI to support reform, led to the legalisation of abortion under certain conditions in 1978.

By the early seventies the Italian feminist movement had developed a considerable organisational presence together with a wide range of activities. Judith Hellman in her book on feminism in five Italian cities shows both how widespread the women's networks were and what different forms they took in different areas. She also describes what was to become one of the most distinctive features of Italian feminism – the attempt to take feminist ideas and forms of organisation into the trade unions.[35] Though this encountered great difficulties it had a lasting effect. Thus in five years Italian feminism had to a large extent succeeded in one of its original aims: to establish 'alternative reference points' for the debate on women.

One of the most striking features of Italian feminism is its apparent ability to combine opposites. Although conflicts among feminists have at times been bitter, cultural feminism and socialist feminism, which in many countries have been separately identified, seem in Italy to be contained within the broad scope of radical feminism – or within the 'liberationist movement' as Italians prefer to call it. Similarly, Italian feminists seem able to accommodate the idea of women's 'difference' – which is seen not as fixed but as something constantly changing – with the need to make direct challenges to male assumptions and state power. As Lesley Caldwell puts it, Italian feminism combines two strategies: the analysis of subjectivity 'through sustained intellectual and personal work' and a commitment to the tradition of political militancy. Sometimes one dominates and sometimes the other, but neither can be abandoned.[36] This, together with a great openness to other cultures, laid a basis for continuing debate and action.

This example illustrates both the commonality of the feminist experience and also the way national culture and forms of struggle inflect the movement. It suggests obvious points of contact but also clear differences in priorities, style and organisation. However, although feminism in Europe was nationally shaped it was by no means nationally contained. A level of transnational activity therefore remained a real possibility.

The continuing legacy

These then were some of the ideas and organisational forms developing within feminism across the member states of the EC during this period. They represented an enormous increase in the level and visibility of women's collective activity and in the vigour and passion with which issues to do with women were debated. Feminists on the whole rejected the demand for equality and sought to replace it with a multi-faceted project designed to explore all the aspects of being a woman. This reversed 'the flight from the body' and put issues to do with sexual relations and the family at the heart of the investigation. In some cases this exploration involved a turning away from the political arena; in others the political challenge was renewed using new strategies and with a different agenda.

On the whole, though diversity among women was recognised, this was not the prime concern. Feminists were discovering what they had in common, not what separated them. As a result and over time, the interests and priorities of certain types of women came to dominate without this having necessarily been the intention. Nevertheless, the breakthroughs achieved during this period began to alter the way women were perceived, and thus opened up space for broader and more diverse groups to become active. Sara Evans's assessment of the American movement in the late seventies applies equally to Europe:

> As the women's movement dispersed, splintered, formed and reformed, its importance lay less and less with the specific groups who initiated it and more with the response it made possible . . . The experiences which had provoked and formed a feminist consciousness in the first place, re-created themselves not only beyond the new left, but beyond the middle class as well.[37]

Neither in Italy nor in the other member states of the EC was this activity targeted, except in the rarest of cases, at EC institutions or policy makers. This was despite the fact that the EC was already an important forum for economic and political decision making in Europe and was beginning to debate the need for a policy on women. In general, the distance from formal politics remained immense. Nevertheless, second-wave feminism did have a considerable impact in the member states and effects from this were felt at EC level. The result was to open the doors of the EC Commission to 'reasonable feminists' like Evelyne Sullerot, who suddenly seemed like valuable intermediaries. The emphasis in their work on labour market participation rather than sexual politics suited the orientation of EC policies and the thinking of Commission officials.

Notes

1 Viola Klein, *Women Workers – Working Hours and Services*, OECD, Paris, 1965; G.H.S. Kok, *Report on the Political, Social and Civic Position of Women in Europe*, Council of Europe, Strasbourg, 1967; and OECD, *Employment of Women*, Paris, 1970.

2 Françoise Picq, *Les Années-Mouvement Liberation des Femmes*, Seuil, Paris, 1993, pp. 26–7.

3 Elizabeth Wilson, *Only Half Way to Paradise – Women in Postwar Britain: 1945–1968*, Tavistock, London, 1980, pp. 162–86.

4 Evelyne Sullerot, *Histoire et sociologie du travail féminin*, Editions Gonthier, Paris, 1968.

5 Evelyne Sullerot, *Women, Society and Change*, Weidenfeld, London, 1971. This was originally published in French under the title *La femme dans le monde moderne*, Hachette, Paris, 1970.
6 Sullerot, *Women, Society and Change*, p. 75.
7 For these and other relevant statistics see Eurostat, *Social Indicators for the EC*, 1984, and Eurostat, *Women in Europe – their Economic and Social Positions*, 1987.
8 Sullerot, *Women, Society and Change*, p. 17.
9 OECD, *Employment of Women*, p. 16.
10 Kok, *Political, Social and Civic Position of Women*, p. 33.
11 More recent figures are given in Appendix 4.
12 OECD: *The Role of Women in the Economy*, 1975; *Equal Opportunities for Women*, 1979; and *The Integration of Women into the Economy*, 1985.
13 M. Acklesberg, I. Diamond, 'Gender and Political Life – New Directions in Political Science', in B. Hess and M. Ferree, eds, *Analysing Gender*, Sage, London, 1987, p. 520.
14 Pippa Norris, *Politics and Sexual Equality – the Comparative Position of Women in Western Democracies*, Wheatsheaf, Brighton, 1987, pp. 142–8.
15 Frigga Haug, 'Lessons from the Women's Movement in Europe', *Feminist Review*, no. 31, spring 1989, p. 109.
16 Drude Dahlerup, ed., *The New Women's Movement – Feminism and Political Power in Europe and the USA*, Sage, London, 1986, p. 2.
17 Joni Lovenduski, *Women and European Politics*, Wheatsheaf Books, Brighton, 1986.
18 See Teresa de Lauretis, 'Upping the Anti (sic) in Feminist Theory', in M. Hirsch and E.F. Keller, eds, *Conflicts in Feminism*, Routledge, New York/London 1990; and Sandra Harding, 'The Instability of the Analytical Categories of Feminist Theory', in H. Cowley and S. Himmelweit, eds, *Knowing Women*, Polity Press, London, 1992.
19 For more detail on these events see Michelene Wandor, ed., *The Body Politic – Women's Liberation in Britain 1969–1972*, Stage One, London, 1972, pp. 249–60; June Levine, *Sisters*, Ward River Press, Dublin, 1982; and Picq, *Les Années-Mouvement*, pp. 16–17.
20 A riveting description and analysis of this play is given in Teresa de Lauretis, *Technologies of Gender – Essays on Theory, Film, and Fiction*, Macmillan, London, 1989, ch. 5. The quotation is from de Lauretis.
21 Frigga Haug, 'The Women's Movement in West Germany', *New Left Review*, no. 155, 1986, p. 60.
22 Sheila Rowbotham, Lynne Segal and Hilary Wainwright, *Beyond the Fragments – Feminism and the Making of Socialism*, Merlin Press, London, 1979, ch. 2, part 1; Michèle le Doeuff, *L'Etude et le rouet*, Seuil, Paris, 1989, especially part 4.
23 Petra de Vries, 'Feminism in the Netherlands', *Women's Studies International Forum*, vol. 4, no. 4, 1981, pp. 389–407.
24 Rowbotham, *Beyond the Fragments*, pp. 53–5.
25 De Lauretis, *Technologies of Gender*, pp. 1–7.
26 For a detailed demonstration of changing perceptions in the US, see Cynthia Harrison, *On Account of Sex – the Politics of Women's Issues 1945–1968*, University of California Press, Los Angeles, 1989.
27 S. Djikstra, 'Simone de Beauvoir and Betty Friedan – the Politics of Omission', *Feminist Studies*, vol. 6, no. 2, summer 1980, pp. 290–303.
28 Vivid recent histories include Picq, *Les Années-Mouvements* and Sheila Rowbotham, *The Past Is Before Us – Feminism in Action since the 1960s*, Pandora Press, London, 1989.
29 Robert Lumley, *States of Emergency – Cultures of Revolt in Italy from 1968 to 1978*, Verso, London, 1990. I am grateful to Lesley Caldwell for help with this section.
30 Lesley Caldwell, 'Italian Feminism – Some Considerations', in Z. Baranski and S. Vinall, eds, *Women and Italy*, Macmillan, Basingstoke, 1991.
31 Lucia Chiavola Birnbaum, *Liberazione della donna – Feminism in Italy*, Wesleyan University Press, Middletown, Connecticut, 1986.
32 Paola Bono and Sandra Kemp, *Italian Feminist Thought – a Reader*, Blackwell, Oxford, 1991, pp. 33–5.
33 Bono and Kemp, *Italian Feminist Thought*, pp. 40–59.

34 Ellen Cantarow, 'Abortion and Feminism in Italy', *Radical America*, vol. 10, part 6, 1977.
35 Judith A. Hellman, *Journeys among Women – Feminism in Five Italian Cities*, Polity Press, Oxford, 1987.
36 Caldwell, 'Italian Feminism', p. 111.
37 Cited in Rowbotham, *The Past Is Before Us*, p. xii.

3

The Adoption of Article 119 on Equal Pay

It is unlikely that feminism alone, despite its widespread impact in the seventies, would have been enough to generate a policy on women's rights at the European level. This political impetus, however, was given a focus by the already existing presence of Article 119 on equal pay in the Treaty of Rome. As will be shown in the last section of this chapter, Article 119 owes its unusual impact to the fact that during the negotiations it was switched from a position in the economic core of the Treaty to the Title on social policy. Thus, in its very history and terminology, Article 119 raises questions, always central to EU development, about the relation of the economic and the social, and about whether it is possible to construct an economic market without a social content.

To explore these issues further, and provide some background to the EU's development and particular characteristics, this chapter will take a step back to the fifties and sixties. The first section will look at the political foundations of the EC, and the second at how European social policy began to be constructed in this context. The final section will examine, against this backdrop, the concerns and priorities which led to the inclusion of Article 119, and to its particular formulation.

The Political Foundations of the EC

Both the European Coal and Steel Community (already discussed in chapter 1) and the European Community were from the beginning politically inspired institutions fulfilling economic functions. The main purpose was to create a framework within which France and Germany could compete and cooperate, precluding any further recourse to war. The Americans favoured these developments, seeing them as helping to create a bulwark against any extension of Soviet power and influence. The leading European politicians for the most part agreed with this, but there was an underlying feeling that Europe needed a stronger identity to deal with both superpowers – the United States as well as the Soviet Union. The creators and facilitators of the EC were all men, as can be seen from the photographs of the time. They are accurately referred to as 'the founding fathers'.[1]

During the fifties, the political roots and implications of these moves to economic integration were consistently down-played, a trend that has continued ever since. However, a corollary of this was the acceptance from the start that any real integration between the economies of six such distinct entities would require a transfer of power to the centre. Thus, at the time of the formation of the ECSC, a balance was struck between the central authorities of the Community, with powers of initiation and implementation, and the policy makers in the individual member states, who retained final control both over the Community decision-making process, and over enforcement at the national level. This created a dynamic tension between supranational and national elements which while varying over the years has remained the pivot of Community policy making. In the course of effecting this balance, the need for democratic controls and modes of representation at European level was largely ignored.

By 1955 the ECSC was operating successfully. However, attempts to create a similar level of European cooperation in defence and security had collapsed amid recriminations. Fearing a renewal of Franco/German hostility, the smaller countries, Belgium, the Netherlands and Luxembourg, proposed a further expansion of economic cooperation, following the strategy which had already proved successful.

France and Germany agreed to open negotiations on these proposals, but the leaders of both made it clear that there was to be no discussion of political union and no increase of supranational powers.[2] Paul-Henri Spaak, the Belgian foreign minister, coordinated both the preliminary work and the direct negotiations which led eventually to the signing of the Treaty of Rome in 1957. His main aim was to open the way for deeper integration in the economic sphere while not overtly breaching the conditions set out by the two major powers. In 1956 the negotiations took place against a background of French anxieties and sense of weakness, and of growing instability in Paris as a result of the Algerian war and the crisis over Suez.[3]

Robert Marjolin, who was a key member of the French delegation, describes vividly the difficulties the French negotiators faced, given the general hostility in France to the removal, even by stages, of the ring of protection which had been constructed around French industry. As a result, at the beginning of the negotiations, the French team submitted a new set of demands which they saw as providing compensation for the inevitable lowering of tariffs. These demands included the acceptance across the Community of the principle of equal pay.[4]

The other negotiators responded to these demands diplomatically – incorporating what they could, and standing out against any provisions which they saw as damaging to the emerging common market. Spaak was well aware of the need to make concessions to the French that could be represented in Paris as a victory. He was also anxious to complete the negotiations quickly – while a government favourable to the idea of European cooperation was in power in Paris. Many of the loose ends and anomalies in the Treaty (and certainly the inclusion of the provisions on equal pay) can be attributed to these pressures.[5]

What comes out of accounts of these deliberations is the determination of the principal negotiators to go beyond a free trade area or a customs union to a structure which is variously called a 'common market' or an 'economic union'. The implications of this were that economic integration among the six states would involve not just the removal or alignment of controls on trade but the creation of a common economic space. Within this space it was envisaged that barriers to a wide range of economic activities would be lifted and joint action encouraged. It was assumed at the beginning of the negotiations that some degree of harmonisation of social provisions (and hence of costs) between the six would be necessary to achieve these objectives; by the end, the need for this was being increasingly down-played.

It was in this political context that a reference to gender difference (through the provisions on equal pay) came to be included in the Treaty of Rome, albeit in a half-hearted and ill-considered way. The urgency of the last stages of the negotiations together with the need to conciliate the French were crucial factors. In order to consider equal pay in the Treaty the drafters had to conceptualise it as an issue likely to distort competition between states; at this stage its implications for women's status were regarded as matters for the individual member states.[6]

To understand the implications of this, it helps to look in more detail at the elements that make up social policy, and how these articulated with both national and European interests during these early stages of the EC's development. Although in the end social provision was given a low priority in the Treaty, the issue of what kind of social policy was appropriate to what kind of economic union was debated right through the negotiations and in the years that followed – as it has been ever since.

The Social and the Economic in EC Development

The many facets of a country's social policy play a crucial role in determining how a society is constructed, who participates on what terms – and what values, objectives and strategies are endorsed.[7] Social policy helps to create society and build the state and provides channels for redistribution; it also acts as a powerful force for social control. Although all of society is affected by social policy, it acts most directly on those not in paid work.

Social provision by the state results from social pressures and conflict, a central focus of which is whether such provision should be limited to the minimum requirements necessary to the functioning of economic markets, or should be expanded in response to social needs. The fact that conflicts over social provision have historically been focused on the nation state helps to explain the differences in forms and levels which exist, even among states as similar as those within the EU.

At international level, cooperation between states has been dominated in the social sphere by economic motives and purposes. This is a reflection of the national focus of social and class organisation and of the difficulties already discussed in chapter 1 of extending such activity in international arenas. The same pattern can be seen within federal systems. In the United States, for example, the federal government's powers under the 'commerce clause' of the Constitution were for decades seen in narrow economic terms and social policy was left to be regulated by individual states. Only after the growth of strong labour organisations, and the election of Roosevelt, was there an acceptance in the thirties of federal regulation of labour law and industrial relations.[8]

This suggests that there is likely to be a significant time-lag between a process of economic integration and transnational control of social policy. It also suggests that, because paid labour is more directly involved in the market, the regulation of provisions concerning or springing out of the employment relationship will precede those which affect the population as a whole. In the past, it was assumed that any transnational harmonisation of social policy would be in an upward direction. Since the eighties, such an assumption is no longer valid, and one of the attractions of social harmonisation for states in the future may well be the possibility it provides for levelling down welfare provision. In this context, the degree of organisation of labour and social movements at the international level will be of key importance.

Issues of social policy are always extremely sensitive in that they concern the allocation of resources and the transmission of ideology. Changes in social policy can affect the political base of any regime since it is through social policy that a large part of the population most directly experiences the actions of the state. Raymond Rifflet, who was for many years concerned with social affairs in the European Commission, points out ruefully how precisely the 'social' pinpoints the political sensitivities of governments. As a consequence, national politicians have in general been extremely reluctant to transfer any real responsibility in this domain to the European level.[9]

Social policy measures

These preliminary remarks help to explain the way in which social policy issues were handled during the negotiations which led up to the Treaty of Rome, and in the decade which followed.

At the time of the negotiations, three types of European measure were in theory possible:

1. Measures of the *society-creating* type discussed above, involving the transfer of some of the social protection/social control functions to the European level. In respect of the workforce, this might involve European protection for basic employment rights, or, more ambitiously, some European involvement or guarantee in the provision of social security. The effect would be to begin to develop common social regimes across the Community, with a likely long-term effect on the formation of social groups and social activity more generally.

2. Measures aimed at *harmonising* social costs for employers (or at least removing obvious distortions) primarily for economic reasons and to assist the development of conditions of fair competition across the member states. Examples would be measures to standardise the length of paid holidays or sick pay entitlements (especially the part paid by employers) in all of the member states.

3. Measures necessary to achieve certain economic objectives considered essential to the *functioning* of the common market – for example, the creation of a mobile and flexible labour force.

For convenience, I have labelled these three types of social policy 'society-creating', 'harmonising' and 'functional', although there is obviously a great deal of overlap and slippage between them.[10]

In the mid fifties in Europe, the nature of the coalition pressing for integration (political elites mainly from centrist and social democratic parties, civil servants and some industrialists) made it highly unlikely that bold steps towards society-creating social policy would be taken.[11] In fact, as Alan Milward makes clear, the rebuilding of the nation states in Europe at this point required that they remain the primary focus for the handling of social conflict and for the provision of social policy.[12] Thus, the Spaak Report, which laid the basis for the negotiations, stated clearly that it would be 'unnecessary, because irrelevant' to interfere with arrangements giving help to individuals not in the productive sector, and that 'redistributive benefits used as instruments of social policy should remain entirely a matter for states'.[13] The agreed gloss on this, later enshrined in Article 2 of the Treaty, was that while social progress was undoubtedly one of the aims of the Community, it would occur naturally as a by-product of economic integration. Provisions at EC level would therefore hardly be necessary and the management of that social progress would be a matter for states.

However, there were some, both inside and outside the negotiations, who would have preferred a more populist tone to the Treaty, and who felt that social policy could play a part in that. This was particularly so since the earlier ECSC Treaty had at least recognised the role of social groups (for example, unemployed miners) and paid some attention to industry-wide living standards.[14]

Documents relating to the negotiation of the Treaty of Rome show that very late in the day (January 1957) an approach was made directly to Spaak by representatives of labour organisations and members of the Assembly of the ECSC. They asked that more emphasis be given to social policy and to the representation of workers in Community decision making.[15] Spaak seems personally to have supported this move and as a result an already existing, vaguely-worded text became what is now Article 117 of the Treaty, in a separate Title on social policy. Article 117 repeats the commitment in Article 2 to social progress (but specifies that the concern here will be with workers) and goes on to suggest that this will come about from the 'procedures' of the EC as well as from its 'functioning'. Harmonisation of social systems appears as an objective and it is clearly stated that this should only take place in the context of improved working conditions and living standards.[16]

Article 117 is given precision by Article 118 which was also added early in 1957. Article 118 suggests areas in the social field with which the EC can be concerned and gives some examples (but not an exhaustive list) of what these might be.[17] The provisions of Article 118 were subject to much debate, and in the end the European Commission was given very limited powers of implementation: it could only promote 'close cooperation between member states' and develop research and consultation on the topics covered.

Despite everything, there is a whiff of society-creating social policy in these two articles, and they suggest that it might be possible in the future to develop Community provisions for workers based on a more progressive view of what economic necessity required. They also go beyond the assumption discussed earlier that social progress will occur naturally as a result of the operations of the common market.

Harmonisation

The main debate on social policy which took place during the negotiations concerned the necessity for the harmonisation of social measures and, in particular, the extent to which the creation of the common market required the harmonisation of social costs to the employer in the interests of fair competition. In order to clarify the issues in this debate, the International Labour Organisation (ILO) convened an expert group early in 1955, under the chairmanship of Bertil Ohlin, professor and former Minister of Commerce in Sweden. The conclusion of the group was that little action would be needed by the EC in the case of general social costs as these would tend to even out between member states as the market developed. There might, however, be distortions within a particular industry which would entail some intervention.

It is significant that the Ohlin group mentioned as one of these possible distortions differences in the extent to which the member states applied the principle of equal pay between men and women. To back up their argument, they gave statistics on the differential wage rates between men and women in different economic sectors, and showed how the ratio varied between European states. Overall, however, they concluded that, from an economic perspective at least, few social policy measures would be required to implement the common market.[18]

As a result of these discussions, the EC negotiators were encouraged in this respect also to take a minimalist view of social policy requirements, though the debate continued, especially in France.[19] However, the possibility remained alive that in certain circumstances measures to harmonise social costs might be appropriate, and it was under this heading that the negotiators were able to accommodate French demands when the need arose. This was the rationale for including articles on equal pay, and on the equivalence of paid holidays, as Articles 119 and 120 of the Treaty.

In the end, it was only on 'functional' social policy measures (those necessary to achieve essential Community objectives) that there existed any consensus, or any real willingness to give effective powers to the Community institutions. The two areas where an agreement was possible under this head concerned measures to encourage the free movement of labour, and measures to establish a funding body to assist workers in adjusting to economic change. Both of these were areas already covered by the ECSC and where there was experience to draw on.

The free movement of labour was viewed in the context of the liberalisation of factors of production in the common market. If goods were to circulate freely, then it was seen as 'profitable' in economic terms to enable those who produced them to do so also. Measures to ensure such free movement were included, not in the section on social policy, but in an earlier section on the foundations of the Community. However, it was clear that strong social provisions would be required, both to persuade workers to move and to break down the measures which favoured nationals in the labour markets of the member states. In an attempt to achieve this, Articles 48–51 entitled the migrant to access to the labour market and placed a ban on discrimination in employment on grounds of nationality in the Community as a whole. At the same time, the Treaty stated that migrants should be given the right to aggregate and transfer social security benefits irrespective of where in the Community they had been acquired. Significantly, the European Commission was given strong powers to implement these measures.[20]

The European Social Fund (ESF) was set up under Articles 123–8 of the Treaty to 'improve employment opportunities for workers'. The experience of the ECSC had helped to establish that the availability of a Community fund to finance the retraining of workers and encourage mobility was valuable in creating a more flexible labour force and cushioning change. A similar fund was envisaged for the EC, but the emphasis was less on protection and more on galvanising the workforce and providing incentives for innovation and change.[21]

This then is the sum total of social policy measures in the Treaty of Rome: a whiff of society-creating measures in Articles 2, 117 and 118; a gesture towards harmonisation in Articles 119 and 120; and a strong element of functional social policy to encourage the mobility of labour, and the retraining of workers through the ESF. It is noticeable that only in the case of the last category, and to some extent with regard to Article 119, were any real powers accorded to the Commission.

A perceptive analysis of these provisions was made in 1958 in the French labour movement journal, *Informations Sociales*, in an issue which also contained a survey of the situation in European countries with regard to equal pay. The preface to the issue argued that the EC *did* require a social policy, because of the way social security systems were based on economic frontiers, and to consolidate popular sentiment behind the whole endeavour of European integration. If the new Common Market's social concern was limited to encouraging the free movement of labour, then effectively people would be being treated as though they were goods.[22]

This article reflected a clear worry about the lack of social measures in the Rome Treaty, and the effect this would have on the future development of the Community. Looking back from the nineties, we can see that this absence (together with the down-playing of the political, discussed earlier) shaped the EC in particular ways which have proved hard to change.

Consolidation in the sixties

Developments in the sixties confirmed these early trends. Social provisions to promote the free movement of labour were implemented firmly and effectively over the next decade. Once the framework was established, access to benefits was provided by coordinating the systems of the member states (i.e. linking them in the interests of the migrant worker) rather than by the harmonisation of levels or standards.[23] The coordination was effective in the sense that, at least in legal terms, the migrant worker was not disadvantaged in comparison with the worker of the host country. As will be discussed in more detail in chapter 9, it was assumed from the beginning (although the Treaty provisions did not say so) that these measures would only apply to migrant workers who were nationals of a member state. Non-citizen workers, mainly from the peripheries of Europe or from former colonial territories, were excluded.[24]

Despite the limitations of the Treaty, during the late fifties and early sixties the Commission did not restrict itself in the social policy area to proposals on functional measures only. This was a period when Commission activity was expanding, and when officials felt confident in their role as innovators and initiators. They believed that out of the hints and asides in the Treaty, some sort of a broader social policy programme could be put together. Both Doreen Collins and John Holloway have examined in some detail the attempts to do this, showing how the Commission first tried to move on the issue of social costs to employers, then envisaged a grand harmonisation of benefits, and finally ended up desperately searching for any measure in the social policy field upon which agreement might be reached.[25]

All to no avail. The contest between 'economic' and 'social' interpretations of the Treaty reflected those between the Council and the Commission, and between the representatives of the employers and of labour. Those who favoured an extension of social policy at the European level were defeated by 'the magnitude of the goal . . . and the paucity of the powers' accorded to the Community institutions.[26] The EC still, at this stage, functioned primarily as 'an organisation of states not a community of peoples'.[27]

By the mid sixties, however, any discussion of advancing social policy became entangled in the constitutional crisis which hit the EC in 1965–66. Accusing the Commission of over-stepping its power, De Gaulle withdrew his delegation from the Council of Ministers, proclaiming the sovereignty and autonomy of France. In the negotiation and compromise which ensued, the Commission emerged with its essential powers intact, but with its exuberance and confidence badly dented and with some specific limitations placed on its ability to act directly within the member states.[28] One of the aspects of Commission activity which had particularly alarmed member states was the development of direct links between the Commission and non-governmental organisations on issues relating to social policy.

Pursuing social policy initiatives, after these events, had few advocates in the Commission. Ironically, however, the compromise which ended the crisis came only two years before the dramatic upheavals of 1968 when students, at times in a powerful alliance with labour movements, organised direct actions across Europe. Such upheavals can, to some extent at least, be attributed to the failure of the states of Western Europe to meet people's social expectations after a period of growing prosperity. When 'normality' returned at the beginning of the seventies, social policy was high on the agenda at both national and European levels.

The period of the negotiation of the Treaty and the decade immediately afterwards thus set a pattern where, despite the magnitude of the structural changes being made in the economic field, social policy at the European level was kept to the minimum, and was regarded not as parallel to, or as setting a framework for, economic measures but as subordinate to them. This removed from the Community enterprise some of the dimensions which over the years might have begun to create societal changes commensurate with the new economic forms. Given this balance of policies, any success the Community achieved, or turbulence it experienced, would for the most part be processed through national channels, and interpreted in terms of national culture and preoccupations.

Negotiating Article 119

The negotiation and early implementation of Article 119 needs to be situated within the context discussed above, although its trajectory differed markedly from that of social policy generally. However, it also owed its existence and particular shape to two main factors not yet considered: first, the debate on equal pay which took place in international organisations at the end of the war, and second, the situation of women in France in the forties and fifties, which prompted French demands for equal pay to be included on the EC agenda.

The ILO

Equal pay for men and women formed part of the broad span of human rights given international definition in the forties. It was recognised as a principle which needed to be implemented in the constitution of the International Labour Organisation (ILO), and it was included in the UN's Universal Declaration of Human Rights. The commitment in the ILO constitution led to intensive debate and eventually to the adoption in 1951 of an ILO Convention (No. 100) and Recommendation on 'equal remuneration between male and female workers for work of equal value'.[29] The ILO Convention (from now on referred to as ILO 100) was important as a backdrop to Article 119 and serves to introduce some of the debates and practical issues which are implicit in the concept of equal pay.

In the forties and fifties (and in some cases much later) it was common throughout Europe to have a 'women's rate' and a 'men's rate' of payment for the same job. The rationale for this was on the one hand that the woman worker was worth less to the employer because of factors like absenteeism and a fragmented working life, and on the other that her 'needs' were less. The main aim of ILO 100 was to shift the emphasis in wage setting from valuing the person to valuing the job, and to establish the principle that if a job of the same value was being carried out, then the same wage should be paid. This raised important issues about the way value was established and the criteria used.[30]

It seems likely that in using the formulation 'work of equal value' (rather than 'equal work') the initial intention was to emphasise the fact that the valuation should rest in the job. However, it very quickly became apparent that this formula also made it possible to compare a wider range of jobs – if it could be argued that the value was the same. It is this latter aspect of the definition which has become important in subsequent debate. The term 'remuneration' was used to indicate that the equality principle should be applied to everything the employee received from the employer – not just basic pay.

Jenks states that ILO 100 is 'a policy and promotional rather than a strict obligation convention'.[31] It was recognised that the introduction and maintenance of free collective bargaining was an important issue in many countries, and that in any case wage setting was a highly sensitive area. In these circumstances, the Convention sought to establish the principle of equal remuneration, while leaving open the way in which this was implemented. The Recommendation went further, however, and suggested procedures for the 'progressive application of the principles' laid down in the Convention. In particular, it was proposed that priority should be given to action in the public sector, and that where there were difficulties the differential between women's and men's rates should be reduced by stages.[32]

As a result of these debates, the relevant ministries in the countries negotiating the Treaty of Rome would have been familiar with some of the issues surrounding equal pay – even if these were not always well understood. It was presumably this familiarity, together with the direct involvement of the ILO, that led the experts who drew up the Ohlin Report to use equal pay as an example of an area where different levels of regulation might distort competition in the EC. Michel Gaudet, who was present at the negotiations, confirms this impression. 'The other governments would not have accepted equal pay just because France wanted it', he maintains. 'It was already a legitimate issue and in the public domain.'[33]

Equal pay in France

France adopted provisions on equal pay much earlier than other comparable countries. The reasons for this, and the role that women played in this development, are hard to disentangle and any interpretation must be tentative. It would seem, however, to be the result both of specifically political factors, and of the contradictory ways in which women were seen after the war in France – on the one hand as emancipated workers and wartime resistance partners, and on the other as traditional mothers, the embodiment of 'family' values.

Equal pay was certainly an issue in France in the thirties. One woman trade unionist asserts that it was the struggles of women workers that brought it to the fore, and that after the war the trade unions 'remembered their principles'. She claims that these actions were at least partly responsible for both ILO 100 and Article 119.[34] When the war ended, equal pay formed part of the programme developed by the left, which aimed at greater social equality, the raising of living standards and the relief of family poverty. Claire Laubier describes the desperate situation of the French working class at this point, and how the position of women was seen as pivotal, both as workers who would help regenerate the economy and as mothers who would replace the population lost in the war. She claims that without the role of women in the strikes and bread riots of 1946–47, these reforms might never have been implemented.[35]

If provisions on equal pay came early in France, votes for women came late. Women won the vote in France only in 1944, much later than in other comparable countries. For a short while at least, this had the effect of increasing awareness and the salience of women's issues. Jane Jenson maintains, however, that the extension of the vote represented, not the recognition of women as a new category, but rather a decision to give more status to the role of 'mother'.[36]

Whatever the reasons, a number of provisions which in a formal sense at least embodied the concept of equal pay were introduced in France in the period up to 1950. These included: the adoption in July 1946 of a decree which abolished the reductions in women's pay which had been permitted up to then; the preamble to the Constitution of October 1946 which guaranteed women equal rights 'in all domains'; and the law of February 1950 which, while reintroducing free collective bargaining, stipulated that the previous decrees affecting wages must be respected, and that collective agreements 'capable of extension' must incorporate the principle of equal pay. Perhaps most important, the minimum wage (SMIG) introduced in France in 1950 had a single scale for men and women.[37]

Tribolati is doubtful about the effectiveness of all of this especially as so few women workers were covered by collective agreements. Equality, she says, only really existed at the level of the minimum wage.[38] Nevertheless, implemented or not, this legislation was enough to alarm French employers, especially when they saw that no similar measures existed in the other states negotiating with France over the terms of the Treaty of Rome. It seems to have been this that persuaded the French government to include the issue of equal pay in the set of demands on harmonising social costs which, as we have seen, were tabled by the French delegation before and during the negotiations.

The text

The six member states negotiating the Treaty had different attitudes to and experiences of equal pay between men and women.[39] The Dutch had the most difficulties – mainly it would seem because there were few women in the labour force and equal pay was not an issue taken up by the trade unions. In these circumstances, it was seen as acceptable in the Netherlands to increase family wages by paying the breadwinner (assumed to be male) a higher rate. At the same time, Dutch employers in certain sectors such as textiles were able to gain advantage by employing low-paid female workers.[40] As a result, Dutch officials tried hard to narrow the scope of what was agreed. Other delegations appeared at different times confused, complaisant or indifferent – but willing to make compromises in order to satisfy the French.

Tracking the textual development of Article 119 is by no means easy, even with access to documentation on the *travaux préparatoires* of the Treaty of Rome.[41] There seems to have been an early text in which action on equal pay (and other matters) is associated with concern about differences in social costs. This draft imposed no direct obligation on states but left the European Commission to make proposals for implementation to the Council of Ministers.[42] Only in the autumn of 1956, when the French renewed their pressure, was equal pay considered separately and provisions developed in any detail.[43] At this point it seems to have been agreed (for the reasons discussed earlier) that it was necessary to conciliate the French, and that equal pay was the area where this could be done most easily. From then on debate centred on the exact wording of the text, and the earlier version was abandoned.

The *travaux préparatoires* show that by the time the Foreign Affairs Ministers of the six met in October 1956 to review progress, a very short draft for an article on equal pay already existed (as yet unnumbered). The text was as follows:

> Each member state government will take all the measures necessary to ensure, during the first stage, the application of the principle of equal pay for men and women for equal work and for work of equal value. (my translation)

This text uses the French '*salaire*' rather than '*rémunération*' but endorses the ILO formula by including work of equal value as well as equal work.[44] It is significant that this new text does now make the application of equal pay a direct obligation on states – and sets some kind of a time limit.

In November this text was approved by the heads of the negotiating teams, but with a reservation on the phrase 'work of equal value'. At this point the French were asked exactly what was meant by the principle of equal pay. Their answer specified that equal pay must apply both to piecework and to hourly rates, a formulation that was incorporated in the final text. The problem was then passed to a sub-group of social affairs experts who were given a resumé of the issues and asked to come up with a text 'in line with the ILO Convention'.

It is this sub-group that seems to have played the major role in devising the final text. In their version, the firm obligation is retained, but the controversial phrase 'work of equal value' is removed. As though to compensate, the scope of the term 'pay' is considerably increased by the use (in French) of the term '*rémunération*' instead of '*salaire*', and by the adoption, in line with ILO 100, of a broad definition: namely, that remuneration includes everything the employee receives 'directly or indirectly, whether in cash or in kind' from the employer in connection with employment. They then add the French reference to piecework and hourly rates on at the end.

By the beginning of February 1957, this text had been labelled Article 46 and included in a section of the Treaty (later suppressed) which dealt with distortions to competition. The new provisions on equal pay (still as Article 46) were formally approved by the heads of delegation on 20 February, and constitute the text as finally adopted (see Appendix 1).

What happened after that is by no means clear. It seems likely, however, that it was the need to strengthen the social policy section after the pressures on Spaak already discussed, that caused the equal pay provisions to be shifted to that Title of the Treaty and relabelled Article 119. Either before or after that decision, the whole section on distortions to competition was deleted, and replaced by Article 101 which gave the Commission general powers to deal with such matters.

This transfer goes some way to explaining the unexpected force of Article 119 by comparison with the other social policy articles: it was drafted for a different section of the Treaty and was therefore expected to create stronger obligations. This is exemplified by the obligation to take action 'in the first stage', a phraseology which ties Article 119 to the implementation of the common market, the timetable for which is set out in Article 8. This move from competition to social policy was crucial to the 'bridging' function of Article 119 discussed earlier. It made it possible to direct some of the legal obligation being developed to strengthen the process of economic integration into the arena of social policy.

What is particularly striking about what we know of the debates and manoeuvres which produced Article 119 is the level of abstraction at which they took place. At no time are the interests of women considered even obliquely or the issues of social justice raised. The distance from the reality of work or any real struggle seems complete. However, the potential for a stronger implementation of equal pay was embedded in the history of the article and, paradoxically, in the history of the EC itself. It took activist women to realise these possibilities – and switch the debate from one of economic rationality to a demand for rights.

Notes

1 For accounts of this period see Derek Urwin, *Western Europe Since 1945 – a Political History*, Longman, London, 1989, chs 7–9; and F.R. Willis, *France, Germany and the New Europe, 1945–1967*, Oxford University Press, Oxford, 1968, chs 8 and 9.

2 Pierre-Henri Laurent, 'Paul-Henri Spaak and the Diplomatic Origins of the Common Market 1955–56', *Political Science Quarterly*, vol. 85, 1970, pp. 373–96.

3 Paul-Henri Spaak, *Combats inachevés*, Fayard, Paris, 1969, vol. 2, ch. 39.
4 Robert Marjolin, *Le travail d'une vie*, Editions Robert Laffont, Paris, 1986, ch. 4.
5 Laurent, 'Diplomatic Origins'; Spaak, *Combats*, ch. 39.
6 Interview, Michel Gaudet, Paris, 27 June 1994. Gaudet, head of the legal service in the ECSC, was one of the legal drafters of the Treaty of Rome.
7 Social policy is a blanket term used to describe the kinds of decisions that governments take which affect the welfare of groups and individuals in society. Central to social policy are provisions which deal with income maintenance, housing policy, health care, employment protection, education and family policy. Other policies, for example on immigration and nationality, while not dealing directly with welfare, also have clear social effects and implications.
8 Brian Bercusson, *Human Rights and the European Community: Towards 1992 and Beyond*, European University Institute, Florence, 1989, pp. 9–10.
9 Raymond Rifflet, 'Bilan et evaluation de la politique social communautaire', in *Pour une nouvelle politique sociale en Europe*, J. Vandamme, ed. Economica, Paris, 1984.
10 Using Wolfgang Streeck's terminology discussed in chapter 1, n. 54 this volume, the first would be 'state-building' and the last two 'market-making'.
11 For a personal account which emphasises the pragmatic ethos of the negotiators see Pierre Pescatore, 'Les travaux du "Groupe Juridique" dans la négociation des Traités de Rome', *Studia Diplomatica* (Brussels), vol. XXXVI, 1981, pp. 145–61.
12 Alan S. Milward, *The European Rescue of the Nation State*, Routledge, London, 1992, ch. 1.
13 Doreen Collins, *The European Communities: the Social Policy of the First Phase*, Martin Robertson, London, 1975, vol. 2: The European Economic Community 1958–72, p. 9.
14 Collins, *Social Policy*, vol. 1: The European Coal and Steel Community, pp. 14–23.
15 Archives of the Council of Ministers, Brussels. File CM3/0245. This file details the history of Articles 117–120 as they passed through the negotiating process. A note headed *Dispositions relative à la politique sociale dans le Traité sur le Marché Commun* was sent by Spaak to the Heads of Delegation on 19 January in response to labour movement and other pressure.
16 The full text of Article 117 is as follows:

> Member states agree upon the need to promote improved working conditions and an improved standard of living for workers, so as to make possible their harmonisation while the improvement is being maintained.
>
> They believe that such a development will ensue not only from the functioning of the common market, which will favour the harmonization of social systems, but also from the procedures provided for in this Treaty and from the approximation of provisions laid down by law, regulation or administrative action.

17 The areas specified include: employment conditions, vocational training, social security, health and safety at work, and collective bargaining. For the Commission's attempts to use this Article to expand its competence over issues of migration policy, see chapter 9 this volume.
18 International Labour Organisation, *Social Aspects of European Economic Integration* (Ohlin Report), International Labour Office, Geneva, 1956.
19 See André Philip, 'Social Aspects of European Economic Co-operation', *International Labour Review*, September 1957, pp. 244–56.
20 Philippa Watson, 'Social Security and the European Communities', in G. Whyte, ed., *Sex Equality, Community Rights and Irish Social Welfare Law*, Trinity College, Dublin, 1988, pp. 60–77.
21 Doreen Collins, *The Operation of the European Social Fund*, Croom Helm, Beckenham, 1983, ch. 1.
22 *Informations Sociales* (Paris), September 1958. See especially D. Cépède, 'Les aspects sociaux du Traité de Rome'.
23 Philippa Watson, *Social Security Law of the European Community*, Mansell, London, 1980, ch. 3.

24 Christopher Greenwood, 'Nationality and the Limits of the Free Movement of Persons in Community Law', *Yearbook of European Law*, 1987, pp. 185–210.
25 Collins, *Social Policy*, vol. 2, 1975; John Holloway, *Social Policy Harmonisation in the European Community*, Gower, Farnborough, 1981.
26 Holloway, *Social Policy Harmonisation*, p. 22.
27 Collins, *Social Policy*, vol. 2, 1975, p. 161.
28 John Newhouse, *Collision in Brussels – the Common Market Crisis of 30 June 1965*, Faber, London, 1967.
29 C. Wilfred Jenks, *Human Rights and International Labour Standards*, Stevens, 1960, ch. 6. The full history of ILO 100 has yet to be written. Some glimpses are given in Carol Riegelman Lubin and Anne Winslow, *Social Justice for Women – the International Labour Organization and Women*, Duke University Press, Durham and London, 1990; and in John Mainwaring, *The International Labour Organization, a Canadian View*, Ministry of Labor, Canada, Ottawa, 1986.
30 International Labour Office, 'Equal Remuneration for Men and Women Workers for Work of Equal Value', Report V (1), Geneva, 1949.
31 Jenks, *Human Rights*, p. 92.
32 For texts of the Convention and the Recommendation see *International Labour Conventions and Recommendations 1919–1981*, International Labour Organisation, Geneva, 1982, pp. 43–6.
33 Gaudet, interview, 1994.
34 Madeleine Tribolati, 'Salaires féminins dans les pays du Marché Commun', *Informations Sociales*, September 1958.
35 Claire Laubier, ed., *The Condition of Women in France: 1945 to the Present – a Documentary Anthology*, Routledge, London, 1990, ch. 1.
36 Jane Jenson, 'Changing Discourse, Changing Agendas: Political Rights and Reproductive Policies in France', in M. Katzenstein and C. Mueller, eds, *The Women's Movements of the United States and Western Europe*, Temple University Press, Philadelphia, 1987, pp. 64–88. See also Claire Duchen, *Women and Politics in France 1944–58*, Loughborough University, 1991.
37 See the section on France in the European Commission's 1965 report on equal pay, *Rapport de la Commission au Conseil sur l'état d'application au 31 décembre 1964 de l'article 119 et de la résolution*, V/COM(65) 270 final, 7 July 1965, pp. 21–32. I am grateful to Fabrice Spenninck, formerly of Warwick University, for help with this material.
38 Tribolati, 'Salaires féminins'.
39 The dates on which countries ratified ILO 100 is some indication. Belgium ratified in May 1952 and France in March 1953. Italy and Germany both ratified in June 1956 just as the negotiations on the Treaty of Rome got under way. Luxembourg did not ratify until August 1967 and the Netherlands (along with Britain) not until June 1971.
40 Information from interviews: Joyce Outshoorn, Amsterdam, 23 May 1984; and Evelyne Sullerot, Paris, September 1984.
41 Well organised and referenced documentation on the *travaux préparatoires* exists in the archives of the Council of Ministers in Brussels. One set of files follows the textual history of each article in the Treaty through the various meetings at which it was discussed. Another documents each of these meetings in more detail. Unless otherwise referenced, the material in these pages is taken from the section on Article 119 in file CM3/0245, entitled *Conference intergouvernementale: Historique des articles 117 à 120 du traité instituant la CEE*. I am grateful to the archivists, and especially Mme. Huego and M. Stols, for directing me through the dossiers.
42 S. Neri and H. Sperl, *Traité instituent la Communauté Economique Européenne*, Cour de Justice des CE, Luxembourg, 1960, pp. 299–302.
43 *Le Monde*, 8 September 1956.
44 Debate at this point was complicated by the fact that the nuances and possibilities of the terms were different in the different languages being used. See Roland Van Lint, 'L'egalité des rémunérations entre les travailleurs masculins et les travailleurs féminins pour un même travail', *Cahier du Droit Européen*, vol. 5, 1969, pp. 375–403.

4

The Involvement of Women

Article 119 was rescued in the late sixties from ten years of ineffective implementation by two kinds of activism both generated by women and both located in Belgium. The first came out of direct struggle by women in the munitions factory at Herstal, who tried to use Article 119 in their campaign for equal pay. The second came from the determination of a Belgian advocate and academic lawyer, Eliane Vogel-Polsky. She argued as an academic for a strong definition of Article 119 and then attempted to test out her contentions in the courts. These two events taken together constitute the founding moment of the EU women's policy. Before this combination took effect, however, there had been some developments at the level of the EC institutions on policy towards equal pay.

EC Policy on Equal Pay

As was shown in chapter 3, Article 119 was adopted for tactical reasons and not for its content or the results its application might achieve. It is therefore not surprising that there was no rush to apply it once the Treaty came into force. Even when the Commission was pushing on social policy, there was no particular concern with equal pay. Although some new thinking did take place on Article 119 in the early sixties, this was again for tactical rather than substantive reasons.

Article 119 contained the commitment to ensure application of the principle of equal pay during 'the first stage' of the creation of the common market. When in May 1960, the Council of Ministers agreed to accelerate the first stage (due to end in December 1961) by speeding up the rate at which internal tariffs between the six would be reduced, there was a sudden embarrassment when it was found that nothing had been done to honour the commitment on equal pay and very little on social policy generally.[1]

The Commission used the excuse of acceleration to increase its push on social policy and establish a programme for the application of Article 119. Looking at the personnel involved, we can see that this was still an almost entirely male endeavour. The directory for the social affairs divisions of the Commission shows that all the executive and management posts were held by men; during the same period there seems to have been only one woman on the Social Committee of the European Parliament. The EC's Economic and Social Committee (ESC), formed especially to advise on issues of this kind, had only two women members out of a total of 101.[2]

However, even at this point there are signs of a more significant women's involvement. One of the women on the ESC was Maria Weber from the German trade union federation DGB (*Deutscher Gewerkschaftsbund*) who later played an important role in developing equal treatment policies in both Germany and the EC. And Emilienne Brunfaut, the formidable Belgian trade unionist, later recounted how in 1960 she was invited by François Winck, then one of the Commission officials dealing with social affairs, to an 'informal' meeting to discuss equal pay policy.[3]

Given the degree of incoherence and divergence on the issue of equal pay, the main concern of the Commission seems to have been to devise an acceptable interpretation of Article 119 and a feasible programme of action which could be agreed by all states. In order to set this in motion, Commission officials drafted a Recommendation which was sent to the Council of Ministers in July 1960.[4] The Recommendation quietly sidestepped the 'minimalist' interpretation of Article 119 being favoured by some countries. Instead it embodied an interpretation in line with that of ILO 100 and put the emphasis on direct forms of pay discrimination, particularly those set out formally in collective agreements, minimum pay provisions and administrative instruments. The terms used made clear that the concern here was with situations where there were different men's and women's rates for the same job and where stereotypical assumptions about women were used to justify this. No mention was made of equal pay for work of equal value, faith being kept on this issue with the compromises negotiated at the time of the drafting of Article 119.

The Recommendation was directed at member states and its implicit assumption was that Article 119 conferred a strong obligation on the governments concerned – but nothing more. In 1960 it was not yet clear what the legal force of Treaty articles would be, though the European Court of Justice (ECJ) was on the verge of the classic rulings of the sixties in which it established both the direct applicability of European law and its supremacy over national law.[5] In the event, the Commission took a cautious view and directed its efforts at trying to persuade governments to take the required national action, if possible within common parameters. This caution with regard to the legal force of Article 119 persisted in the Commission and certainly coloured the interventions of its legal staff well into the seventies.[6]

The Commission's Recommendation asked for notification by June 1961 of action taken by governments. By this date not a single reply had been received. A report on equal pay by the European Parliament, which gave a synopsis of the situation in each country, suggests some reasons for this. Not only were the structures (and indeed the cultures) within and through which equal pay provisions had to be enforced extremely diverse, but official reactions to the Recommendation suggested a bewildering array of attitudes on the issue on the part of both bureaucrats and politicians.[7]

Still the problem of the first stage remained, and with governments complaining that the requirements of the Recommendation lacked factual support the Commission decided in June 1961 to set up a special 'Article 119 group'. This consisted of government and Commission representatives, assisted by expert working parties of jurists and statisticians. The documentation does not reveal who the members of these groups were, but since even ten years later few women were involved, it seems highly likely that they were almost entirely male. The reports available suggest that in the early stages at least these groups were for the most part ineffective, with the jurists declaring that it was not their job to interpret Article 119, and the statisticians arguing at length about what kinds of surveys and research might be both appropriate and feasible.[8]

As 31 December came closer, still nothing effective had been done. Yet the matter could not be dropped because the French government was unwilling to allow the move to the second stage of the common market unless there was a more overt commitment on equal pay. A hastily conceived 'political' solution was therefore devised, which involved the governments of the member states formally adopting their own intergovernmental Resolution on equal pay.[9]

In content, the Resolution in the main followed the terms of the Recommendation, setting out limited but apparently 'clear' objectives with regard to direct pay discrimination in formal agreements. On enforcement, however, while maintaining the assumption of member state responsibility, it went further than the Recommendation in proposing a staged timetable for equalising discriminatory wage rates, and for removing discriminatory clauses in collective agreements and other instruments. The process was to be completed by 31 December 1964. The idea of closing the gap between women's rates and men's rates by stages followed both French provisions, the ILO's recommended strategy and, perhaps most significantly, the Community's own experience with regard to the equalisation of tariffs. The Resolution stated, more clearly than the Recommendation, that governments must adopt 'appropriate measures' for the application of Article 119, and that these must be capable of being 'upheld by the Courts'. The drafters also showed some awareness of the kinds of avoidance strategies which might be used if employers really felt under pressure, and made clear that the systematic downgrading of women workers and the application of criteria irrelevant to the job would be incompatible with the terms of the Resolution.

With the Resolution to point to as evidence of good faith on the issue of equal pay, there was general agreement that the transition to the second stage could be made. The Commission was then asked to report at each stage of the timetable set out in the Resolution on the progress achieved. Once the urgency had passed, however, the lack of any real economic or social impetus prevented anything more than a superficial implementation.

The 'Article 119 group' continued to meet – and sometime in the early sixties Brunfaut became a permanent member representing Belgium. Its proceedings became more effective and gradually more accurate material and better statistics were produced. The European Parliament also produced its own surveys on the situation with regard to the implementation of the new provisions. The result was that by 1966 Jacques Ribas, then in charge of social security for the Commission, could begin to make a typology of how states dealt with the issue of equal pay, citing some documentation.[10]

The Commission, in its report after the 'final' 1964 deadline set in the Resolution, stated that there had been 'remarkable progress'. It qualified this, however, by pointing out that in no country was application complete (even in the rather limited terms of the Resolution) and that, in particular, neither Belgium nor the Netherlands had yet established the overall provisions required or a suitable means of judicial remedy.[11] The tone of the report is pleading, and very soon after it was published the Commission became embroiled in the constitutional crisis described in chapter 3. This prevented any immediate follow-up.

The effect of the provisions

What then had been achieved (or revealed) by the mid sixties by this attempt to give some application to the provisions of Article 119? The Recommendation and the Resolution sought to limit the remit of the Article to the issue of direct pay discrimination in formal agreements, and having done that to clarify the definitions and set some precise targets. But even in these definitional terms the issues seem to escape the neat packaging and there is a curious air of unreality in both documents. As a result, and because there appeared to be no enforceable rights at stake, there was little incentive for effective application.

In fact by the mid sixties the political will behind these provisions, never very strong, was actually weakening. The economic justification for social policy (which lay behind the harmonising forms of social policy discussed in chapter 3) was no longer being argued even by France, for the very good reason that French industry was beginning to flourish in the newly deregulating market and had little to fear from competition.[12] The Italian government was certainly pressing on social policy but resented what it saw as the 'over emphasis' on equal pay in what had been agreed.

At the same time, it is abundantly clear from contemporary accounts that at this stage no positive trade union voice was being heard in the European institutions on the issue of equal pay.[13] Since trade unions, inadequately organised as they were at the European level, provided the channels through which in the EC the interests of workers were expected to be expressed, such a silence was damaging. Part of the reason was lack of organisation and insufficient procedures for reaching consensus between the different trade union centres but, as the following section on the Herstal strike demonstrates, equal pay was almost always a difficult issue for trade unions to accommodate. This was particularly true in countries where the unions were heavily implicated in the existing wage structures and workplace practices.

The fact that equal pay provisions were developed as far as they were at this stage at the level of the EC was due partly to the procedural requirements described above and partly to the fact that the (male) social reformers in both the Commission and the Parliament wanted to push forward on social policy generally and saw equal pay as an issue where some movement was possible. However, the lack of real commitment meant that the equal pay provisions constituted an 'add on' and were not incorporated centrally into EC policy. The EC's influential and quite progressive Medium Term Economic Programme issued in 1967 makes no mention of any EC commitment to equal pay, although it does comment quite extensively on the increasing involvement of women in the labour market.[14]

These attempts to define and apply the principle of equal pay – limited in all the ways we have seen – nevertheless began to make it clear that challenging direct pay discrimination, even if effective measures were introduced, was only the start of the process of eradicating gender inequality. The steps already taken, if nothing else, helped to reveal some of the more subtle strategies that were being used to devalue women and their work, and the deep roots of discrimination.[15] It was these realisations, increasingly taken up by those who cared about the substance of the issue, which laid the basis for the expansion of the EC's equal treatment policy in the seventies.

Thus by 1965–66 some of the arguments around equal pay had been rehearsed in a rather academic fashion and a skeleton policy existed at European level for 'tackling' direct pay discrimination. The combination of package deals, procedural demands and inadvertent goodwill had by this stage carried the policy as far as it could go. Real involvement by the supposed beneficiaries (women) was needed to carry it further. This was beginning to develop – symbolically in Belgium itself, at the heart of the EC.

The Herstal Equal Pay Strike

The situation in Belgium in the mid to late sixties with regard to equal pay illustrates some of the changes sparked off by the Europeanisation of political processes. In the sequence which follows, one can trace an almost perfect circular connection between provisions at the EC level, their national impact, the political processes thus produced, and the effect of these on subsequent EC policy making. One striking change from events discussed previously is that for the first time individual women and groups of women are serious players in the game.

The sixties were a time of traumatic change in Belgium. In June 1960, its huge African colony, the so-called 'Belgian Congo', became independent in circumstances which were perceived as wounding both to Belgian pride and economic prosperity. Public humiliations associated with developments in the Congo continued till 1965 and beyond, and can be seen as partly responsible both for the deteriorating relations between the Flemish and Francophone (Walloon) communities in Belgium itself and for the shaky coalition governments which held power during that period.[16]

This crisis situation was compounded by the fact that Belgium's traditional industries were in decline, and that prosperity, such as it was, was shifting from the Francophone areas in the south of the country to Flanders in the north. In these circumstances trade union militancy was high, and the period was racked with industrial disputes during which time the separate interests of the Flemish and the Walloons began to be articulated. In these circumstances both of the main unions, the socialist *Fédération Générale du Travail de Belgique* (FGTB) and the Catholic *Confédération des Syndicats Chrétiens* (CSC), oscillated between direct action on the one hand and a quite high level of cooption on the other.

In Belgium, wage and salary levels were generally fixed through sectoral negotiations between the employers and the trade unions – 'the social partners'. These were then consolidated in national, regional and local collective agreements. The orthodoxy was that government did not intervene but there were various conciliation procedures built into the process which could in the end involve government mediation. The need to respect 'the autonomy of the social partners' was the justification used by the Belgian government to explain why it had not introduced measures to implement Article 119.[17]

However, despite the failure of the government to give an open lead, certain changes were coming about in the way women workers were graded and paid. Both Belgium's ratification of ILO 100 and Article 119 seem to have been influential in this. Employers could see the way policy was developing and were beginning to act to cover themselves without giving too much away. The trade unions were playing the field, sometimes representing the status quo and male workers and sometimes using the equal pay issue as a bargaining counter. Whatever the reason, there is no doubt that the trend in collective agreements in the late fifties and early sixties in Belgium was away from separate men's and women's rates for the same job and towards a single scale for both sexes (*barème unique*). Often, however, this represented little more than a camouflage for the continued downgrading of women's work.[18]

In the engineering sector, of which the Herstal factory was a part, the national agreements drawn up at the end of 1962 had recommended, as an implementation of the principle of equal pay, a single scale for unskilled workers comprising eight grades.[19] Acceptance of this was voluntary but enterprises not complying were urged to achieve the results in other ways. The criteria used in this grading meant that virtually all women would be found in the lowest three grades – and in fact there seems to have been an informal understanding (*hors convention*) that no adult male worker would be placed below grade four.[20] At the end of 1965 this agreement was 'denounced' by the trade unions who opened negotiations by demanding from the employers that the wage rates of the lowest three grades should be raised to that of grade four – a belated implementation of the staged rises proposed in the EC Resolution of 1961.

The management at the Belgian arms factory *Fabrique nationale d'armes de guerre* (FN) in Herstal had not accepted or implemented any of these agreements and furthermore refused dialogue at factory level while national negotiations were going on. Thus the Herstal strike came about, not so much because the situation was unchanging, but because in a situation of some change the expectations of a particular group of women workers had been dashed. That they were aware of this injustice was due in no small part to the international and European developments discussed earlier.

The Herstal equal pay strike took place between 15 February and 9 May 1966. It received widespread publicity and at its peak involved 3,000 women and caused 4,500 other workers to be laid off. Big demonstrations were held in Herstal on 7 April, in Liège on 25 April, and in Brussels on 2 June, after the strike was ended. Women who participated in these events remember them vividly even today and had the feeling that they were involved in something new.[21] At the Brussels demonstration it is said that placards were carried calling for the 'application of Article 119'.[22]

The strike started in the FN factory and then spread to other factories in the region of Liège. Conditions at FN were well known to be appalling: 'women worked in oil and came home black'.[23] Evelyne Sullerot cites the example of Herstal in her books, pointing out that before the strike 'a skilled operative (female) attending three machines earned less than the male yard sweeper and the messenger boy'.[24] Coenen states that the real issue was the undervaluing of women's skills, and that the main reason for the strike was the 'desire of the women to be recognised as skilled workers and graded accordingly'.[25]

The authors of *Grèves féminines*, analysing the origins of the strike, comment that at this stage 'women were not well integrated either at work or in the union'. There was therefore nothing for women 'between the international provisions and the experience of discrimination'.[26] However, although women may not have been integrated into the unions in the sense of being part of the negotiating structures, the FGTB at least was beginning to provide a framework for activity that more specifically represented women's interests.[27]

One consequence of this was that the women's committee of the FGTB held a seminar on 'the problems of women' in Brussels in September 1965. The details of this seminar are not recorded but certainly Article 119 was discussed and certainly women from the FN were there.[28] When they returned they set up a women's committee at the factory. It was this committee which called the strike.

The strike initially was unofficial and activated a quite wide and mainly Francophone women's network (*groupements d'intêrets féminins*) which went well outside the confines of the labour movement. The local FGTB tended to be suspicious of this outside involvement but quite quickly the unions were forced to make the strike official. The authors of *Grèves féminines* give a detailed account of the interaction between the union officials and the women's committee in the factory and of the dynamic between direct action on the one hand and negotiation on the other. The tactics of the women – most of whom were unionised – of acting autonomously and generating new kinds of support, and then bringing that power back into the negotiating process, represented something new in Belgian trade union history.

No breakthrough was possible, however, until conciliation procedures were invoked and the Ministry of Labour became involved. At this point the management gave way. In the end the women won a single grading system, an increase of two francs per hour for all women workers on return, and further wage rises in three stages to October 1968. Brunfaut and Vogel emphasise the shock of this victory which 'only involved women' but which they claim had its effect on the trade unions, on the political and judicial elite and on the European Community itself.[29]

All of this took place amid huge publicity. The strike was widely reported in the French language press and questions were asked and motions submitted in both the Belgian and the European Parliaments.[30] A glimpse of the mood of some trade union women at this point is given at the beginning of Anne-Marie Lizin's book of conversations with Emilienne Brunfaut. Here Lizin describes how she first met Brunfaut 'sitting out on a terrace with other women' during a seminar on trade union strategies in Europe. They were discussing the famous victory at Herstal and the absolute need to spread the action to women 'who had no knowledge of the extent of their exploitation both at home and at work.' Lizin (now a senior politician and former Secretary of State) records how deeply affected she was by this demonstration of women's activism.[31]

The Case of Gabrielle Defrenne

Watching these developments was the Belgian lawyer, Eliane Vogel-Polsky. As a young advocate, specialising in social and labour law cases, she was fascinated by the relation between international labour provisions, Belgian domestic law and collective bargaining. The Herstal women, who seemed to be directly claiming rights under European law, stirred her imagination.[32]

In April 1967, Vogel-Polsky wrote an important article in a Belgian legal journal in which she asked the question: 'should Article 119 be considered as self-executing?'[33] She compared Article 119 with Article 95 (dealing with discriminatory taxes on goods) which the ECJ in the recent *Lütticke* case had ruled gave individuals enforceable rights in national courts if the member states had not taken implementing measures by the specified deadline.[34] What was the difference, she asked? Both articles were clearly worded, established a principle and set a timetable for states to take implementing action. The answer seemed to be that Article 95 dealt with matters considered central to the EC's operations (fair competition and the free circulation of goods), but also that some individuals had cared enough to bring cases demanding their rights. She ended the article with an appeal:

> Why are women who are victims of unequal pay hesitating to invoke Article 119 of the Treaty of Rome, and take action against those discriminations in laws, provisions and collective agreements from which they suffer? (my translation)

One reason for the hesitation became clear as she went round the trade unions suggesting the bringing of a test case. The unions were unwilling to use the law to override the collective agreements which they had helped to negotiate and saw such a tactic as setting a dangerous precedent. Lawyers in the European Commission seem to have been equally discouraging. Even Brunfaut, who had worked hard for the Herstal women and who had a great personal regard for Vogel-Polsky, opposed this tactic.[35]

Meanwhile the Belgian government was in the process of revising all the legal provisions to do with women's paid work, particularly those concerning protection and arrangements for maternity. In the course of this exercise the issue of equal pay was raised – and the necessity to comply with Article 119. Rather than establish a firm commitment to the principal of equal pay in Belgian law, it was agreed to include a brief statement (Article 14) to the effect that 'in conformity with Article 119' all women workers had the right to bring actions in the Belgian courts to apply the principle of equal pay. Belgium would rely on 'jurisprudence and interpretation' from the ECJ rather than attempt its own definitions.[36] Thus just at the time when Vogel-Polsky was searching for her test case, the Belgian government eased the path of legal action on equal pay, in accordance with EC provisions and partly at least in response to her arguments.[37]

In the end Vogel-Polsky found her case not through the big unions in manufacturing, as she had hoped, but in the service sector among air hostesses working for the Belgian state airline, Sabena. Air hostesses were becoming militant about their conditions, and when the main union for airline staff refused to take up women's issues, they consulted a Belgian lawyer, Marie-Thérèse Cuvelliez, about the possibility of forming a separate union.[38]

Cuvelliez reports that the air hostesses were extremely angry about their terms of work with Sabena. Although direct discrimination in basic pay had ended in 1966, their contracts stated that air hostesses must retire at 40 while male cabin crew who did identical work could continue to 55.[39] Apart from the assumptions about women's role which this provision revealed, it also entailed what Vogel-Polsky later called 'a cascade of discrimination'. Retiring at 40 meant that air hostesses lost status and pay, had to search for alternative work at a vulnerable age, and suffered proportionate cuts in severance pay and pension entitlement. This discrimination was later aggravated by an agreement reached in 1969 which gave 'any member of the air crew *except air hostesses*' (my italics) a special deal on pensions amounting to what was virtually full salary on retirement.[40]

The militancy of the women arose from the fact that the stereotypical view of the air hostess as an attractive young woman working for the glamour was ceasing to fit – if indeed it ever had. They were women professionals who felt acutely the loss of status and economic independence which retirement at 40 involved. They may also, given the international character of civil aviation, have been influenced by the actions being taken by air hostesses in the USA against similar degrading assumptions and discrimination.[41]

In February 1968, Gabrielle Defrenne, an air hostess who had worked with Sabena since 1951, was forced to resign, having reached her fortieth birthday. The experience of losing a valued job and facing material insecurity induced in her a profound depression – and anger at the way she had been treated. At the request of Cuvelliez and Vogel-Polsky she agreed to allow her name and her experience to form the basis of a case against Sabena, citing Article 119. She asked, however, that she should not be involved any further once she had briefed the lawyers on her situation.[42]

The *Defrenne* judicial saga started in the Brussels labour court (*Tribunal du travail*) on 13 March 1968.[43] Here Defrenne claimed compensation for loss of earnings in three respects – for salary lost as a result of the discriminatory pay scales in operation before 1966, and for reduced severance pay and pension entitlement due to the different retirement age for women.

The tribunal was clearly unsympathetic and Cuvelliez recalls the advocate for Sabena arguing, to general agreement, that surely it was reasonable for an air traveller (assumed to be a man) to wish 'to have his whisky served by an attractive woman'.[44] The tribunal took more than two years to reach a decision (delays and postponements were frequent in the *Defrenne* cases) and when it did, on 17 December 1970, all the claims were dismissed as unfounded. The case then went on to the labour appeal court (*Cour du travail*) where it was stalled for four years.

While they were waiting for the tribunal judgment, Cuvelliez and

Vogel-Polsky decided to launch another case, this time against the Belgian state for the annulment of the special pensions scheme for air crew adopted in 1969, on the grounds that it was contrary to the provisions of Article 119.[45] This case went direct to the Belgian Administrative Court (*Conseil d'Etat*). Because, as we have seen, there was no direct statement on equal pay in Belgian labour law, Article 119 was the only law which could be cited. The Administrative Court (with remarkable speed in this instance) decided to refer the matter to the ECJ in December 1970. Thus by a fluke this second case, where the substance was less clearly related to pay and to the content of Article 119, in fact reached the ECJ before the main case which had been started two years earlier.

References to the ECJ from national courts had already by this stage become an important part of the implementation of Community law. This procedure (established under Article 177 of the Treaty of Rome) allows a national court, when issues of EC law arise, to suspend a case to pose precise questions to the ECJ. The national court then decides the case in the light of the ECJ's response.[46]

The Administrative Court, when it formulated its questions for the ECJ, did not ask as it might have done if Article 119 was directly applicable or self-executing, either because it assumed that Article 14 of the Belgian law had made it so, or because it did not want to know the answer. Instead its questions concentrated on the scope of Article 119 and in particular whether the phrasing of the article, with its emphasis on the employer/employee relationship, could cover a pension scheme which was part of the general social security system and established by national statute.[47]

The mood of the Court

This case (from now on referred to as *Defrenne 1*), centring on the 1969 pension scheme, was lodged with the ECJ at the end of 1970 and went through written and oral proceedings in the early months of 1971.[48] It found a Court of seven judges from different national jurisdictions and from different branches of law.[49] These judges, who shared the formative experience of the second world war, appear to have been united in their determination to give reality to the process of European integration and to do so through the development of law. As one of the judges then on the Court said:

> this was not a Court engaged in conservation and reaction – the mood was progressive. . . . The events of 1968 did not disturb us very much, we felt we were already acting in the spirit of 1968 . . . We were more concerned about the fact that Britain had been twice refused entry.

Another one said:

> We saw it as our role to keep the Community project together after de Gaulle.

In order to create this strong legal system at the European level, the ECJ had been establishing the supremacy of European law and direct applicability through rulings like that in the *Lütticke* case discussed by Vogel-Polsky. Since the main initial focus of the Community was on the removal of barriers to the free movement of goods, most of its decisions at this stage dealt with tariffs, quotas and taxes. However, the judges had also been concerned to strengthen the rights and benefits of EC nationals working in other member states, and in a general sense to uphold human rights.[50] Thus by the early seventies the Court was already familiar in its jurisprudence with concepts of freedom, non-discrimination and rights – but not till this point had it had to consider how these might be applied to the situation of women in the labour market.

In fact, the *Defrenne 1* reference seems to have taken the members of the Court by surprise. This case involved neither the subject matter nor the personnel with whom they were familiar. However, the Court officials seem to have been intrigued and to have gone out of their way to help the applicants. Cuvelliez recalls that they were helpful and fair and took trouble to explain the procedures. Both the judges I interviewed remembered that she was an effective advocate – and even many years after the case, one recalled that she had worn black trousers in Court! On the whole the judges and the legal officials of the Court seem to have been sympathetic to the case – and critical of the Belgian authorities. There were doubts, however, as to whether Article 119 could really be stretched that far.

No such friendly contacts seem to have been established with the legal service of the European Commission, although the Commission had the right to submit its opinion to the Court on the issues in the case. A woman lawyer, who was a junior member of the Commission team at this point, later admitted that she felt the need for professional reasons to keep her distance from the 'feminist' stance of Defrenne's advocates.

The *Defrenne I* case hinged on the definition and scope of Article 119. The pension scheme complained of was part of the statutory social security regime for employed people and, although both employer and employee paid into it, it was managed by the state. It did however apply to workers performing a particular function – that of air crew. The questions at issue were therefore whether a pension counted as pay, and whether this particular scheme could be regarded as something the employee received 'directly or indirectly from the employer' as Article 119 specified.

Defrenne and her lawyers argued that pensions constituted 'deferred pay' or a 'social salary' and that because of the contributions and the link to the job the scheme fell within the scope of Article 119. The advocates for Belgium argued that employment and social security constituted separate regimes and that there was no clear link between the employer's contribution and the payments made. The Commission lawyers argued the same way, maintaining that Article 119 did not establish a general principle of equality and that neither social security nor pensions came within its remit.

The judgment

These arguments were assessed by the French Advocate-General, Duthcillet de Lamothe.[51] Clearly moved by the case (and unable to resist pointing out that air hostesses in France could never be treated in this way) he ended up by making a tight legal argument. Pensions could be pay within Article 119 if they were paid 'directly or indirectly' by the employer and if they were 'in respect of employment'. Having concluded that pensions paid through a statutory social security scheme fell outside this definition, but that occupational or supplementary schemes might very well fall within it, he proceeded to analyse the scheme in question. Reluctantly (it would seem) he came to the conclusion that this too fell outside, chiefly because the link with the employers' contribution was too distant. In the course of his Opinion he made clear, however, both that he considered Article 119 to be directly applicable (with or without Belgium's Article 14) and that he, personally, wished to see it applied to the maximum.

The Court followed his reasoning and the final and very bare judgment stated that pay as defined in Article 119 did not include benefits from statutory social security schemes nor from special schemes within them, and that therefore discrimination resulting from those schemes was not covered by the article. The Belgian Administrative Court had no difficulty in applying this ruling and consequently dismissed the case.

These judgments, however, left an uneasy feeling. The discrimination in the provision in the Sabena contract was clear, and as Dutheillet de Lamothe had pointed out, the competition element, which had been France's reason for insisting on Article 119 in the first place, was not dead. Article 119, which was drafted in an expansive way, had in effect been given a restrictive reading. Both Vogel-Polsky herself, and the distinguished French lawyer Gérard Lyon-Caen, in comments on the ruling, showed quite clearly how a more progressive judgment might have been arrived at.[52]

As one of the judges in the case commented when interviewed: 'an audacious Court might have ruled that retirement age and pensions are part of deferred pay, but we were not ready to take that decision then.' The question remains, why? For this *was* an audacious Court, as its previous decisions make clear. The answer would seem to lie along two lines – the attitude to women and the attitude to the law.

As Cuvelliez found, the atmosphere in the Court was relatively open – certainly when compared to Belgian procedures. Commenting frankly on the case one of the judges stated: 'We understood the reasons for the Sabena provision, but we felt they were out of date.' This probably sums up the mood fairly well. The judges were aware that attitudes which they held, or were accustomed to, were becoming less acceptable. However, they were unable or unwilling at this stage to move from that to see that rights for women could be a peg upon which they could hang a further extension of European law.

Despite or because of all this, it is clear that the Court was not entirely happy with its decision in *Defrenne 1*. *Defrenne* was 'unfinished business' and when *Defrenne 2* finally came before the Court in 1976 (five of the judges were the same) it made a particularly forceful ruling. But this was after the scope of the EC women's policy had been expanded and second-wave feminism had made its mark. More immediately, when two cases involving a regulation which it was alleged discriminated against women working for Community institutions came before the Court in 1972, the judges overturned the Advocate-General's Opinion to rule in the women's favour.[53]

The *Defrenne 1* judgment did not receive a great deal of publicity – neither Sabena nor the women concerned wished to publicise the outcome. Nevertheless, there is evidence that it was politically important and helped to lay the base for the extension of EC legislation on women's rights in the seventies. For, on the one hand, it made clear that an expansion in the scope of Article 119 was needed if its objectives were to be achieved, and on the other, that given more appropriate legal questions the Court was likely to rule that Article 119 was directly applicable, thus opening the way, as in fact happened, for a stream of new cases.

The case provided a jolt for the Commission, which appeared to be in danger of being outflanked in both legal reasoning and policy development by autonomous and 'unpredictable' women's initiatives. Paradoxically, this opened the way for women within the Commission's own bureaucracy to push for a stronger policy. The judgment also alerted the

Commission to the fact that even if statutory social security schemes were not included as pay under Article 119, occupational schemes might very well be.

Finally, both the Herstal strike and the *Defrenne* saga exposed a level of discrimination against women in employment which blew apart the self-serving platitudes of governments, routinely made at both national and European level during the sixties. What was true of the FN factory and of Sabena was undoubtedly replicated in different ways in workplaces across the EC. This as we have seen was one of the factors which caused second-wave feminism to explode in the member states of the EC in the early seventies – in just those months in fact when the European Court was pondering on the submissions before it in *Defrenne 1*.

Notes

1 An overview of the policy on equal pay during this period is given in Doreen Collins, *The European Communities: the Social Policy of the First Phase*, vol. 2: The European Economic Community 1958–72, Martin Robertson, London, 1975, pp. 84–9.

2 *First General Report on the Activities of the Community* (1 January to 17 September 1958), Brussels, 1958. The full membership of the ESC is given in Annex C, pp. 133–43. Figures given in Appendix 5 of this book show that even today there are few women staff in the top echelons of the Commission.

3 Interview, Emilienne Brunfaut, Brussels, June 1983. She stated in the interview that she received the invitation because 'Winck knew her father'.

4 For text see *Bulletin of the ECs*, no. 6/7, 1960, pp. 46–7.

5 For the political and legal significance of these 'classic rulings' see Joseph Weiler, 'The Transformation of Europe', *Yale Law Journal*, vol. 100, 1991, pp. 2413–19. The main question at issue was whether a Treaty provision was automatically incorporated into domestic law, and thus 'directly applicable', or whether it required implementing legislation from the member states. The ECJ through its jurisprudence gradually ensured that the former rather than the latter principle was applied in the case of European law.

6 See letter to governments from Walter Hallstein, the President of the Commission, 'explaining' the Recommendation. (Archives, Council of Ministers, Brussels, file CM2/1960. Letter dated 28 July 1960.)

7 Bertrand Motte, *Rapport intérimaire sur l'égalisation des salaires masculins et féminins*, Assemblée Parlementaire Européenne, Document 68, 11 October 1961.

8 Motte, *Rapport intérimaire*, p. 10 and *Rapport de la Commission au Conseil sur l'état d'application au 31 décembre 1964 de l'article 119 et de la résolution*, V/COM(65) 270 final, 7 July 1965.

9 For more detailed accounts of these developments see Bernard Fleury, 'A quoi sert l'article 119 du Traité de Rome?', *Directions* (Paris), vol. 99, October 1963, p. 1037; and Ernst Heynig, 'L'égalité des salaires des travailleurs masculins et des travailleurs féminins dans le Marché Commun', *Revue Marché Commun*, 1965, pp. 194–7. The text of the Resolution is given in *Bulletin of the ECs*, no. 1, 1962, pp. 8–10.

10 Jean-Jacques Ribas, 'L'égalité des salaires féminins et masculins dans la C.E.E.', *Droit Social* (Paris), November 1966, pp. 556–61.

11 *Rapport de la Commission*, July 1965.

12 Robert Marjolin, *Le travail d'une vie*, Editions Robert Laffont, Paris, 1986, p. 303.

13 Fleury, pp. 1037–9. For a more general and later account of trade union action at the European level see J. Megret et al., 'Politique Sociale', in *Le Droit de la Communauté Economique Européenne*, Editions de l'Université de Bruxelles, Brussels, 1973, vol. 7.

14 *Premier Programme de politique économique à moyen terme*, Communautés Européennes, Brussels, 1967. pp. 1552–3. See also further discussion in chapter 6 this volume.
15 See Alessandra Codazzi, 'Problems of Equal Pay for Men and Women Workers' in *The Employment of Women – Report of a Regional Trade Union Seminar*, OECD, Paris, 1970 (French original 1968), pp. 131–61.
16 For this whole period see Els Witts and Jan Craeybeck, *La Belgique politique de 1830 à nos jours*, Editions Labor, Brussels, 1987, chs 3 and 4.
17 For the social context in which the struggle for equal pay took place in Belgium see Emilienne Brunfaut and Eliane Vogel, 'Le droit à l'égalité des rémunérations', *Revue du Travail* (Brussels), November 1968, pp. 1505–55. The best descriptions of the strike itself are given in 'Les grèves féminines de la construction métallique et la revendication pour l'égalité de rémunération', *Courrier Hebdomadaire* (Centre de Recherche et d'Information Socio-Politiques – CRISP), nos 325–6, 24 June 1966, pp. 1–52; and in Marie-Thérèse Coenen, *La grève des femmes de la F.N. en 1966*, Pol-His, Brussels, 1991. I have drawn substantially on these works in the account which follows in the text.
18 *Grèves féminines*, pp. 6–8.
19 Collective agreement 26 December 1962 covering the electrical, mechanical and metal-working industries.
20 *Grèves féminines*, p. 9.
21 Interviews: Marijke Van Hemeldonck, Brussels, June 1986; Janine Niépce, Paris, September 1984; Marie-Thérèse Cuvelliez, Brussels, April 1994.
22 *Grèves féminines*, p. 46; interview, Niépce, 1984. I have not, however, been able to find any photographic evidence of the use of this slogan.
23 Evidence from Pierre Verjans, University of Liège; Coenen's *Femmes de la F.N.* gives telling evidence on women's work conditions, pp. 96–9. These were 'not considered a priority' by the social partners.
24 See, for example, Evelyne Sullerot, *Women, Society and Change*, Weidenfeld, London, 1971, p. 128.
25 *Femmes de la F.N.*, p. 104.
26 *Grèves féminines*, p. 17.
27 This seems to have been as a result of Emilienne Brunfaut's greater influence by this stage within the union.
28 *Grèves féminines*, p. 17, n. 2; interview, Eliane Vogel-Polsky, Brussels, June 1983.
29 Brunfaut and Vogel, 'Le droit à l'égalité des rémunérations', pp. 1544–6.
30 One of those who raised the matter in the European Parliament was the Dutch MEP, Henk Vredeling. In the late seventies, when he became EC Commissioner in charge of social affairs, he went out of his way to support further EC legislation in favour of women.
31 Anne-Marie Lizin, *Emilienne Brunfaut*, Archives de Wallonie, Charleroi, 1987, pp. 9–10.
32 Interview, Brunfaut, 1983.
33 Eliane Vogel-Polsky, 'L'Article 119 du traité de Rome – peut-il être considéré comme *self-executing*?', *Journal des Tribunaux* (Brussels), 15 April 1967. By using the term 'self-executing' she was implying that Article 119 should be seen as conveying direct rights to individuals which could be argued in the national courts. It was this view of European law that the ECJ was in the process of developing – but not so far with regard to Article 119.
34 *Lütticke*, ECJ Case 57/65, 1966.
35 Interview, Brunfaut, 1983.
36 The full text reads:

> In accordance with Article 119 of the Treaty establishing the European Economic Community, adopted by the Law of 2 December 1957, any woman worker may institute proceedings in the competent court for the application of the principle of equal pay for men and women workers.

This Article was later incorporated as Article 47bis into a previously existing law on the protection of remuneration (*loi du 12 avril 1965*). This accounts for the fact that Article

14 is normally now given the date of 1965. I am grateful to Jean Jacqmain for sorting out this anomaly for me.
37 The revisions were eventually issued in *Arrêté royal No.40*, 24 October 1967. This included the text of an accompanying memorandum and explanations for the individual articles.
38 This was achieved in 1971 with the formation of the Belgian Corporation of Flight Hostesses (BCFH). An English name was adopted to sidestep the Flemish/Walloon linguistic dispute and to emphasise the international character of the profession. The BCFH was immediately involved in a long-running dispute with Sabena about recognition.
39 Interview, Marie-Thérèse Cuvelliez, Brussels, 20 September 1989. See also Cuvelliez, 'Les femmes ont intérêt à être emmerdeuses' (Women ought to be bloody minded), *Bulletin, Maison des Femmes*, Brussels, February 1978.
40 Eliane Vogel-Polsky (Case note on the *Defrenne 1* judgment), *Journal des Tribunaux*, 1973, p. 92. The pension exclusion is detailed in Article 3 of *Arrêté royal*, 3 November 1969.
41 Flora Davis, *Moving the Mountain*, Simon and Schuster, 1991, pp. 16–25. I am grateful to Fred Halliday for pointing out this possible connection.
42 Interview, Cuvelliez, 1989. Cuvelliez states that Defrenne was not the first air hostess to be forced to resign, 'but was the first to resist'.
43 In 1969 Vogel-Polsky was appointed to a full-time post at the Free University in Brussels. From then on she was unable to appear in court, although she continued to help in the preparation of the cases.
44 Interview, Cuvelliez, 1989.
45 They were particularly angry that this new piece of legislation continued and reinforced discrimination even though the issue of women's rights at Sabena had already been raised. Had this scheme not excluded women it would have made a huge difference to Defrenne's circumstances on retirement.
46 These rulings have the effect of publicly clarifying aspects of EU law which can then be applied by the courts in other member states. The aim is to achieve a 'uniform application' of EU measures. This process, which welds the national and European legal systems together in the implementation of Community law, has been important in expanding the scope of the EC women's policy. For further discussion see Weiler, 'The Transformation of Europe', 1991, pp. 2420–22.
47 The questions were in fact badly drafted and in the case of the last two inappropriate. This is an indication of the newness of the reference procedure and the lack of experience of even the higher courts in dealing with the ECJ.
48 *Gabrielle Defrenne* v. *Belgian State*, ECJ Case 80/70, 25 May 1971. For a full report including the Advocate-General's Opinion see *European Court Reports*, 1971, pp. 445–62.
49 I have drawn substantially in this section on interviews with two judges then on the Court.
50 See Pierre Pescatore 'Les droits de l'homme et l'intégration Européenne', *Cahiers de Droit Européen*, 1968, pp. 629–73.
51 The job of the Advocate-General is to summarise the facts of the case and assess the legal arguments. S/he presents a formal Opinion to the judges, which they can follow, amend or reject. The Opinion is printed with the official report of the case and often provides the most coherent guide to the facts and the issues.
52 Vogel-Polsky, Case note, 1973; Gérard Lyon-Caen, Note, *Revue Trimestrielle de Droit Européenne*, 1972, pp. 110–12.
53 Sabbatini, ECJ Case 20/71, and Chollet, ECJ Case 32/71, 1972. The rationale seems to have been that the EC must not treat its own civil servants worse than they would be treated if they were working for a member state.

5

Negotiating the Equal Pay Directive

The events discussed in the last two chapters laid a base for further developments in EC policy making on women's rights. These took place amid the effervescence generated by second-wave feminism and were given effect during the seventies after a prolonged series of negotiations in Brussels. The result was three Directives, one on equal pay, one on equal treatment at work, and one on equal treatment in social security.[1] These still today encapsulate the essence and particular nature of the EU's policy on women.

Negotiations on these Directives were initiated in a period of political upheaval at both national and international level. This had the effect in the EC of shaking up accepted attitudes and structures, and introducing new personnel into the bureaucracies. One of the effects of this was to alter the balance between social and economic policy which, as was discussed in chapter 3, had been set in the early years. This balance changed again in the mid seventies as economic crisis tightened the purse strings, and political consensus fell away. In the midst of this three new member states, Denmark, Britain and Ireland, joined the Community.

Of all the EC initiatives proposed in the early seventies in the social field, it was those on women's rights which were most fully implemented. Proposals to support migrants or improve industrial democracy lost momentum much sooner. It is the argument of this chapter and the next that part of the explanation for this success lies in the way in which in this period the external force of second-wave feminism acted to empower lone women (and some lone men) within the EC institutions and in national delegations, who were then able to make use of the particular shape of Article 119 to achieve practical gains.

This chapter will first examine the characteristics of this 'new look' Community of the seventies, and then consider the substance of the Equal Pay Directive and how it was adopted. This means looking at the extent of the consensus between states on this issue, the involvement of women, and the nature of the bargains struck. The chapter will end with an examination of the ECJ's judgment in the second *Defrenne* case – the culmination of this phase of policy development.

The New Context for Social Policy

The late sixties/early seventies was a crucial period both for the member states of the EC and for the Community itself. The judges in the ECJ may have taken the events of 1968 in their stride, but this was not the general view. For many in the intelligentsia, the attack on accepted values, the ruthless unveiling of the down side of the 'economic miracle', and most of all the alienation of youth, came as a shock.[2] The signs of financial instability already clear in the US and in France contributed to this malaise.

The effect of this at the level of the EC is illustrated by the Declaration published on 1 July 1968 by the President of the European Commission, Jean Rey, on the occasion of the achievement of the Customs Union. The Declaration, cast in emotive terms, talked of the 'profound economic and social crisis' and of the need for Community action.[3] Raymond Rifflet, writing of the Hague summit of December 1969, refers to the 'anguish' which gripped the Heads of State and Government as they met together, faced with monetary instability and growing socio-economic divisions.[4]

Despite or perhaps because of this, there was a determination to set the EC off on a new course, and in contrast to the earlier years social policy was seen as a necessary element in the package. Part of the reason for this emphasis was undoubtedly the coming to power of the German Social Democratic Party (SPD) late in 1969. The new German Chancellor, Willy Brandt, who had spent the war years in exile in Norway and espoused a much more Scandinavian view of welfare policy, saw his role as healing 'the cracks in the social state' and encouraging a wider participation in industrial and political processes.[5] This affected his input into EC as well as national policy.

The year 1969 also saw de Gaulle finally retire to be replaced by the smooth banker and skilled negotiator Georges Pompidou. Pompidou although irrefutably of the right and well ensconced in power, knew that France's commitment to the EC needed reestablishing, and unlike his predecessor was willing to bargain and accept compromises. He knew too that a revitalised EC was important to France and was willing to lift the ban imposed on British entry in return for certain concessions.[6]

The Hague summit was timed for the point at which the Community was due to move from its transitional stage into full operation. Despite the disarray and considerable awkwardness between the leaders, the summit took some important decisions.[7] It was agreed to open negotiations with the three applicant countries (British membership had been twice vetoed by de Gaulle in the sixties) and to plan by stages the expansion of the Common Market into an Economic and Monetary Union (EMU). The leaders made clear that they realised the Community had reached a turning point and that any further development would require a new political consensus. Social policy was seen as part of this and it was agreed to reform the European Social Fund (ESF) 'in the context of a close coordination (*concertation étroite*) of social policy'.[8] Rifflet commented that it was 'no longer a question of considering the social as a byproduct of the economic' but that competition itself demanded the practical achievement of harmonisation and a proper balance between revenues and the 'diverse national manifestations of the welfare state'.[9]

The close link between the economic and the social was emphasised in a different way in the interim 'Werner' Report which in May 1970 set out the plan for EMU. The report recognised the need for cooperation between unions, employers and social organisations, and stated that 'the combined effect of market forces and of policies devised and implemented by the authorities' should produce growth, employment, stability, the 'narrowing of regional and social disparities' and the protection of the environment.[10] This clear statement of the linking of the economic and social seems finally to have galvanised the Commission into producing in the following year 'Preliminary Guidelines for a Community Social Policy'. Among other things this committed the Commission to making further proposals on 'equal wages' and to taking additional action on women's employment needs.[11]

These advances led to the much more upbeat summit of EC leaders in Paris in October 1972. The summit was called by Pompidou and prepared with extreme care, and it included the heads of the three states due to join in 1973. The summit was designed to demonstrate the 'relaunching of Europe' and both the agenda and the outcomes were effectively controlled by the triumvirate of Brandt, Pompidou and Edward Heath, now representing Britain. A strong commitment to a renewed social policy at the level of the EC was made and the final communiqué stated that 'vigorous action in the social sphere . . . [was] just as important as achieving EMU.' The Commission was instructed to produce an action programme in the social field 'providing practical measures and the means for them' before 1 January 1974.[12]

Significantly, no change was made at this point to the weak Treaty provisions on social policy (and indeed Treaty amendment of any kind does not seem to have been on the agenda), nor were any additional powers given to the Commission. Thus the effective implementation of any new programme would require sustained commitment from the political leadership in the Council of Ministers. There was also considerable ambiguity as to whether these new moves on social policy were due, as Rifflet suggests, to a recognition that further economic integration required greater social coordination (i.e. still harmonising measures) or whether they represented a first attempt to establish a more freestanding social dimension to the EC, which might well include some social measures of the society-creating type discussed earlier.

The Social Action Programme

Denmark, Britain and Ireland formally joined the Community on 1 January 1973. This coincided with the installation of a new Commission, led by François-Xavier Ortoli, which had to incorporate at all levels an adequate number of representatives from the new states. This influx particularly affected DG V where the Irish politician, Patrick Hillery, became Commissioner for Social Affairs, and Michael Shanks, a British economist and author, took over as Director-General. This parachuting in of new personnel to senior positions seems to have caused some disaffection among those already there. However, the new people came with much less baggage from the past, and with in most cases a refreshing attitude to the blockages which had restrained social policy development in the sixties.[13]

The immediate task of DG V was to take up the challenge of the summit and produce an action programme on social policy. Ideas were taken from the 1971 guidelines and at the same time a wide range of people inside and outside the Commission were asked 'what would you like to see done?' One insider commented that the main issues that were highlighted in this process were the needs of women and of non-Community migrants.[14] The newcomers in the Commission seem initially to have been infuriated when told that Community social policy was effectively restricted to employment issues, and the Irish concern with the 'underdog' and with tackling poverty gave a new emphasis. The shake up in personnel and the new mandate created a buzz, and a feeling that social policy had now acquired an autonomous writ and was no longer strictly tied to economic requirements. Guidelines representing a range of ideas were produced in April 1973, and the full Social Action Programme (SAP), proposing actions for the years 1974 to 1976, was adopted by the Council of Ministers on 21 January 1974.[15]

Michael Shanks, who wrote a book on his experiences in Brussels, commented that the SAP represented 'a somewhat disparate package of measures covering a very broad canvas'.[16] Since no additional powers had been given, decisions about what to include were pragmatic. Any major proposal had to be separately argued through the Council of Ministers (where each state effectively had a veto) and thus broad political support was essential. The Paris Summit and the Resolution approving the SAP recommended that Article 235 should be used where necessary as a legal base. Although this in theory would allow measures to be adopted which went beyond the strict remit of the Treaty, each use of Article 235 would require the unanimous agreement of the Council.[17]

Despite these limitations, the SAP proposals took a relatively bold stance, namely that economic expansion was not an end in itself and that it was legitimate for the EC to be involved as appropriate in issues concerning the distribution of resources and the maintenance of social stability. The aim was not to impose uniform social systems on member states but to involve the EC level in establishing minimum standards and ensuring consistency.

Inevitably, given the constraints discussed above, the main emphasis in the SAP was on employment. However, within that focus, the programme put a much clearer emphasis than before on participation, both in the labour market and in industrial relations, and this emerged as the clear theme of the document. Thus, part of the programme involved measures to encourage the participation of excluded groups – for example, women, the handicapped and migrants – while another put the emphasis on measures to improve the quality of the employment experience, and to maintain standards, particularly in the area of health and safety. The stress on the involvement of migrants was particularly striking, and an action programme was envisaged which would improve the position of all migrants and their families, whether Community citizens or not, and 'promote consultation' on immigration policies in general.[18]

Particular emphasis was also given to provisions aimed at giving workers and workers' organisations more rights in, and more information about, the management of industry and of the economy in general. There were also provisions to encourage the greater involvement of the social partners in decision making. The SAP went on to raise more controversial issues (since they fell outside the field of employment) and to propose in particular a Community programme to identify and alleviate poverty; it also sought in a more tentative way to extend the notion of the 'social' to broader areas of policy, for example, social protection, health, education and housing.

The SAP was approved early in 1974. This was before the consequences of the growing recession, exacerbated by the oil crisis of October 1973, had really taken effect. Indeed social measures, including as we shall see the Equal Pay Directive, were passed without too much difficulty in 1974 and in 1975.[19] But from this point on, the twin concerns of inflation and unemployment became all-absorbing, and many of the remaining provisions of the SAP (together with the plans for EMU) were tacitly abandoned. It did not help matters that by the middle of 1974 all three of the leaders who had put together the 1972 package were out of power, and thus both the rationale for the new emphasis on social policy and the commitment to it were more easily forgotten.[20]

So for a brief while, the popular discontent at the end of the sixties accompanied by a particular political conjuncture led to a new emphasis being placed on European social policy. Although this change was quickly undermined, it broadened the scope of what could be contemplated, and established a set of objectives which, however impractical in the new circumstances, laid the basis for Commission action on social policy throughout the seventies and the early eighties. This sequence of events makes clear once again the controversial nature of the 'social' as a component in Community policy.

Against this background definite advances in the women's policy were made. In contrast to other areas of social policy where the debate on legislation was basically between the Commission and the Council, in this case different elements entered in. The fact that quite strong measures in favour of women were adopted in 1976 and 1978, well after the barriers against social measures went up in the Council, clearly indicates that some new combination of factors was affecting the outcome.

The Terms of the Directive

One of these new factors was undoubtedly the existence of committed individuals, mainly women, either in the EC institutions, or doing work for them – lone women as I have called them. One of these was Evelyne Sullerot, the French sociologist whose position and work were discussed in chapter 2. In the mid sixties, Sullerot pioneered the academic study of women's work, teaching courses in Paris and Brussels, and producing in 1968 her influential text *Histoire et sociologie du travail féminin*.[21] This activity brought her to the attention of the Commission, and in 1968 she was asked to prepare a report for DG V on women's employment in the six member states of the EC. This was to be *une étude transversale* (a cross-country study) which would break with the country by country format, normally used, to produce an assessment of overall trends.[22] In the preface to the final report, François Winck, at that point Director General for Social Affairs, wrote that the intention had been to establish 'a Community perspective' (*réflexion Communautaire*) on which to base future policy initiatives.[23]

Drawing on her previous and ongoing work Sullerot fulfilled this brief. She produced a synthesis of existing information and a trenchant analysis. Much of what she said has now become orthodoxy, but at that point and certainly in the EC, she broke new ground by emphasising the structural nature of women's disadvantage, the need for society as a whole to take more responsibility for reproduction and childcare, and the importance of breaking the pattern of job segregation which corralled women in low-pay, low-status jobs. Identifying once again the expanding service sectors as the major present and future employers of women, she commented tellingly that services required servants, and that society had conditioned women to accept that role and status.[24] Her conclusions were that the EC policy must be broadened out from a narrow concern with equal pay, and that women must be 'dispersed' throughout the economy, up all the hierarchies and across every sector.

The report had considerable impact both in the Commission and outside. For the first time a study concerning women was written by someone with expertise who cared about the subject. Nevertheless, looking back from the nineties we can see that there were some crucial absences in the report, reflective of the time and of contemporary consciousness, and thus important in explaining the way EC policy developed. In particular, the limitation of EC social policy to the employment function of women (thus avoiding contentious issues such as male violence, sexuality and abortion) was not challenged, nor were the differences between women, and the implications of these for policy development, examined in any detail. The behaviour of men was not directly discussed, nor the extent to which the demands being made would require substantial changes to men's life patterns and expectations. The report, then, was 'of its time' and geared to push the current thinking forward rather than to challenge it. At EC level it helped to authorise a broader approach to women's employment issues and provided a considerable resource for policy development in the seventies.

The Sullerot report, together with the new concern for social policy, created openings and opportunities in a number of directions. Not surprisingly the fastest movement came in the area of equal pay, where at least some of the issues had been aired and where the political dimensions were well understood.

As so often, in these circumstances it needed someone on the spot to identify possibilities and produce a coherent agenda. In the case of equal pay, the person most clearly responsible for turning opportunities into concrete gains was Jean Boudard, a French official in the division of DG V concerned with wages policy. A mathematician and a jurist, he was well equipped to develop a more forceful stance on equal pay when circumstances allowed.

A comparison of the Commission's 1970 report on equal pay with that produced in 1973 – after the Paris summit and the commitment to a Social Action Programme – illustrates the change.[25] The 1970 report adopted a country by country approach, and every paragraph demonstrated the stalemate then existing on this issue between the Commission and the member states. By contrast, the 1973 report (mostly written it would seem by Boudard) contained a punchy, 'transversal' analysis of the issues – in the Sullerot mode. Adopting a positive not to say combative style, the final section of the report on the one hand threatened that the Commission would take 'infringement actions' against recalcitrant member states, and on the other proposed 'a new Community instrument' to clarify the application of Article 119.[26]

Boudard and others in the Commission's legal service still firmly believed that Article 119 was not directly applicable as between individuals, and that legislation at the national level was required to cover continuing gaps and inadequacies. To force governments to adopt such legislation and to ensure consistency would require an EC Directive – despite the fact that Directives had never before been considered in the social field. However, since the new President of the Commission had let it be known that he favoured 'social' Directives, and since equal pay with its lengthy history was a good issue to start on, a project for a Directive on equal pay was included as a priority item in the 1974 Social Action Programme.[27]

The 1973 report also announced, in a gesture that was to cause alarm to the newly participating British government, that as a result of the *Defrenne 1* case, information on occupational social security schemes in each of the member states would be collected and examined.[28] As has been noted, the Commission (and Boudard in particular) felt that the wording of the *Defrenne 1* judgment meant that occupational schemes (and thus a significant part of pension provision) came within the definition of pay under Article 119, and would therefore be covered by the equality provisions. Thus began the long-running saga, which ended only recently with the *Barber* case and the special Protocol to the Maastricht Treaty, over whether and to what extent different kinds of pension regimes came within the scope of Article 119.[29]

The 1973 report was made public just after the three new member states joined the EC. It announced that an additional study was already being drafted on the situation with regard to equal pay in those states.[30] Since no special transition arrangements in respect of Article 119 had been agreed, they were in fact already bound by the existing policy.

They would also be full participants in any negotiations on future developments.

The proposal

The Commission agreed, therefore, to propose and negotiate for a Directive to carry further the principle of equal pay. Use of a Directive implied the harmonisation of national legislation rather than its replacement with a directly applicable Community regulation. The Directive had to set out clearly what the member states were required to achieve, and establish the minimum standards around which harmonisation was to take place.[31]

These requirements were not something the Commission could agree on its own. The decision to aim for a Directive involved invoking the unique structures set up to develop binding legislation through the EC. These called into play procedures blending the supranational 'European' arenas (principally the Commission and the Parliament) with the more intergovernmental forums (mainly the Council of Ministers with its working groups and special committees).[32] Essentially there were at this time four main stages to the adoption of a social affairs Directive: the preparation of a draft in the Commission (including consultation with relevant 'expert' committees, in this case the Article 119 group); the submission of 'opinions' from the European Parliament (EP) and the Economic and Social Committee (ESC); discussion in the social affairs working group of the Council; and finally decision in the influential Committee of Permanent Representatives (COREPER) and in the Social Affairs Council itself.

This then was the procedure within which the Equal Pay Directive (from now on referred to as the EPD) was discussed, amended and eventually agreed.[33] Looking at the process overall, it is clear that there was a high level of agreement on the adoption of a Directive. The stalement at EC level had gone on for too long and in the new circumstances there were advantages in clarifying the obligations and actions required. A development of this kind was also seen as being advantageous politically, given the greater visibility of women in the domestic political arena and the need to give some recognition to the part women were now playing in the labour force.[34] At a more immediate level, the designation by the United Nations of 1975 as International Women's Year seems to have created a certain sense of urgency. It would be useful for the EC to have 'something to say' at the inaugural conference being held in July in Mexico City.[35]

Parallel with these developments, and for some of the same reasons, there had already been moves on the domestic front to give greater effect to the principle of equal pay. So Britain had adopted carefully guarded legislation in 1970, due to come into effect in 1975, and France had passed a full equal pay law at the end of 1972.[36] Already having their own legislation, these two countries would not be averse to seeing others bound by the same requirements; their main concern would be to ensure that nothing adopted at EC level went beyond their own commitments.

The direct involvement of women in the different stages of policy making was not great. There were certainly more women attending the Article 119 group and Brunfaut was now an experienced member representing the Belgian FGTB. Maria Weber from the German DGB was responsible for putting together the ESC opinion, and women like Sullerot had some influence in the Commission. There were also more women in the national delegations and back home in the ministries. Eliane Vogel-Polsky in addition to her job at the university was now a member of the cabinet of the Belgian Minister of Employment, the socialist Ernest Glinne.

The extent to which this greater involvement made a difference varied with the country, the degree of autonomy accorded, and the people involved. There seems little doubt, however, that most women who participated responded differently to the subject matter from their male colleagues. Both Antonietta Ravasio from the Italian Ministry of Labour, and Claude du Granrut, who remembers shuttling between Paris and Brussels to attend a variety of meetings on equality issues, say that for them pursuing equality for women at this level 'was always more than a job'.[37] Sometimes women speaking out were able to carry a controversial point through commitment and 'the shock factor'. Elizabeth Haines, then a member of the new unit dealing with women's equality in the German Federal Ministry for Youth, the Family and Health, describes how she argued with officials from the Ministry of Labour about whether they should agree to the term equal pay for work of equal value being included in the EPD. In the end the officials gave in: 'they were surprised,' she says, 'by a young thing feeling so strongly.'[38]

Men were still in control, especially in the top echelons of the Commission, in COREPER and at the Council. The 'feel' of equal pay negotiations had, however, changed. No longer was equal pay seen as part of a package deal and no longer were the perspectives entirely male. Women even if not physically there, were for the first time 'a presence'.

The bargains

So to the bargains. The Commission made public its draft for the EPD on 14 November 1973, after consultation with the Article 119 group.[39]

Given general agreement on the adoption of a Directive, the two main points at issue were the scope of the prohibition on discriminatory wage rates and the means adopted for implementation and enforcement. These two aspects were important, since the measures adopted would determine whether the EPD remained an instrument embodying formal equality only, or went beyond this to begin to tackle the substantive problems which created inequality in the first place.[40]

On the question of scope, the main issue was whether to make clear that the equal pay principle embodied in the EPD included equal pay for work of equal value. This was a crucial debate since only if the expanded definition were incorporated would the EPD clearly authorise the comparison of *different* jobs, and thus help to reveal the systematic way in which women's skills and roles were undervalued in traditional pay structures.[41] The Herstal strike, discussed in chapter 4, where the real issue was not equal pay for equal work but the value given to women's jobs, demonstrates the importance of this. The fuller definition was deliberately excluded in 1957 in the negotiations on the wording of Article 119. Were the member states willing to adopt it now – and if so, why?

The term 'work of equal value' was not included in the Commission's draft. The Commission was loyal to the 1957 decision and considered that the 1961 Resolution (which adopted a broad definition while not actually mentioning equal value) was guidance enough. However, the demand for equal value to be included came forcefully from the trade union representatives in the Article 119 group (with Brunfaut in the lead), from the ESC in its opinion (but not from the EP), and from some of the government experts and representatives in both the Article 119 group and in the social affairs working group.[42] By the time the issue came before COREPER, only three governments (Britain, Denmark and Germany) were opposing the inclusion, and by the time of the Social Affairs Council only Britain was standing out. In the end the British representatives gave in and accepted a slightly modified text ('work to which equal value is attributed') in the belief or hope that this would mean that the British Equal Pay Act would not require modification.[43]

There seem to be three main reasons why the member states took this decision. The first concerns clarity and efficiency. There were at the time a number of definitions in being as to what the scope of 'the equal pay principle' was – these were contained in ILO 100, Article 119, the 1961 Resolution, and any domestic provisions which applied. The 1972 French equal pay law, for example, did include an equal value provision, while Article 119, by which they were also bound, did not. It would on the face of it seem to be 'reasonable' for there to be as much congruence as possible between these instruments, if only for the sake of those devising national measures of implementation.

This factor alone would certainly not have proved decisive, if counter considerations had been strong. However, the more expansionist view seems also to have been endorsed by those with a some practical experience of applying such measures, namely the majority of the trade union representatives and some at least of the government experts. Neither the Commission nor the EP seems to have drawn on this kind of experience in making its recommendations.

However, even this would not have been decisive if senior government representatives had opposed the measure for strongly held political or financial reasons. But in fact there does seem at this stage to have been a real, if limited, desire to do something about (if not *for*) women, and in this sense the evidence about the new role of women in the labour market may well have been important. It must also be remembered that this was 1974, when mainly social democrat governments were in power, all of whom had been shaken by the social unrest of the sixties. Even the more right wing French government had already conceded the issue of equal value in its domestic legislation. There seems to have been sufficient understanding in the delegations, and perhaps this was where the greater involvement of women was most significant, that without the reference to equal value, the measure would have a much reduced significance. Even the British representatives, displaying already the compulsive preoccupation with detail for which they were later to become famous, in the end were willing to compromise.[44]

The other main issue concerned implementation and enforcement. Initially the Commission seems to have thought in terms of a fairly simple Directive supplemented by a European framework agreement (*accord-cadre européen*) to be negotiated and approved by the trade unions and the employers.[45] This proposal, which it was hoped might mark the beginning of collective bargaining at the EC level, had to be abandoned when it was met with hesitation on the part of the trade unions and opposition from the employers.[46] This established a pattern that was to be repeated with great consistency over the next twenty years.

In the end, enforcement and monitoring had to be fully covered in the EPD itself. The Commission's initial proposals were strong and required governments to ensure application and judicial remedy, to provide for information, monitoring and sanctions, and to prevent victimisation. A great deal of debate occurred over each of these items. Here the governments were much less willing to be generous, especially as they knew that whatever they did agree would be enforced through the strong system of Community monitoring. In the end a much greater degree of flexibility was introduced, allowing governments to achieve these objectives 'in accordance with their own national circumstances and legal systems'. The arguments appeared rational, given that the EPD was to be applied in nine different jurisdictions, but it was also clear that any dilution of strict and precise requirements ran the risk of enmeshing the equal pay provisions in just those structures which had produced and maintained inequality.

The EPD was adopted on 17 December 1974 and states were given one year in which to comply with its provisions.[47] In many ways the EPD seemed an appropriate addition to Article 119: embodying both its economic and social origins and continuing the contestation between patriarchal and women-centred types of agency. On the other hand, it had been adopted in what was virtually a closed system involving only very indirect forms of consultation and representation – a fact that would undoubtedly affect its usefulness to women. It is also relevant that those most involved in the negotiations were professional women with only limited links to other strata and groups.

The Second Defrenne Case

While the EPD was being negotiated and adopted, the second *Defrenne* case (from now on referred to as *Defrenne 2*) was working its way through the Belgian appeal system. This case, as explained in chapter 4, was in fact the first case that Vogel-Polsky and Cuvelliez initiated, and dealt with loss of earnings suffered by Defrenne as a result of a variety of discriminatory practices. After four years the Belgian *Cour du travail* rejected all claims except that concerning the sum of 12,716 Belgian francs lost by Defrenne between 1963 and 1966, because of the different wage rates for men and women then applied by Sabena. Since this claim referred to a period before Belgium's Article 14 came into force, the Court made reference to the ECJ asking whether Article 119 was directly applicable and, if so, since what date. This case thus gave the ECJ the chance, if it so wished, to complete the 'unfinished business' of *Defrenne 1*.

Defrenne 2 was heard in very different circumstances from the earlier case, and Cuvelliez comments that this second case appeared from the beginning to be being taken much more seriously.[48] The judges were influenced by the EC's new emphasis on social policy and by the fact that by the time they made their final ruling two additional Directives on the subject of women's equality had been adopted by the Council. The Court was still in expansionist mode both in the area of protecting human rights and in its concern to give real implementation to Community provisions. As in the first case, the subject matter and the fact that women were involved aroused an emotional response. One of the judges recalls how at the oral hearing the air hostesses sat in the front row in their blue uniforms. 'Judges are impressionable people' was his comment.

In ECJ proceedings, not only the Commission but also the member states have the right to make submissions. It is striking that in *Defrenne 2* none of the original six took advantage of this, and that of the new members only Britain and Ireland did so. The defendants, Sabena, appear to have made no submissions until the oral hearing. Thus in the written evidence, the opposing arguments were made by Defrenne on the one hand (represented by Cuvelliez in consultation with Vogel-Polsky) and the representatives of Britain and Ireland on the other. The Commission stood somewhat uneasily in between, not wishing to be associated with the restrictive arguments of the new member states but by no means supporting the Defrenne side either.

The arguments for Defrenne rested on the contention that she had an individual right to equal pay based on the direct applicability of Article 119 and on the Belgian Article 14. This was justified on the grounds set out by Vogel-Polsky in her 1967 text, namely that Article 119 was 'clear and simple' and that the Court's jurisprudence in other cases implied direct applicability. Underlying all of the arguments made here was the demand that issues to do with women should be given equal importance to other areas of the Treaty and be treated with similar legal rigour.

Britain and Ireland argued exactly the reverse, that the adoption of the EPD had confirmed that Article 119 created obligations for states only and that it could not therefore be considered directly applicable in any sense. Both states also claimed that any attempt to make direct rights under Article 119 retrospective would have disastrous economic consequences.[49]

In response to this debate the Commission stuck to its long-held view that Article 119 was directed principally at states and could not therefore be directly applicable. It did, however, seek to modify this somewhat by saying that it could create rights for individuals who were employed in the public sector (vertical direct effect).[50] In arguing in this general way, the Commission seems to have been influenced by the importance of the EPD so recently adopted, and its desire not to see this achievement downgraded.

These then were the arguments with which the Advocate-General, Alberto Trabucchi, had to deal. He opened his opinion by referring both to the 1972 Paris Summit (where the social purpose of the EC had been demonstrated) and to the concern of the Court to protect human rights within the Community. In so doing he was clearly flagging up the change in the political climate. He also emphasised the position of Article 119 in the social policy section of the Treaty and argued from this that it must be considered to have a social as well as an economic function. The central question then, as he saw it, was whether Article 119 was 'clear enough and sufficiently precise' to be directly applicable. On this point, he accepted the Vogel-Polsky argument, while noting that because of the relatively narrow scope of Article 119 the circumstances in which direct applicability could be used would be limited. Finally, he was very rigorous on dates of application. The direct effects of Article 119 would apply from January 1962 for the original members and from January 1973 for the new ones. Trabucchi was not swayed by the appeals from Britain and Ireland. 'Arguments of this kind, however pressing on grounds of expediency', he said, 'have no relevance in law.'

In its judgment, delivered on 6 April 1976, the Court developed and expanded this Opinion and in one very important respect reversed it. There is a clear sense here that the 'social' is being taken seriously and a chance being seized to expand both the field of action of the Court and of the EC itself. By this stage there was no reluctance on the part of the Court to use women for this purpose and the judgment in this case can be classed as audacious. It should be noted, however, that the Court was responding to events and trends and consolidating them, rather than establishing a new direction, as has sometimes been argued.

The judgment itself is well known. The Court ruled that Article 119 was directly applicable, that it had both economic and social relevance and formed 'part of the foundations of the Community'. The Court went on to make a distinction between 'direct and overt' discrimination which could be distinguished using Article 119 alone, and 'indirect and disguised' discrimination which would need further implementing measures. Direct applicability would prohibit the former but not necessarily the latter, though no clear line was drawn.

The judgment agreed with Trabucchi's Opinion thus far but then parted company on the issue of retrospection. Raising the question of 'legal certainty', the judges took the Commission to task for misleading both states and individuals by maintaining that Article 119 was not directly applicable, and by failing for so long to bring Article 169 proceedings (infringement actions) against recalcitrant states. Thus the 'parties concerned' might well have been misled into thinking that they could continue with practices contrary to Article 119, if this had not yet been incorporated into national law. As a result of these circumstances, the Court decided to limit the retrospective effect of the ruling, and thus of Article 119. Direct applicability would apply only to cases brought after the date of the judgment, except for those who had already initiated claims.

The Court here seems to have been attempting to achieve a balance. The judgment itself was radical and far-reaching, and justified Vogel-Polsky's ten-year-long campaign. The decision to find Article 119 directly applicable established a legal base which helped the policy survive in the difficult years to come. It also broke new ground in making European social law directly binding on relations between individuals. Walter Van Gerven, later himself an advocate-general in the ECJ, wrote that in his opinion this judgment had a constitutive impact (*un effet constitutif*).[51]

Although it was unusual to set limits on retrospection in this way, the decision to do so appears to have been a political act to ensure acceptance of the judgment. It seems likely that the judges used the assertions of Britain and Ireland as a convenient rationale for doing this, without necessarily accepting their predictions about the economic consequences of retrospection. In all of this it is quite clear that the judges, however impressionable, were more concerned about the need to make a 'balanced' judgment than they were to protect the rights of women who, it could be argued, had equally been misled by the Commission's statements. In this connection it is important to note that from all her three cases, Gabrielle Defrenne, despite the manifest discrimination from which she had suffered, received only the sum of 12,716 Belgian francs (approximately £240), finally awarded to her by the Belgian courts after this judgment.

The issue of equal pay has one very important characteristic and that is that it is wholly conceptualised within the field of employment. It involves and affects only those engaged in paid work. As such it is a relatively easy issue to be taken up through the EC, although as we have seen it still raises contentious issues. During the course of the equal pay negotiations there were constant reminders from Sullerot, the Commission and in the end even the Court, that this was not a sufficient policy to tackle women's inequality. It needed to be expanded. The next two Directives, while remaining within the employment field, went much wider and began to raise issues such as childcare and dependency, which crossed the public/private divide and were therefore more controversial.

Notes

1 Directive 75/117/EEC (equal pay); 76/207/EEC (equal treatment at work); 79/7/EEC (equal treatment in social security). See Appendix 2 for full references.

2 For a thoughtful retrospective on the significance of May '68 see Daniel Singer, 'Twenty Years On – May '68 Revisited', in J. Trumpbour, ed., *The Dividing Rhine – Politics and Society in Contemporary France and Germany*, Berg, Oxford, 1989, pp. 29–46.

3 The full text of the Declaration is given in *Bulletin of the ECs*, vol. 1, no. 7, July 1968, pp. 5–8. For an analysis of the changing role of the Commission during the sixties see Christoph Sasse et al., *Decision Making in the European Community*, Praeger, London, 1977, ch. 4.

4 Raymond Rifflet, 'Bilan et evaluation de la politique social communautaire', in J. Vandamme, ed., *Pour une nouvelle politique sociale en Europe*, Economica, Paris, 1984, p. 21. Rifflet states that he attended the Hague summit, presumably as part of the Commission delegation.

5 Willy Brandt, *My Life in Politics*, Penguin Books, London, 1992 (German edition 1989), chs 2 and 4.

6 For an account of Pompidou's background and attitudes at this point see Jean Charlot, *The Gaullist Phenomenon*, Allen and Unwin, London, 1971, pp. 178–86.

7 The full text of the summit communiqué together with other relevant documentation is given in *Bulletin of the ECs*, vol. 3, no. 1, January 1970, pp. 7–18. For an evocative account of the summit itself see Uwe Kitzinger, *Diplomacy and Persuasion – How Britain Joined the Common Market*, Thames and Hudson, London, 1973, pp. 68–72.

8 The agreement to reform the ESF was in response to a long-standing demand from the Commission. The reference to *concertation* was something new.

9 Rifflet, 'Bilan et evaluation', p. 22.

10 'The Establishment by Stages of Economic and Monetary Union in the Community', (interim Werner Report) *Bulletin of the ECs*, Supplement no. 7 of 1970, p. 7. When the final report came out, however, the unions noted that no social measures were actually included in the plan.

11 *Bulletin of the ECs*, Supplement no. 2, 1971, pp. 46 and 60.

12 An account of the preparations for the summit and the text of the final communiqué are given in *Bulletin of the ECs*, no. 10, 1972, pp. 9–26.

13 Information in this and the following paragraph is drawn from interviews with senior Commission civil servants working in DG V in the seventies.

14 It is typical of Community thinking at this point, and indeed until very recently, that there appears to have been no awareness of the fact that there was an overlap between these two categories, in the sense that inevitably some 'women' would also be 'non-Community migrants'. See chapter 9 this volume for a fuller discussion.

15 For full texts see *Bulletin of the ECs*, Supplements no. 4 of 1973 and no. 2 of 1974.

16 Michael Shanks, *European Social Policy Today and Tomorrow*, Pergamon Press, Oxford/New York, 1977, p. 10.

17 The full text of Article 235 reads:

> If action by the Community should prove necessary to attain, in the course of the operation of the common market, one of the objectives of the Community and this Treaty has not provided the necessary powers, the Council shall, acting unanimously on a proposal from the Commission and after consulting the European Parliament, take the appropriate measures.

18 *Bulletin of the ECs*, Supplement 2/74. pp. 8 and 23–5. It should be remembered that the SAP was drawn up well before the entry of Greece, Portugal and Spain into the EC and that at this stage the term 'non-Community migrants' covered migrants from those countries as well as those coming from further afield.

19 Shanks, *European Social Policy*, pp. 15–16.

20 Heath was defeated in the February elections, Pompidou died of cancer in April and Brandt resigned in May after a spy scandal. The British Labour Government which came to power in 1974 was far too preoccupied with renegotiating the terms of Britain's entry into the EC to be concerned with the implementation of social policy.

21 Evelyne Sullerot, *Histoire et sociologie du travail féminin*, Editions Gonthier, Paris, 1968.

22 Interview, Evelyne Sullerot, Paris, September 1984.

23 Evelyne Sullerot, *L'emploi des femmes et ses problèmes dans les états membres de la Communauté Européene*, CEC, Brussels, 1970. English summary, no date, probably 1973.

24 Sullerot, *L'emploi des femmes*, pp. 44–5.

25 *Rapport de la Commission au Conseil sur l'état d'application au 31 décembre 1968 du principe d'égalité entre rémunérations masculines et féminines*, SEC (70) 2338 final, 18 June 1970; 'Report of the Commission to the Council on the Application of the Principle of Equal Pay for Men and Women: Situation on 31 December 1972', SEC (73) 3000 final, 18 July 1973.
26 Report of the Commission, 1973, pp. 44–5. Under Article 169 of the Treaty of Rome, the Commission can take infringement actions (including recourse, if necessary, to the European Court) against member states for failure to comply with Community obligations. Infringement actions had been used in the sixties, but infrequently; they seem never to have been contemplated with regard to Article 119 until this point.
27 Interview, Edwin Fitzgibbon, Brussels, September 1986.
28 Report of the Commission, 1973, pp. 13–14.
29 *Barber*, ECJ Case C-262/88, 17 May 1990. In this case the ECJ finally ruled that occupational pensions did constitute pay within the meaning of Article 119. In the Protocol to the Maastricht Treaty, 'Concerning Article 119', the member states preempted a further ruling by the Court, by stating that this decision only applied to benefits accruing for periods of work *after* 17 May 1990, except for people who had initiated claims before that date. By this means they ensured that the effects of the judgment would only be felt gradually over a period of some forty years.
30 This report when published showed a high level of wage rate discrimination in Britain and Ireland, much less in Denmark. 'Report of the Commission to the Council on the Application of the Principle of Equal Pay for Men and Women in Denmark, Ireland and the United Kingdom: Situation on 31 December 1973', SEC(74) 2721 final, 17 July 1974.
31 For more information on the use of Directives in this context see John Usher, 'European Community Equality Law: Legal Instruments and Judicial Remedies', in C. McCrudden, ed., *Women, Employment and European Equality Law*, Eclipse Publications, London, 1987.
32 For a detailed account of how this 'blending' took place in the early seventies see Glenda Goldstone Rosenthal, *The Men Behind the Decisions*, Lexington Books, London, 1975. Not a woman is mentioned from beginning to end of the book and the title is thus well justified.
33 The analysis in this section relies heavily on interviews (some of which were off the record) and on access to semi-restricted material, for example, minutes of the social affairs working group.
34 Niels Ole Anderson who was Denmark's labour and social affairs attaché in Brussels from 1973, comments that in general equality legislation went through more easily than other areas of social policy 'because of the strength of the women's movement at that point'. (Interview, Copenhagen, April 1983)
35 Jacqueline Nonon is insistent upon the importance of this for at least the first two Directives. (Interview, Paris, September 1984)
36 Equal Pay Act 1970, printed as Schedule 1 in Sex Discrimination Act 1975; *Loi no. 72–1143 du 22 décembre 1972 relative à l'égalité de rémunération entre les hommes et les femmes.*
37 Interviews, Claude du Granrut, Paris, January 1984, and Antonietta Ravasio, Rome, September 1983. The pattern of Ravasio's participation in the negotiations is interesting. She attended both the Article 119 group and the social affairs working group for the ministry. She 'advised' the Italian representative at COREPER but was not present at the final Council meeting.
38 Interview, Elizabeth Haines, Bonn, May 1983.
39 Proposal for a Council Directive on the Approximation of the Laws of the Member States concerning the Application of the Principle of Equal Pay, COM(73) 1927 final, 14 November 1973. The legal base was given as Article 100 rather than Article 235 as proposed in the SAP. This underlined the fact that equal pay was being seen as an integral part of the common market, and not as something tacked on.
40 For a discussion of the distinction see Jeanne Gregory, 'Formal or Substantive Equality: the Future of Protective Legislation', Middlesex Polytechnic Occasional Paper, no. 3, 1981.

41 For a full discussion of the significance of the work of equal value definition in the EC context see Beverley Jones, 'Working Document in Connection with the Memorandum on Equal Pay for Work of Equal Value', Equal Opportunities Unit, CEC, February 1993, V/6108/93.
42 *Official Journal*, No. C 13/5/74 pp. 43–7, (EP Opinion); *Official Journal*, No. C 26/7/74 pp. 6–9, (ESC Opinion).
43 The British representative read into the Council minutes this understanding. This did not prevent the Commission at a later date bringing a (successful) infringement action against Britain on the issue of equal value.
44 It seems also that the British were anxious to see the Directive go through as on their understanding of the relevant law this would postpone the need to comply with Article 119 from January 1973 when they entered the EC to February 1976 when the EPD came into force.
45 See 'Proposal for a Council Directive', p. 3 and 'Report on Denmark, Ireland and the UK', p. 52.
46 This was made clear, for example, at the consultative meeting of the Article 119 group on 29 October 1973.
47 Council Directive of 10 February 1975. For full reference see Appendix 2.
48 Interview, Marie-Thérèse Cuvelliez, Brussels, September 1989. For the full proceedings of the case, including the Advocate-General's opinion, see *Gabrielle Defrenne* v. *Société Anonyme Belge de Navigation Aérienne* (Sabena), ECJ Case 43/75, 8 April 1976, *European Court Reports*, 1976 1, pp. 455–93.
49 Britain claimed that the textile industry would be devastated, and Ireland that the amount equal pay would cost was equal to three years of Ireland's allocation from the Community Regional Fund. The dilemma for the two countries was that the more they emphasised the costs involved the more they revealed the widespread nature of discrimination.
50 The ECJ by this stage had begun to develop its line of argument which established that even Community provisions that were not in themselves directly applicable could have some direct effects and create certain rights for individuals. A distinction was made in this respect between vertical direct effect in the public sector where the state was the employer, and horizontal direct effect between individuals in the private sector (for example, between employers and employees). The Commission was here suggesting the former but not the latter.
51 Walter Van Gerven, 'Contribution de l'arrêt Defrenne au développement du droit communautaire', *Cahiers de Droit Européen*, 1977, pp. 131–43.

6

Extending Equality

The two important European Directives on equal treatment for men and women at work and in social security were negotiated and adopted between 1974 and 1978.[1] This same period saw the consolidation and extension of the women's movement across Europe, and the continuation of its many-pronged attack on the interlocking cultures and structures of male domination. As discussed in chapter 2, this developed in a variety of forms, ranging from small group work and consciousness-raising to dramatic and striking public events. The main emphasis in this activity was on sexual politics, and in particular on issues involving violence against women and reproductive rights.

Although none of these concerns directly entered into the negotiations for either Directive (nor would have been considered particularly relevant) it seems likely that the decision-making process was indirectly influenced by this publicly demonstrated anger. The account of feminist politics in Italy, given in chapter 2, gives some indications of the effects at national level. Thus the political environment created by the vigour of the women's movement should be seen as providing at least part of the explanation for the continued expansion of the EC level women's policy. This momentum was especially significant since the late seventies was a period when the impetus behind European integration was generally in decline.[2]

The two new Directives, dealing with working conditions and social security, were firmly rooted in the concept of equality – or equal treatment as the EU prefers to call it – and incorporated a ban on both direct and indirect discrimination. Equal treatment and non-discrimination were already familiar EC concepts, and lay at the base of the whole attempt to create the common market.[3] The concept of indirect discrimination, applying to situations where apparently neutral measures produce discriminatory effects, was by the early seventies being developed and applied by the European Court of Justice (ECJ).[4] Law based on equality or equal treatment may need to provide for derogations or exceptions to its provisions. The EC practice up to this point in the spheres of trade and free movement had been to draw such exceptions as narrowly as possible.

To a certain extent, therefore, the new Directives fitted into an already existing framework, and used terms and a conceptualisation which would have been familiar to the negotiators. Nevertheless, extending these principles to deal with discrimination on grounds of sex and gender constituted a significant expansion in scope, the implications of which remained unclear. Applying equal treatment to goods was sufficiently complex: applying the same principle to living human beings with direct connections to the political arena became instantly more tangled and the outcomes less predictable.

John Pinder, writing in 1968, described the emphasis on the removal of barriers and on non-discrimination in the early actions of the EC as 'negative integration'. In a perceptive essay, he predicted that unless the Community proved also able to develop 'positive integration', which would involve the adoption of common policies and a 'planning ethic', the project would become distorted. The effect would be that the consequences of market integration and planning for growth would either be left to the individual member states or be patched together through intergovernmental bargaining. He saw political will as crucial for the development of positive integration, and believed it to be in most instances and on most issues lacking.[5]

This analysis has relevance for the development of the women's policy. These first three Directives are based on the principles of equal treatment and non-discrimination, which are given the relatively strong formulation which had proved necessary to remove barriers and create a free market in the economic sphere. However, a positive policy towards women's generally subordinate role in the field of employment would involve, in addition to the removal of barriers, some forms of special treatment: for example, positive action and transitional measures to compensate for past disadvantage, together with a careful consideration of policy towards maternity and the role of men and women in childcare.

As discussed in chapter 1, the balances to be struck between equal and special treatment in a strategy for women's empowerment raise questions which have been the subject of debate and controversy among feminists, and to which there are no easy answers. Suffice to say for the moment that, in accordance with the paradigm put forward by Pinder, the EC negotiators showed little willingness at this stage to develop 'positive' policies for women alongside the 'negative' ones concerned with non-discrimination and the removal of barriers. However, because of the degree of mobilisation, pressure for such policies surfaced at various points and in various ways both during the negotiation of these

Directives and after. It was, indeed, this conflict that was primarily responsible for the deadlock over policy making on the women's programme in the eighties.

Some of the major controversies on these issues arose as a result of the decision to include social security within the scope of the equality principle. This sprang directly from the ECJ ruling in *Defrenne 1*, which took the position that statutory social security schemes fell outside the scope of Article 119, thus requiring action by secondary legislation. For occupational schemes to be included, but statutory schemes not, seemed to the Commission to be untenable and thus social security was included in the initial drafts for a further Directive. The area of social security was by no means unknown in EC policy making since the free movement of labour already required equal access to social security benefits for migrant workers under Article 51 of the Treaty of Rome.[6] Nevertheless, the Commission's proposal to include social security in sex equality legislation proved deeply controversial, and both enactment and implementation were substantially delayed.

The negotiations for these Directives followed the pattern set out in chapter 5. However, the issues, the balance of interests, and above all the changing context, made for significant differences.

The Equal Treatment Directive

In the debates on the Equal Pay Directive, the link between the proposed measures and women's actual or potential labour market participation was never directly articulated, perhaps because equal pay was an established issue and the arguments were well rehearsed. In the case of the Directive on equal treatment at work (from now on referred to as the Equal Treatment Directive or ETD) the situation was somewhat different. This was a new measure and its rationale needed to be spelled out. Its roots in the changing labour market situation, and in the perceived need to expand and maintain the participation of women workers, were explicit and can be traced. The fact that such an analysis could now be made owed a great deal to the activities of 'reasonable feminists', discussed in chapter 2. From this point of view, the move from equal pay to equal treatment constituted a change in emphasis from a concern with the situation of women already in the labour market, to what was needed to attract more women in.

The origins of the ETD go back to the Medium Term Economic Programme (MTEP) referred to earlier. This, written in 1967, and drawing on the kind of material discussed in chapter 2, stated quite clearly that encouraging women into the labour market constituted the best way in the medium term to increase the supply of workers, and that a policy should be developed to enhance this and make it easier for women to transfer from one type of activity to another. The Programme noted tax and social security measures which discouraged women from working, and recommended better childcare facilities and the development of part-time work to enable married women 'to reconcile family responsibilities with professional activity'.[7]

It seems to have been this analysis and the interest it aroused which eventually led the employment division in DG V to commission the Sullerot report, discussed in chapter 5. Sullerot put considerable emphasis on women's caring responsibilities and on what was needed to enable women to manage these while taking up paid work. This emphasis was echoed by Winck in his preface. Developing the theme of women's 'double burden', he suggested that initiatives should be taken at EC level 'to improve the integration of women in economic life, in particular mothers who desire economic activity'.[8]

The person who took responsibility for this issue in the employment division of the Commission, and who became increasingly *engagée* in the process, was Jacqueline Nonon, a French official who had been with the Commission since 1958.[9] When Sullerot was asked, soon after the publication of her report, to submit policy proposals to the Commission, it was Nonon that she consulted.[10] What exactly they proposed is not recorded, but it was presumably their influence, and that of the report itself, which led the 1971 guidelines on social policy to include for the first time a view of women's work which went beyond equal pay. The section on 'better employment' listed a range of measures which needed to be adopted to improve the employment situation for women, including those which, echoing the MTEP, would allow 'work away from home to be reconciled with family life'.[11]

This use of the term 'reconcile' to link the two sides of women's lives seems to have been adopted here to stress the employment orientation of any policy initiatives which appeared to impinge on or take a position towards the domestic sphere and family life. In the Social Action Programme the same term was used twice, once in a more gender-neutral sense (directed at *all* those with family responsibilities) and once with reference to women only.[12]

By this stage the policy options were becoming clearer. Women's participation in paid work could be increased and enhanced, it seemed, by going beyond the issue of pay, and prohibiting discrimination on grounds of sex in areas such as selection procedures, training provision, social security entitlement, dismissals and so on. Such measures could be supplemented in two ways: by various forms of positive action (for example, schemes to train women for non-traditional jobs) and by special measures which would help 'reconcile' paid work with family responsibilities (for example, measures to encourage parental and family leave or the provision of childcare facilities). These latter measures could be designed primarily for women, or be geared more generally to encourage men to participate in caring. The drive behind the policy at this stage came from the fact that it seemed both to satisfy the needs of planners and contribute to women's growing demand for independence. However, the measures became increasingly controversial the further they moved away from a fairly narrow definition of equal treatment in the workplace.

Not till after the SAP was approved was there talk of a second Directive. Nonon was surprised, as till then she had been thinking of at most a Resolution. Once more the need to have a programme for UN International Women's Year seems to have been of crucial importance. Nonon's personal agenda at that stage, she recalls, was to encourage action in the field of training and over childcare facilities.[13]

The 'ad hoc' group on women's work[14]

In order to prepare for a Directive, Nonon needed a group to consult with – a body similar to the Article 119 Group, but dealing more generally with women's work. Since no such group existed, it was necessary to construct it from scratch. Normal procedure was for the Commission to request governments to nominate representatives for such 'ad hoc' groups, usually independent experts or civil servants from appropriate departments. In this case, Nonon used her influence to try to see that as many as possible of those nominated were women, and had a genuine interest in the issues.

In this she was largely successful. Out of eighteen national representatives, only four or five were men, and there were few passengers. Some of those nominated were women who were at the same time involved in the equal pay negotiations – for example, du Granrut, Haines and Ravasio. Vogel-Polsky, from her position in Glinne's cabinet, was one of the representatives from Belgium. New faces included Nancy Seear from the UK and Karen Dahlerup from Denmark. The group held four meetings during the course of 1974. The meetings were chaired by a senior Commission official – always a man.

In general, trade unions active at the EC level were hostile to the formation of this group, feeling that it should have been set up as a sub-group of the Standing Committee on Employment, a powerful body primarily consisting of representatives of the social partners.[15] The feeling seems to have been that 'allowing' women separate representation in this way would lead to a take-over by professional women and to a loss of labour movement solidarity. The real concerns behind this view tended to be invalidated by the failure of European trade unions in general to respond to women's rising expectations, or to recognise the complex intersections in this period of gender and class interests. The openly expressed opposition at this point marked a rift which was to have far-reaching consequences.

The ad hoc group on women's work (as it was eventually called) exchanged information, compared statistics and created useful horizontal links between women dealing with the same issues in the different member states.[16] The mood seems to have been relaxed and issues debated in terms of the needs of women rather than the interests of governments. The group fully endorsed the view that women needed special as well as equal treatment to gain access to the labour market, and that the double burden must be tackled. A draft Directive which tried to blend the two was submitted by Vogel-Polsky at the third meeting of the group. This referred to equal opportunities (*égalité de chances*) as well as equal treatment (*égalité de traitement*), a formulation which was intended to combine equality and non-discrimination with some forms of positive action.[17]

After this third meeting in June 1974, Nonon was given the task of drawing up a draft for the new Directive and for an explanatory Memorandum to go with it. In this she was advised by the Commission legal service, and consultations were held with the social partners. The policy issues at stake seem to have provoked considerable controversy within the Commission, and the Memorandum in the end went through nine revisions.[18]

The controversy centred on how far it was possible in an EC legislative instrument to go beyond the straight 'equality in the workplace' formula. However, as so often in the Commission, arguments about what was appropriate merged very quickly into considerations about what would be acceptable to the member states. Doubts on the one score were often concealed as pragmatism on the latter. Nonon's position was to expand policy outwards from equal pay, and 'stretch the elastic as far as it would go'.[19]

As might be expected, it was the issue of childcare and what to do about reconciling family responsibilities with job aspirations which caused the most debate. Some senior Commission officials turned out to have very traditional views on these subjects. Positive action also became problematic when it was realised that this would have legal, financial and political implications. The Memorandum in its final version stated that the Commission was not concerned 'with family policy as such', and that the only aspects of caring which could be considered were those which directly affected 'women working outside the home'.[20]

Thus, in theory at least, EC provisions on issues like parental leave and the provision of childcare facilities could be considered, as long as they were seen as employment-related benefits. On positive action the main thrust of the Memorandum was to urge the adaptation of the guidelines of the European Social Fund to make it more open to training for women.[21]

Negotiating the text

A draft for the Directive was attached to the Memorandum.[22] This followed a relatively narrow line of thinking, apparently on the advice of the legal service. It was better, the lawyers argued, to aim at this stage at something effective for women in the workplace, rather than attempt to go wider, and risk endless delay and argument about Community competence. Thus no mention was made in the draft of measures to reconcile family responsibilities, and positive action was included only obliquely. The legal base was given as Article 235, thus making clear that new measures were being proposed, going beyond the scope of Article 119. Significantly, the preamble used the language of Article 117, talking of 'the harmonization of living and working conditions while maintaining their improvement'.[23] This suggested that for the first time in the equality field measures were being proposed which contained elements of the society-creating model for social policy discussed in chapter 3.

The draft dealt with equal treatment in the areas of access to employment, vocational training, promotion, and working conditions (including social security). The emphasis was on formal rules, and states were required to abolish, amend or review contrary laws, regulations and administrative provisions. Equal treatment was defined as:

> the elimination of all discrimination based on sex or on marital or family status, including the adoption of appropriate measures to provide women with equal opportunity in employment, vocational training, promotion and working conditions. (Article 1/2)

Thus very deftly, the definition of equal treatment itself was broadened to include the idea of positive action ('appropriate measures') which would make equality more of a reality. Indirect discrimination was not mentioned at this stage.

Rather surprisingly, the text did not include the usual sex equality derogations, for sex-specific jobs and for pregnancy and maternity provisions.[24] This was an indication of how new this area was to those involved, and also of the Commission's suspicion in general of derogations. Protective legislation (provisions, for example, prohibiting certain types of nightwork to women) were to be reviewed and withdrawn when 'no longer justified'. The draft contained basically the same provisions for application and enforcement as were agreed in the EPD.

This draft was approved by the Commission and then went to the Council's social affairs working group for detailed examination.[25] This working group, which consisted in the main of the social affairs attachés from the member state delegations in Brussels, represented a key arena for negotiation and bargaining. At this level, there seems to have been a fair degree of consensus over the need for a Directive, and pressure to adopt it in 1975 – International Women's Year. Nevertheless, debate was keen since states with legislation already drafted (like Britain) were anxious not to go an inch beyond it, while states with virtually no provision (like Germany) were anxious to limit the potential damage. All the principal representatives in the working group at this point were men. Nonon, though present, was considered too junior to represent the Commission and found herself having to brief more senior Commission men who were neither so well informed nor so committed.

The Directive emerged from this discussion – which went right up to a final full Council meeting in December 1975 – much amended. The particular points at issue concerned the definition of equal treatment, the scope of the provisions and the extent of derogations.

In discussing the definition, the attachés immediately jumped on the reference to 'appropriate measures', and asked what it meant. Very quickly they decided it was too vague and agreed to delete it. All encouragement for positive action was thus removed, and it was only as an afterthought that a paragraph *permitting* such measures was included.[26] As if to compensate, however, the concept of indirect discrimination was introduced into the definition, if in a rather ambiguous form, apparently at the suggestion of the British representative.[27] As a result, the final version read:

> For the purpose of the following provisions, the principle of equal treatment shall mean that there shall be no discrimination whatsoever on grounds of sex either directly or indirectly by reference in particular to marital or family status. (Article 2(1))

Thus, it seems the attachés were able to accept the notion of indirect discrimination, a concept already familiar in EC discourse and practice, but balked at the idea of positive action, which they did not understand and which appeared to go against the neo-liberal ethos of the market.

As far as scope was concerned, the aim of the member state representatives at this stage seems to have been to keep this as limited as possible. A reference to 'general education' in the context of equal treatment in vocational training (intended to refer to option choices and careers advice in schools) was deleted on the grounds that the Community had no competence in the field of education. The inclusion of social security provisions was also controversial, raising as it did the likely requirement to equalise retirement and pension ages. In the end, it was Barbara Castle, the British Secretary of State for Social Services, and the only senior woman present at the Council meeting in June, who insisted that they must be removed. Her arguments (and she has given her own account of the occasion) made no reference to advantages or disadvantages for women, but were based on a purely governmental view of the likely costs and disruption.[28] The Commission here fought an effective rear-guard action and insisted that if the social security provisions were removed at this stage, a firm commitment must be made to include them in a subsequent measure. This was agreed.

The issue of derogations was difficult, the representatives having realised, somewhat belatedly, that any special treatment not specifically exempted would be prohibited by the application of the equality principle. In the end, the usual derogations for sex-specific jobs and maternity provisions were inserted. The Commission, however, insisted that the former should be the subject of rigorous monitoring. Protective legislation was in principle to be repealed but only after a lengthy period of review and consideration. In general, Community practice and the firmness of the Commission kept derogations to the minimum. There are far fewer in the ETD than in the British Sex Discrimination Act, adopted at almost the same time.

The Directive was adopted in December 1975.[29] As with the EPD, it set minimum standards upon which the harmonisation of national provision could be based. States were given until August 1978 to comply.

Implications

The ETD emerged, after all the debate and negotiation, as a measure which dealt centrally with the issue of equal treatment in the workplace. Though the provisions were strong, the elastic had not been stretched as far as Nonon might have hoped. A cynic might take the view that all that had been achieved by the discussion of family measures, positive action and social security, had been to give (in turn) the Commission, the social affairs working group and the Council something to delete, thus leaving the central core intact.

However, allowing this to happen was not without cost. In its final form the Directive appears thin with most of the rich texture of the earlier versions gone. The failure to include measures on positive action and family responsibilities made the objectives ambiguous. As Michael

Rubenstein points out, it is not obvious whether the aim of the legislation is to treat women like men when they *are* like men, i.e. challenge inaccurate stereotyping and labels, or actually to revalue and accommodate gender differences.[30] Thus the legislation as it stands does little to challenge the 'male norm' against which women are rated, or to bring pressure on male lifestyles. It is this narrowing which has allowed the ETD to be used by the ECJ in the *Kalanke* case referred to earlier to curb the growing movement towards quotas and/or preferential treatment for women in the process of selection.[31]

The pattern of the negotiations discussed above demonstrates how reluctant those with power were to allow EC policy to 'spill over' from the public to the private. This reluctance, which has been demonstrated many times since, goes back to the debate about the economic and the social and to what is considered 'appropriate' for regulation at the EC level. The consequence has been that the aspects of women's employment policy which link into the domestic and the family, have been regulated in very different ways by the individual member states, thus perpetuating conflicting policies and standards in relation to caring and unpaid work.

There is a clear gender division in the dichotomies discussed above (public/private, economic/social), and the predominance of the 'male' elements in each was achieved by the 'imposition of hierarchy'. The negotiation of the ETD is particularly revealing in this respect since (unusually) women were dominant in the early stages of the process. The discussion in Nonon's ad hoc group, even though most of the women were government employees, seems to have been qualitatively different from that in the Council's social affairs working group. This was because the women took the issue seriously, and had some knowledge of the situations being discussed, whereas by and large the men did not. This kind of difference is only likely to occur when a fairly large number of women are involved. Isolated at the Council meeting and entrenched in her role as Minister, Barbara Castle, unusually for her, acted as a 'system woman' – though she played the role with some panache.

The ETD was published in February 1976. In April, the ECJ reached its ruling in *Defrenne 2* which was discussed in chapter 5. The judges were influenced by the fact that the women's policy was continuing to develop, and in turn their action rendered the ETD more meaningful. In between these two happenings a significant event took place in Brussels. In March 1976 an International Tribunal on Crimes Against Women was held in the city. This brought women together from all over Europe and from the United States, and was one of the first attempts at an international public hearing to be made by feminists. Delegations were asked to bear witness and to bring issues for debate. The Tribunal's proceedings centred on domestic violence, sex-trading and abortion rights.[32]

The Tribunal received a great deal of publicity, particularly for excluding male journalists from its proceedings. It is unlikely that those who negotiated the ETD, even if they heard about the Tribunal, considered its proceedings at all relevant, or that those who came to the Tribunal knew a Directive on equal treatment for women had just been enacted. If measures to do with family responsibilities and positive action were too much for the Brussels bureaucracy to contemplate, how much more so were deep and disturbing issues of sexual politics. Yet the decision to hold the Tribunal in Brussels was significant – a sign that connections were being made. And it may well be that some of the hesitations the negotiators felt about letting women set the agenda, or allowing the EC to 'invade' the private, had their roots in the very issues the Tribunal was discussing.

The Social Security Directive

The debate over the ETD raised issues about family responsibilities and the relation between the public and the private which in the end the negotiators found hard to accommodate. In particular, it highlighted the imbalance which exists in the caring responsibilities of men and women, and the difficulties this poses for a policy based on equality.

The Directive on equal treatment in social security (from now on referred to as the SSD) which followed on from this, raised these issues even more strongly, since it dealt centrally with social protection and the right to benefits. In general, in the EC member states, social security systems have been tied to the employment situation, providing direct rights to the employed worker and derived rights to those engaged in unpaid caring. The effect has been to create or perpetuate situations of dependency and to contribute overall to the lack of power which women possess in both the domestic and the public arena.[33] As a recent ILO study states, reviewing social security means reconsidering 'traditional concepts of women and the value of their work inside and outside the home'.[34] By entering into this field, even by trying to impose on it 'only' a rather crude notion of equality, the EC was moving into a sensitive arena, and one where intervention disturbed national policies of redistribution and social control, and challenged deep-seated assumptions and traditions.

Work on the new Directive went ahead as soon as the ETD was adopted. The main rationale seemed to be the Commission's desire to activate as soon as possible the commitment made in the ETD, and to fill in the gaps left by the *Defrenne* decisions. In general, most people seemed to agree with the view set out in the ETD Memorandum, that by discriminating against women and providing unequal treatment, social security systems were lagging behind 'socio-economic realities'.[35]

In fact the EC was venturing into an area already in flux. Most social security systems in the member states at this stage encouraged and reinforced situations in which women did unpaid caring, marginal paid work, and were rewarded by either derived rights or a low level of personal rights. Inadequate provision in either case was normally topped up by the state in the form of an assisted minimum income, usually paid to the family. Most systems relied on aggregating the wages of the couple (variously defined) which in many cases entailed disincentives for women to take on paid work.

By the mid seventies these provisions were looking increasingly outdated, given the greater demand for women's labour, the pressure from women for more visibility and rights, and the evident unreliability of marriage as a life-long source of protection. A clear indication of the need for change was given by the Federal Constitutional Court in Germany in 1975, when it served notice on the government that the pension position of women was inadequate, and that something must be done over the next ten years to improve women's entitlements.[36] However, perceptions by governments of the need for change were being constantly undercut by concerns about costs and increasing financial stringency.

In comparison with the ETD, women played much less of a role in the negotiation of the SSD and nothing like the ad hoc group was created. However, as though to compensate, there was more activity outside the institutions, and more awareness of what was being discussed. This was partly a result of the timing – the extent of the EC's policy for women was by this time better known – but it seems also to have come from the fact that the issues of autonomy and dependency being addressed struck a direct chord with some of the main concerns of feminists. The Belgian pamphlet 'The Social Insecurity of Women' published in 1974, and containing both a detailed analysis of benefits and personal accounts of their effects, is a good example of this.[37] Sheila Rowbotham gives a vivid account of similar debates in Britain.[38] Feminists did not necessarily have solutions or a policy but the issues were in debate.

Some of the same influences affected trade union women who, led once again by Emilienne Brunfaut, made attempts to influence the outcome.[39] Thus a rather different dynamic takes place with regard to this Directive – the 'women's influence' is outside rather than inside, and more directly focused.

Preparations[40]

At the end of 1976 a Bureau for problems concerning women's work (referred to from now on as the Women's Bureau) was set up in DG V of the Commission. This complemented the Women's Information Service being established in DG X. The Bureau, which was headed by Jacqueline Nonon and had a very small staff, was set up as a department rather than a division (conferring a lower status in terms of the Commission hierarchy) and its main tasks were to see to the implementation of the ETD, to monitor changes in the European Social Fund (ESF), and to develop future policy based on the Memorandum.[41] Equal pay did not come into its remit (remaining with Boudard in the wages policy division) nor did the new concern with social security, although the Bureau kept a watching brief on developments.

Responsibility for preparing the SSD was given to Edward James, a British Commission official then working on the Poverty Programme. This shifted the work away from the labour market experts and towards those with experience of disadvantage, and of social security in the context of free movement of workers. The failure to set up a consultative group to represent women's interests seems one reason why, in contrast to the ETD, no imaginative solutions were presented early on in the proceedings. These might have included the suggestion that caring should be added to the list of insurable employment risks, or a commitment to the individualisation of entitlement to benefits (i.e. the end of the aggregation of a couple's earnings as a base for the calculation of benefits or tax) as the ultimate goal.[42]

Although both of these suggestions would almost certainly have been turned down on grounds of cost, their introduction in the early stages would have helped to establish what an alternative policy might look like. When government experts and representatives became involved they tended to be experts in social security and not in equal treatment, and thus few women were involved here either.[43]

The aim of the Social Security Directive was to follow up the ETD and bring within the scope of the equality policy all social security schemes which insured against the main employment risks of sickness, invalidity, unemployment and old age. The situation in each of the member states was different, provision being based on some combination of contributory, non-contributory and means-tested schemes, covering both social security and social assistance. As a result of this diversity, states had developed different ways of accommodating women to the regimes of work and welfare – and thus different forms of discrimination had developed also.[44] Taking the extremes, by this stage Denmark was well on the way to providing individual entitlement for all, while Ireland was still practising direct discrimination against married women across a range of benefits.[45]

Given this background, the question then was on what basis to construct the Directive. There were many ways in which equality could be viewed, including individualisation of benefits, along Danish lines, which was in general the demand of the women's movement. In the end, the decision was taken not to go for individualisation, even in the long term, but to carry on from the ETD (presumably this was what had been originally intended) and seek to extend the principle of equal treatment between men and women to all employment related social security. According to James, individualisation, or what he called 'decoupling', was considered but ruled out because it would be too expensive.[46] Equal treatment as then envisaged would mean that contributions to and entitlements from schemes would have to be the same for men and women, and that gender neutral terminology would be essential. Aggregation and dependency could continue, but crude assumptions about who was the dependant and who the breadwinner or claimant would have to end.

A draft for the Directive was produced in January 1977 – just as the newly appointed Commission, with the British politician Roy Jenkins as President, came into office. This brought in a Dutch socialist, Henk Vredeling, as Commissioner for Social Affairs, with Nel Barendreght, a former Dutch MP who had campaigned for equal pay, as his *chef de cabinet*. Finding the SSD already in draft, they both gave it substantial support, and it became one of the main pieces of legislation which DG V then sought to have adopted. The Directive was negotiated in an erratic way over the next two years – the main points at issue being the scope of the provisions, the derogations allowed, and the timescale for application.

Scope, derogations, timing

In the original draft of the Directive its scope was broad.[47] It applied to both statutory and occupational social security schemes, covering the normal employment risks of sickness, invalidity, old age, accidents at work and unemployment. It also covered social assistance schemes which supplemented or replaced the above. In the negotiation process occupational schemes were postponed to a further Directive (just as statutory schemes had been postponed from the ETD) following anxiety about the complications of renegotiating the terms of such schemes.

The personal scope of the Directive was confined to the working population, as might be expected, but this was given a broad definition to include people seeking employment, the self-employed and retired workers (Article 2). The same definition of equal treatment was used as in the ETD. Significantly, this included the prohibition on indirect as well as direct discrimination.

The derogations issue was controversial and member states had considerably expanded the list by the end of the negotiations. In the final text there are three sets of derogations: the usual one for maternity provisions (Article 4(3)), derogations supposed to be permanent (on the grounds that they fall outside the employment sphere) for family benefits and survivors' (widows) benefits, (Article 3(2)), and a number of more 'temporary' exclusions, including pensionable age and certain kinds of derived rights (Article 7). These latter ones were 'permissive', in that member states could exclude them if they wished, but the hope was that in the end they would become unnecessary.

As the negotiations came nearer to a conclusion, a certain amount of panic set in, with government representatives beginning to realise what they might be signing up to. Lobbying in the capitals at this stage was carried out by both Barendreght and James, and both comment that they felt some kind of women's network existed that could be appealed to.[48] Resolve may also have been strengthened by the European Court's ruling in the third *Defrenne* case, which was made in June 1978 during the final stages of the negotiations. Although finding against the substantive claim, the Court took the opportunity to affirm that 'the elimination of discrimination based on sex' formed part of the fundamental personal human rights of the Community.[49]

It was at the Council meeting on 27 November 1978 that the decision to remove occupational schemes from the remit of the Directive was finally taken, and the negotiators had then to agree on the date for implementation. In its draft proposal, the Commission had recommended staggered deadlines for different aspects of the Directive. This was abandoned and the question then was, what delay should be put on the Directive as a whole? Observers comment that the Council became like an auction with member states bidding for certain dates and with the German president picking six years out of the air as the date most likely to command general agreement. Thus with the longest date for implementation ever set for a Directive, the text was finally agreed.[50]

Edward James maintains that the adoption of the Directive in this form was something of a triumph, 'especially as none of the three major countries really wanted it'.[51] Emilienne Brunfaut felt on the contrary that the member states had controlled the process. 'Member states dictated their Directive to us', she wrote in a report to the European Trade Union Confederation. 'We must learn to be more vigilant'.[52]

Special or equal treatment?

The SSD is an instrument which deals with the surface aspects of women's disadvantage in social security. As with the ETD, it attacks stereotyping and labelling, but not the substantive problems. However, the subject matter of the Directive is such that it proved more difficult than in the case of the ETD to keep the employment aspects separate from the domestic and private. As must have been rivetingly clear to the negotiators, although as far as one can tell this was never openly admitted, the whole system of social security had its base in women's dependence on men, a dependence with its roots not in employment, but in reproduction and caring.

The derogations and exceptions, the 'special treatment' for women, are much stronger in this Directive than in the ETD. Most of them represent 'advantages' for women, gradually developed as compensation for the caring role, and to preclude or defer more radical change. The dilemma of the negotiators is clear: to do away with these advantages in the interests of equal treatment, without dealing with the situations that made them necessary, would be seriously to disadvantage many women, in a policy that was supposed to make women more 'equal'. This was clearly politically unacceptable, and thus the derogations were inserted.[53]

Keeping such 'advantages' for a transitional period, while taking other measures to deal with the substantive problems women face, in the context of a general commitment to greater individualisation of benefits, would have been a progressive strategy. It is indeed more or less the one advocated in the ILO study cited earlier.[54] However, because the SSD states neither an ultimate goal nor a commitment to supplementary actions, these special measures look like, and indeed can easily become, reinforcements for women's continuing domestic role. The only slight commitment to further action given in the SSD is the statement in the title that the measure forms part of 'the progressive implementation of the principle of equal treatment'. This did lead to a further Directive on occupational pensions, and in 1987 to a proposal for a third Social Security Directive. However, the attempt to state in that text that individualisation was the ultimate goal was cut out very early in the proceedings, and, in the changing political circumstances of the eighties, the Directive itself was never adopted.[55]

In the development of the SSD, as we have seen, the role of professional women is less marked, and the network which operated in respect of both the EPD and the ETD for the most part failed to stretch this far. By contrast, the issues resonated more strongly with trade union women and feminist groups. When the European Network of Women (a feminist umbrella for women's groups) was created in 1983, issues arising from the SSD were the first to be taken up.[56]

For all its limitations and conceptual inadequacy, the SSD moved EC policy into areas which dealt with some of the central issues of women's disadvantage, and thus legitimised discussion of these within the EC context. However, the Directive was adopted at the end of the seventies, and represented the last gasp of the ambitious Social Action Programme. It was implemented in the eighties in very different circumstances. It is a weakness of the Directive that it contains, even with the reference to Article 117, no measures which would prevent states from complying with equal treatment by levelling benefits down or removing them altogether.

The Equal Treatment and Social Security Directives, together with the Article 119 and the Equal Pay Directive, established what Chris Docksey has called 'an advanced legal framework' on equality, with considerable force in European law.[57] The main responsibility for implementation lay with the member state governments who had a duty in respect of the Directives to incorporate the commitments into national law. Once the implementation deadline was reached, these Directives also became subject to the rigorous EC procedures for enforcement and interpretation.

Notes

1 For full references see Appendix 2.

2 Michael Shanks contrasts at this point the level of mobilisation among women and migrants (and at this stage he does not recognise an overlap), both of which were the subject of EC policy making in the seventies. Women's organisations, he says, were much more 'available'. See Shanks, *European Social Policy Today and Tomorrow*, Pergamon Press, Oxford, 1977, p. 86.

3 Article 7 of the Treaty of Rome contains a prohibition against discrimination on grounds of nationality which applies across the board to all the areas in which the EU has competence. In addition, the provisions and policies on competition and on the free movement of labour are both concerned not only to remove direct barriers but also to prevent discrimination, so as to allow goods, services, capital and labour to circulate freely in the market.

4 See, for example, ECJ Case 152/73, *Sotgiu* v. *Deutsche Bundespost*, judgment 12 February 1974; and ECJ Case 61/77 *Commission of the European Communities* v. *Ireland*, judgment 16 February 1978.

5 John Pinder, 'Positive Integration and Negative Integration: Some Problems of Economic Union in the EEC', *World Today*, vol. 24, 1968, pp. 88–110.

6 The provisions of Article 51 by this stage had led both to secondary legislation and considerable jurisprudence in the ECJ. For an overview see Philippa Watson, 'Social Security and the European Communities', in G. Whyte ed., *Sex Equality, Community Rights and Irish Social Welfare Law*, Trinity College, Dublin, 1988 pp. 60–77.

7 CEC, *Premier programme de politique économique à moyen terme* (Medium Term Economic Programme), Brussels, 1967, pp. 1552–3. The ideas in the text were further developed in Annexe II, pp. 10–14.

8 Evelyne Sullerot, *L'emploi des femmes et ses problèmes dans les états membres de la Communauté Européene*, CEC, Brussels, 1970.

9 Interview, Jacqueline Nonon, Paris, March 1983.

10 Interview, Evelyne Sullerot, Paris, September 1984.

11 *Bulletin of the ECs*, Supplement 2/71, pp. 46 and 60.

12 *Bulletin of the ECs*, Supplement 2/74. The first reference comes on p. 8 of the resolution, and the second in Action II(4), p. 23.

13 Interview, Nonon, Paris, September 1984.
14 For an early version of this section and the next see 'Women's Equality and the European Community', *Feminist Review*, no. 20, 1985, pp. 71–88.
15 A version of this trade union view is given in the Opinion of the Economic and Social Committee on the Equal Pay Directive, OJ No. C 26/7/74, p. 8, para 5. In the draft for the Opinion prepared by the Secretariat of the ESC, the formation of the ad hoc group is 'welcomed' (R/CES I65/74, p. 5). For a further comment on this issue see Shanks, *European Social Policy*, p. 86.
16 This account is based on minutes of the first three meetings and interviews with some of those involved.
17 *Document de travail concernant l'adoption d'un instrument juridique destiné à réaliser l'égalité de traitement entre les travailleurs masculins et féminins et à éliminer les discriminations subsistants à l'égard des femmes*. Brussels, V/488/74-F.
18 For the text of the final version of the Memorandum see *Equality of Treatment Between Men and Women* (Communication of the Commission to the Council) COM(75) 36 final, Brussels, 12 February 1975.
19 Interview with Nonon's colleague, Florence Morgan, Berlin, May 1983.
20 *Equality of Treatment*, p. 1.
21 *Equality of Treatment*, pp. 31–4. This was actually achieved quite quickly in Council Decision, 77/804/EEC.
22 *Equality of Treatment*, pp. 5–9.
23 Susan Atkins, Linda Luckhaus, 'The Social Security Directive and UK Law', p. 103, in C. McCrudden, ed., *Women, Employment and European Equality Law*, Eclipse Publications, London, 1987.
24 Sex equality laws require derogations for maternity provisions and sex-specific jobs, e.g. a wet-nurse or a soprano singer. The list of jobs, however, can easily be expanded to suit particular cultural or political interests. The British Sex Discrimination Act, for example, excludes organised religion and the army from its provisions. On the other hand, it allows for positive action by political parties.
25 The account here relies mainly on access to semi-restricted material, in particular minutes of the meetings of the social affairs working group.
26 The paragraph reads:

> This Directive shall be without prejudice to measures to promote equal opportunity for men and women, in particular by removing existing inequalities which affect women's opportunities in the areas referred to in Article 1 (1).

27 The British it would seem played a crucial role here. The Sex Discrimination Act was in the process of being finalised and (largely as a result of American influence) contained quite strong measures on indirect discrimination. The British representatives presumably thought that an equivalent level of protection should be included in the European law also.
28 Barbara Castle, *The Castle Diaries 1974–76*, Weidenfeld, London, 1980, pp. 418–20.
29 For full reference see Appendix 2.
30 Michael Rubenstein, 'The Equal Treatment Directive and UK Law', p. 97, in C. McCrudden, ed., *Women, Employment and European Equality Law*.
31 See chapter 10 this volume for a fuller discussion.
32 For a full account see Diana Russell and Nicole Van de Ven, eds, *Crimes Against Women – Proceedings of the International Tribunal*, Les Femmes, Millbrae, California, 1976. I am grateful to Jalna Hamna of Bradford University for talking to me about the hearing.
33 For an analysis of the way social security provisions affect women and the relevance of European law see: Ina Sjerps, 'Indirect Discrimination in Social Security in the Netherlands: Demands of the Dutch Women's Movement', in M. Buckley and M. Anderson, eds, *Women, Equality and Europe*, Macmillan, Basingstoke, 1988, pp. 95–106.
34 Anne-Marie Brocas, Anne-Marie Cailloux and Virginie Oget, *Women and Social Security*, International Labour Office, Geneva, 1990, p. v.
35 *Equality of Treatment*, p. 30. Interview, Edward James, London, December 1983.

36 Judgment of the German Federal Constitutional Court of 12 March 1975, Reports of the Court (BVerfGE), vol. 39, p. 169.
37 Special Issue, 'L'insécurité sociale des femmes', *Les Cahiers du Grif*, October 1974, pp. 1–88.
38 Sheila Rowbotham, *The Past Is Before Us – Feminism in Action since the 1960s*, Pandora Press, London, 1989, pp. 148–9.
39 Brunfaut describes in '3éme Directive de la CEE', a memo written in 1978 to the European Trade Union Confederation, how trade union and other women went to the President of the Council of Ministers after the adoption of the ETD to press for immediate action on social security. She herself followed the progress of the SSD closely and was in no doubt as to the importance of its provisions for women.
40 For an early version of this section and the next see Catherine Hoskyns and Linda Luckhaus, 'The European Community Directive on Equal Treatment in Social Security', *Policy and Politics*, vol. 17, no. 4, 1989, pp. 321–5.
41 Jacqueline Nonon, 'The "Bureau for problems concerning women's work"', *Memo From Belgium*, 1979, pp. 137–40.
42 Caring has never been seen as a legitimate employment-related risk, a good example of how male life patterns determine social security provision. See Susan Atkins and Linda Luckhaus, 'The Social Security Directive and UK Law', in C. McCrudden, ed., *Women, Employment and European Equality Law*, p. 105.
43 Interview, André Laurent, Brussels, June 1983.
44 Some of these discriminations are listed in the Commission's paper *Unequal Treatment of Men and Women in Matters of Social Security*, CEC, V/444/1/76.
45 Good comparative material on the situation in different countries is given in Jane Lewis, ed., *Women and Social Policies in Europe – Work, Family and the State*, Edward Elgar, Aldershot, 1993. See particularly the chapters on Denmark by Birte Siim and on Germany by Ilona Ostner.
46 Interview, James, 1983. For the implications of individualisation in this context see Linda Luckhaus, 'Individualisation of Social Security Benefits', in C. McCrudden, ed., *Equality of Treatment between Men and Women in Social Security*, Butterworth, London, 1994, pp. 147–62.
47 *Proposal for a Directive concerning the progressive implementation of the principle of equality of treatment for men and women in matters of social security*, COM(76) 650 final, 10 January 1977.
48 Interviews: Nel Barendreght, The Hague, June 1983; and James, December 1983.
49 *Gabrielle Defrenne* v. *Société Anonyme Belge de Navigation Aérienne* (Sabena), ECJ Case 149/77, 15 June 1978, *European Court Reports*, 1978, p. 1378.
50 Its legal base was Article 235 and it made the same use of Article 117 language as had the ETD.
51 Interview, James, 1983.
52 Emilienne Brunfaut, '3éme Directive de la CEE', 1978. See note 39 above.
53 For divergent views among feminists on the subject of these derogations, see Atkins and Luckhaus 'The Social Security Directive', p. 106; and Sjerps, 'Indirect Discrimination in Social Security'.
54 Brocas, *Women and Social Security*, pp. 109–10.
55 Luckhaus, 'Individualisation of Social Security Benefits', p. 154.
56 See *Working Document on Equal Treatment in Social Security*, Report of ENOW meeting, Brussels, 8–9 December 1983, Centre for Research on European Women, Brussels, June 1984.
57 Christopher Docksey, 'The European Community and the Promotion of Equality', in C. McCrudden, ed., *Women, Employment and European Equality Law*, p. 22.

7

Implementing the Directives

The study of political processes involving policy making conventionally focuses on two stages: negotiation and implementation. Implementation in a formal sense suggests a functional, more or less straightforward process for putting law and policy into effect. In fact, in most contexts, and certainly where the EC is concerned, such a conceptualisation is quite misleading. The adoption of an EC Directive is like throwing a rock into a pond: the effects produced are complex and interactive, and any linear progression is quickly distorted. As a result, it is often difficult to track through particular developments. Because of these characteristics and the difficulty of evaluating outcomes, the process of implementation has been less studied than that of negotiation.[1]

Where Directives are concerned, the formal implementation process constitutes the starting point from which other developments take off. The formal process involves two stages: first, the incorporation of the terms of the Directive into national law, and second, their application on the ground and the achievement of practical outcomes. Both of these processes are primarily national, but they are watched over and influenced by the European Commission, the Court, and increasingly in recent years, the Parliament.

The Commission has prime responsibility for monitoring incorporation and for pointing out where states have failed to comply. It also plays a considerable role in application by facilitating transnational links and research, and by setting up its own cross-national groups of experts to provide information and advice. The Parliament shares this latter role, but is more overtly political and concerned to encourage participation and evoke a popular response. Finally, the Court adjudicates on issues of incorporation, and assists in application by issuing authoritative (and often bold) interpretations of EC law, by way of the references which it receives from the national courts.

Such actions and interventions spark off in their turn a multiplicity of side effects and chain reactions which begin to inflect implementation at national level. At the same time, they encourage the establishment of various kinds of policy networks which grow up to influence the outcomes and respond to new developments. Thus national policy makers and bureaucrats have to learn to absorb and accommodate both a growth in transnationalism and a degree of supervision from the Community institutions. They also learn how to retaliate.

All of this applies, though with certain unique features, to the implementation of the equal treatment policy, which began in the early eighties. By way of illustration, this chapter will examine and try to relate three aspects of this: first, the attempts by Germany and Ireland to incorporate the equal treatment measures into national law; second, the development of networks among different groups of women to assist in implementation and plan new policy; and finally some aspects of judicial enforcement and interpretation through the Commission and the Court. Each of these illustrates a very different facet of the implementation process. Taken together they give some idea of what implementing EC policy means in practice, and the ripples and cross-currents which are produced.

The National Level – Germany and Ireland[2]

The necessity to bring national law into line with EC Directives (incorporation) meant that equal treatment and equal opportunities for women came onto the political agenda in all the member states in the latter half of the seventies. In some this created a new policy direction, in others EC requirements supplemented or inflected already existing proposals and provisions. Initiatives from the EC on women's issues were mostly unexpected and not well understood. They frequently met with a mixed response even from those who might be expected to benefit.

The process of incorporation in each country varied according to the starting point, prevailing social norms, traditions in labour market regulation, and the style of women's organisation. The outcomes represented in most cases an attempt at implementation subtly geared to national needs and preoccupations. How this worked out in two contrasting countries, Germany and Ireland, demonstrates this very well. It also begins to show what the effects of these measures were on different groups of women and what kinds of political processes were being set in motion.

Incorporation – the national starting point

In both Germany and Ireland the formal starting point for considering equality for women is the Constitution, and in each case, although equality is clearly stated as a general principle, this right, as far as women are concerned, is qualified in other ways. In Germany, the qualification comes from provisions which ensure the collective autonomy of parties in the labour market and safeguard marriage,[3] and in Ireland from the protection given to women's special role as mothers.[4] Thus, in each case, 'male' priorities or assumptions about women, cut into and inflect the right to equality.

For both countries, the late seventies was a period when reforming governments were on the decline. In Germany, the SPD/Liberal coalition was to lose power in 1982, while in Ireland, the Fine Gael/Labour coalition, which in 1973 had ended sixteen years of Fianna Fàil rule, was in and out of power between 1977 and 1987.[5] Thus the first requirements to incorporate equal treatment legislation came at a time when governments with overt commitments to social change were still in power, but were increasingly affected by political instability and financial constraint.

The women's movement in each country, though very different in style and composition, had produced political shocks in the early seventies. The main campaigns had been on reproductive rights and for the repeal of restrictive laws around marriage and the family.[6] Operating in a small country, with a relatively accessible structure of formal politics, feminist women in Ireland made constant demands on the state, and were able to form alliances across a wide range of groups. German women faced a much more complex and layered system of authority, and there was in addition more separation between the autonomous women's movement, traditional women's organisations and women working within formal politics. Many German women were sceptical about the liberating effects of full-time work, and remained attached to some combination of domestic work and part-time employment.

In both countries incorporation was delayed beyond the due date in areas where the EC provisions were felt to cut too sharply against prevailing norms. In Germany, the main problems came with the incorporation of the employment provisions, in Ireland with social security. In both cases, the reluctance and procrastination of civil servants, reflecting or encouraging political hesitations, were a major factor. Civil servants in both countries subsequently referred to compliance as having been 'piecemeal' in these contested areas.[7]

The initial response from German civil servants to the EC Directives was that 'nothing was needed' by way of compliance. The equality provisions in the Constitution and the right of appeal to the Federal Constitutional Court were seen as providing sufficient protection. However, this view was questioned by some women civil servants. As one remarked:

> My male colleagues say the law is OK – there is no discrimination. But I see it everywhere; it is systemic. The problem in Germany is that work is over-identified with men.

It gradually became clear, however, that the Constitutional guarantees were insufficient to enforce equality in the private sphere (because of the qualification already mentioned) and that some action at least would be needed in this area.

In Ireland, the complexities of applying the equal treatment principle in the SSD to the Irish system, which relied heavily on payments for dependent wives, caught the civil servants unawares. Virtually no preparations were made during the six-year lead-in time (which coincided with three changes of government) and as a result there was no time for a staged implementation or for a rethink of the principles upon which the Irish system was based. As one civil servant commented at the time:

> We didn't realise the full implications of the Directive when it was passed. The concepts of dependency and equal treatment just don't mix. What is needed is a full overhaul of the system with more emphasis on individualisation.

Such an overhaul never took place, and the SSD provisions were incorporated in a rush in ways which caused both political and legal controversy.

Employment

In both countries, despite the inertia of national systems, important changes were made in the field of employment rights. In Germany, news of the European Directives and what was happening in other countries filtered through to domestic politics, and by 1977 the issue was being taken up by the women's sections in the ruling SPD. As a result, proposals were made for a broad anti-discrimination law which, if adopted, would have gone well beyond EC requirements. However, this proposal met with opposition from both trade unions and employers, who saw it as interfering with collective bargaining rights, and also from some sections of the women's movement worried about the emphasis on paid work and on equality.

As a result, no framework law was passed, but in 1980 a piecemeal compliance law, including a blanket ban on sex-discrimination in hiring, promotion and dismissal, a right to equal pay for the same or equivalent work, and a strong 'recommendation' against sex-specific language in job advertisements, was incorporated into the Civil Code.[8] However, employers were still given some leeway in the hiring process, by means of a number of unclear provisions which seemed to allow both exceptions to and justifications for discriminatory practices. Even if discrimination were proved in hiring, the provisions specifically stated (in a way that was to cause controversy later on) that only minimal costs, not damages, could be awarded by way of compensation.

These provisions (from now on referred to as 'the compliance law') were widely criticised and doubts remained as to whether they constituted an adequate incorporation of the EC Directives. However, their adoption meant that for the first time the ban on discrimination in employment applied unambiguously to the private sector. Whether the provisions did or did not comply with European requirements would be up to the Commission and eventually the ECJ to decide.

In Ireland, national equal pay legislation was being developed at the same time as negotiations were going on in Brussels on the terms of the Equal Pay Directive. Care was taken to keep the two in line and the Irish legislation was in fact adopted in 1974, before the EPD was finalised.[9] This was followed by the 1977 Employment Equality Act, adopted to comply with, and in terms very near to, the Equal Treatment Directive. The specific prohibition of discrimination on grounds of marital status in both texts was particularly important in the Irish situation.[10]

Social Security

The incorporation of the Social Security Directive (SSD) caused few direct problems in Germany, if only because the system was already being revised in the light of the concerns of the Federal Constitutional Court.[11] However, once the CDU came back into power in 1982, the debate moved onto a new plane and into the area of family benefits, thus taking it beyond the formal scope of the SSD. Pushed by women in the CDU, and hoping to appeal to women voters, the government moved to increase the status given to childcare by introducing pension entitlements for child-rearing years and a paid parental leave benefit (*Bundeserziehungsgeld*).[12]

Under the parental leave scheme, finally introduced in 1986 though planned much earlier, 600 DM (approximately £250) per month was given for twelve months, to a 'supporting parent', who during that time was either not in paid work or working below 20 hours per week. Unlike the 'additional' maternity leave scheme which it replaced, the benefit was impeccably gender neutral in formulation, and both leave and benefit could be taken by either the mother or the father.[13] So far it has been overwhelmingly taken up by women: by 1993 men made up only 1.5 per cent of beneficiaries.[14]

This benefit has proved to be extremely popular with women, since for the first time it gives 'public' recognition to childcare and meets some immediate needs for cash and status. It has been criticised by some analysts, however, because in the long term it seems likely to reinforce rather than break the nexus between women, domestic work, dependency and low pay. Significant here is the fact that the benefit is not paid to parents who remain in full-time work, that it bears no relation to the actual cost of raising a child, and that so far it has had little impact on male lifestyles. In addition, the length of the leave has been steadily extended, thus paradoxically making more difficult the return to full-time work.[15] After giving a sympathetic account of the attractions of the benefit, Ilona Ostner concludes that in the long run it reduces women's choices and helps to create a 'special category of flexible employees'.[16]

The Irish government was caught unprepared by the need to incorporate the SSD. In the event, it was forced, under great popular pressure, hastily to carry out a piecemeal reform. This was beneficial in the sense that it ended the disparities for married women in access to and levels of benefit. However, the problem for applying equal treatment lay in the fact that under the Irish system all married women had been regarded as dependent on their husbands, even if they were in employment. Thus a married man on benefit automatically received an Adult Dependant's Allowance (ADA) for a dependent wife, whether or not she was in paid work.[17]

Unable, and understandably unwilling, to extend this arrangement to everyone (by treating all men also as dependent on their wives) the government proposed ending the arrangement and imposing a test for 'genuine' dependency, for the purpose of determining entitlement to the ADA. Introduced gradually, with an accompanying rise in basic rates of benefit, this might have been acceptable, and have constituted a move towards greater independence for women. However, introduced in a hurry with no offsetting measures, it caused an outcry, since the net effect was to disadvantage the poorest women and their families.[18]

Under political pressure the government was forced to give 'temporary' subsidies (in fact they lasted until June 1992) to the worst hit families; and create an 'earnings disregard', which meant that spouses (mainly women) could earn up to £50 a week without jeopardising the ADA. This delayed application of the Directive until 1986, well after the deadline. As Rosheen Callender has pointed out, the earnings ceiling tended to reinforce women's dependency while also giving an incentive to employers to offer and women to accept wages beneath the disregard.[19]

Thus in both countries the consequences of the implementation of the SSD, or of attempts to go beyond it, ended up in arrangements which while beneficial in certain ways and to certain groups of women, also acted in other ways to continue dependence and reinforce gender segregation in employment.

Effects and implications

The adoption of these measures led in both countries to an increase in the bureaucratic infrastructure around equality policy, and to facilities which at a certain level at least made it easier for women's issues to be articulated. In Germany, the 'working group on women's issues' (*Arbeitsstab Frauenpolitik*) of the Federal Ministry for Youth, the Family and Health, was increased in size, and given both cross-department authority and responsibility for funding women's projects and disseminating information. It may well be that expanding the unit, rather than creating an independent equality agency at federal level, represented a compromise with the trade unions; certainly the first head of the group was a trade union woman, Marlies Kutsch, appointed while the SPD was still in power.

At the same time, a variety of equality commissions and units were set up at regional and local level with different briefs and resources depending on the political priorities of the authorities concerned. A number of these bodies became active in applying the new equality provisions, and significant case law, often involving the ECJ, began to develop from 1979 onwards.

In Ireland, the 1977 Act set up the Employment Equality Agency (EEA) to monitor law and policy from the perspective of women and play an advisory and research role. As in Germany, a woman with a trade union background, Sylvia Meehan, was chosen to be the first chair. The EEA developed a relatively autonomous role and acted as a stimulant for the implementation and development of policy, but in the employment field only. The existence of the new laws, and a relatively good system of redress, led to a process of conciliation which was on the whole regarded as fair, and to the bringing of some important cases.[20]

What then was the effect of all this on women? An early sign in Germany that the issue of equal pay was becoming more visible came in 1979 with the publicity around the case of the 'Heinze-women' from Gelsenkirchen in the Ruhr. This case, which concerned the payment of overtime allowances to male workers only, zigzagged through the German courts on the legal issue of whether the equality principle took precedence over the right of the employer to autonomy. Finally, in September 1981, the Federal Labour Court in Kassel, following huge demonstrations and media publicity, ruled that the equality provisions must apply to allowances and bonuses as well as to basic rates of pay. European law (and particularly Article 119) seems to have been decisive in tipping the balance this way.[21]

The case did much to publicise the effects of EC law, the judgment coming just after the compliance law had been adopted in 1980. In general, however, the main part of the autonomous women's movement remained separatist, and suspicious both of the idea of equality and of the use of the law. The CDU's concern with women in the home received a sympathetic response from many feminists.

In Ireland, activist women took quickly to the idea of taking advantage of EC law and provisions where possible. Pauline Conroy Jackson comments that EC law helped to prise open the grip which Irish society had on women, just at the point that women themselves were becoming more active and aware.[22] However, the failure of the EC to take a position on sexual violence and reproductive rights, together with the disastrous application of the SSD, dented this appreciation. It demonstrated that while a policy based on equality and limited to the employment sphere had certain beneficial effects, it failed to meet the most urgent needs of the majority of women, particularly those with the lowest incomes.

For the traditional authorities in Ireland, this 'modernising trend' from the EC appeared as a threat. In 1983 a successful move was made to insert by means of a referendum a prohibition of abortion into the Constitution. This can be seen as an attempt to shore up defences against 'unacceptable' changes in the status of women being brought about by a combination of internal pressure and external influence.[23]

This account of incorporation in two states (and it was not dissimilar elsewhere) suggests that the main effect of the Directives was to establish a more comprehensive framework to combat discrimination in the central areas of employment relations, namely pay and conditions. Given the extent to which traditional ideas about women and employment still had force, this was an important development. In the social security field the impact was less clear: upset was caused and attention focused on the situation of women, but the equal treatment approach encouraged cosmetic rather than substantive change. It also, and Ireland is a case in point, allowed governments to carry out what were in effect reductions in benefits, using the need to comply with the EC's equal treatment policy as an excuse.

The examples of Germany and Ireland reveal one interesting common factor, and that is that the authorities or dominant cultural elements in both countries, while being forced to comply with these measures, moved at the same time or soon after to reassert national control in related areas which fell outside EC competence. The Germans did this rather subtly with the parental leave benefit, the Irish more crudely with the abortion amendment. One of the aims in each case seems to have been to make sure that changes induced by the EC did not move policy too far from what were perceived to be the country's basic norms and values.

The experience of incorporation discussed here suggests that at this stage there were certain areas where a broad range of women shared common goals and where effective campaigning could take place. This was particularly true in Ireland where the subordination of women was clear and obvious in many fields. But it also suggests that there were other areas where women were by no means agreed on the policy options and where groups of women and individuals had diverse needs and aspirations. No agreement had been reached, and indeed debate was only just beginning, about what an 'equal' policy might mean in such crucial areas as social security and family benefits.

It was this that made the response from women to the EC measures often uncertain and ambiguous – the provisions met certain needs but not others, and more importantly they were not primarily the product of women-centred debate. The experience with the German parental leave benefit suggests that measures must meet women's immediate needs if they are to receive popular support: but that they need also to be framed in ways which open up the widest possible range of choices in the long term and bring changes to men's as well as women's lifestyles.

As a result of these developments, awareness of the EC level of policy-making increased, at least among some women, and certain new alliances and agencies were created. This meant that there were groups and individuals ready to respond to the fragile but significant infrastructure developing in the European institutions around the women's policy. At the same time, attempts were made to develop transnational links among women, to support, influence and benefit from these new possibilities. Thus there began to be created a 'policy network' around women's issues, springing out of and contributing to the process of incorporation.

Transnational Networking

Charting the creation of a transnational policy network on women's issues across the EC is by no means easy. No one person can hope to identify more than a fraction of the range of contacts and common endeavours which lie behind a strengthened policy input of this kind. For women to become active in EC politics at this point meant crossing all kinds of cultural and practical barriers, and very importantly also, it required resources. Commitment and urgency could overcome these difficulties on a temporary basis, but creating permanent transnational links or regular relations with the European institutions was impossible without institutional or financial backing. To some extent the EC institutions tried to offer this support, but this involved a degree of control that was unacceptable to many.

In order to get a feel for what was happening in these new circumstances, I want to look here at the events leading up to the establishment by the European Commission of the Advisory Committee on Equal Opportunities for Men and Women, at the adoption of the European Parliament's Resolution on the position of women in the EC, and at the attempts to set up more informal networks of both traditional and activist women. All of this begins to indicate the different policy priorities and styles of different groups of women and the nature and extent of the common interest.

The Advisory Committee on Equal Opportunities

Both Germany and Ireland in the course of incorporation established or expanded, though on very different bases, units to deal more specifically with women's issues. This happened in one way or another in the other member states also. By the early eighties, the most experienced units were the French *Comité du Travail Feminin* (CTF) and the British Equal Opportunities Commission (EOC).[24] The EOC, semi-autonomous, comparatively well-funded, and able to assist in the bringing of legal actions, was regarded by the European Commission as a model to which other countries should aspire. As a result, the EOC established at the end of the seventies quite close links with the Women's Bureau in the Commission and with Henk Vredeling, who remained Commissioner for Social Affairs until the end of 1980.[25]

It was from these contacts that the idea came for a Europe-wide conference that would generate 'a new European plan for women'. It was hoped by this means on the one hand to build on the existing Directives and carry them further, and on the other to establish firmer links between the new agencies in each country, and between them and the Commission. After careful planning and selection of delegates the conference was held in Manchester in May 1980.[26]

Four papers were presented at the conference dealing with dependency, occupational segregation, domestic relationships and new technologies. The topics were carefully chosen to stay within the terms of the EC's employment remit, but within that to delve deep. On this basis a real debate seems to have taken place, revealing the extent to which similar proposals (for example, on parental leave or on measures to encourage part-time work) resonated differently with and might have very different effects on women in the various countries.

In the end, agreement was reached to recommend that future EC policy should be based on the individualisation of benefits, positive action to desegregate the labour market, the provision of a wide variety of child-care facilities, and the development of 'appropriate' leave arrangements.

On organisational questions, the conference looked to the strengthening both of the national units and of the specialised structures within the Commission. Trade union women at the conference, while expressing sympathy with the policy proposals, again opposed in principle the separate organisation of women in the employment field.

This conference represented perhaps the height of the achievement of official (lone) women in the European context. The proposals were imaginative and well targeted and had they been even partially implemented would have made a huge difference to the situation of working women. They seem to have been drawn up in the belief that if appropriate proposals were made, the EC member states might be persuaded to adopt in the eighties a further set of Directives to complement those of the seventies. However, what was singularly lacking from the proposals was any programme of mobilisation, or strategy to obtain backing for these proposals from a wider audience of women. Nor was there any apparent realisation of how much the seventies programme owed to the activism of grassroots women and the shock tactics of feminism. Surprisingly, the only person who raised these issues overtly was the Commissioner, Henk Vredeling, in his speech at the end of the conference. In a phrase which must have stunned many of the delegates, he said that women needed to take action, 'possibly violent action', to get what they wanted.[27] He was clearly much more aware than the delegates of the changing mood in the EC Council of Ministers, and the increasing difficulties facing the adoption of social policy measures.

As a result of this conference, the various national equality agencies and units were brought together by the European Commission first as a Standing Liaison Group and then at the end of 1981 as the Advisory Committee on Equal Opportunities for Men and Women. The task of the Committee was 'to advise the Commission on the formulation and implementation of policy' and 'ensure the continuous exchange of information'.[28] Although initially hopes were high that it could act as an effective transmission belt between the European and national levels, and aggregate the strengths of the different units, in practice this seems rarely to have happened. Needing far more resources to be effective, and suffering all the political and cultural difficulties of transnational institutional structures, the Committee seems for much of the eighties to have lacked both commitment and competence.[29] The conclusions of the 1980 conference, however, did provide an important input into future EC policy making.

These developments coincided with one of the periodic moments of change in the Commission. In January 1981, Henk Vredeling was replaced as Social Affairs Commissioner by Ivor Richard, the British former Labour MP. In May, Jacqueline Nonon left the Women's Bureau for a top EC job in Paris. Her successor, Odile Quintin, did not take up her post until early in 1982, and in the interim the Bureau was run by junior women who were also more radical.[30] These changes shifted the kaleidoscope and it took a while for new patterns to emerge.

The Parliament's Resolution

Attending the Manchester Conference was a delegation of five women MEPs from the newly elected European Parliament. According to the written records, they appear to have said very little, and no mention is made in the conclusions of their role. The 1979 European elections were the first to be conducted on direct universal suffrage, and the effect was to increase the proportion of women members from 11 out of 198 in the old Parliament (5 per cent), to 66 out of 410 in the new (16 per cent).[31] Direct elections brought in a right-wing majority – but also confirmed the determination of MEPs to extend the Parliament's powers and role.

This was certainly the mood of many of the women MEPs, who felt not only that new things should be done but that at least some of these should directly involve women. Thus quite soon after the new Parliament met, French and German women MEPs persuaded the Socialist Group to press for the setting up of an Ad Hoc Committee on Women's Rights. That this proposal was accepted by the full Parliament was very largely due to the support given to it by the new President of the Parliament, the French liberal, Simone Veil.[32] The remit of the Committee was to prepare a report on the situation of women and submit a resolution for the Parliament to debate in 1980 – later extended to 1981.[33]

The membership of the Committee covered all political groups and ten of its original thirty-five members were men. The chair was the French socialist, Yvette Roudy, the rapporteur, Hanja Maij-Weigen, a Dutch Christian Democrat. Its active members spanned the spectrum from the Italian Communist, Maria Cinciari Rodano, to the British Conservative, Shelagh Roberts.[34] All of these were politically active women elected very recently to represent conflicting parties and ideologies and bound to a greater or lesser extent by party discipline. They set up the Committee in the conviction that they shared enough common interest to produce a useful report.

The Committee held eleven open meetings during 1980 and its active members prepared papers on different issues. It was decided to hold a public hearing in Milan in October 1980 on two issues, women and social security, and the position of women working in small- and medium-sized businesses and in agriculture. It seems that this was the first time this latter issue (which provided a counterweight to the urban emphasis of the seventies Directives) had been raised in a Community context.[35]

The draft of the report and final resolution caused much debate and some controversy within the group. Roudy states that she was determined that the issue of sexual politics should not be avoided. The two issues she wanted to raise for consideration were the differential availability of abortion across the EC and the continuing practice in some member states of 'allowing' genital mutilation to be performed. In each case she felt there was a genuine reason for comparing practice and inviting an EC response.[36]

This was by no means agreed by all the group, many of whom, whatever they might feel personally about the issue of abortion, felt that reference to it in the resolution would cause problems in getting broader support. Shelagh Roberts wanted to keep the scope of the resolution narrow but deep (in the mode of the Manchester meeting) and she inveighed against the 'ardent and unreasonable feminists' who were with her on the Committee.[37] In the end a compromise was agreed by the group, raising the issue of abortion but not proposing any precise action. The issue of genital mutilation was also included though the reference was amended in the final text.

The report and resolution as presented to Parliament (and they were not much changed) covered a broad scope.[38] The resolution emphasised the importance of implementing the existing Directives and the need to expand choices for women, particularly in the areas of employment, education, and healthcare – it was here that the points were made about abortion. Significantly, the resolution then highlighted the needs of special groups of vulnerable women (particularly immigrant women, women in family businesses and women in thinly populated rural areas) constituting the first substantial recognition in a Community document of the needs of different categories of women.

The debate on this resolution, which took place on 10 February 1981, caused great excitement. It was the first time such an issue had ever been raised in the Parliament. Many male MEPs stayed away. Others came to patronise, a few to support. Most interesting was the debate among women themselves. A number of women belonging to traditional parties spoke out in support of the resolution – although in some cases with hesitation. Marlene Lenz from Germany, speaking for the Christian Democrat group (the European People's Party), expressed very honestly the dilemma as she saw it for traditional women, and the risks involved in the inevitable move which they were making away from the protection of men. She urged in this situation that pay should not become 'the only yardstick for achievement and recognition'.[39]

The women of the social-democratic left emphasised the diversity of women's interests and the need to take account of the situation of women at the base. Communist women challenged the notion of equality which lay at the root of the Directives. Ever the politician, Yvette Roudy was looking to the vote. 'I wasn't listening to what was said,' she recalls, 'I was totting up whether we had enough votes to win.' In her own speech she emphasised that the text was already a compromise – and urged members to vote for it.

In the end the vote was won by 173 to 101, with 24 abstentions.[40] Only a few amendments were adopted: none to the paragraphs on abortion. The result caused huge relief and excitement. A range of observers including some representatives of the feminist press had been invited to share the occasion. Ruth Wallsgrove from the UK's *Spare Rib* admitted, having started off sceptical, that as the vote was declared she felt a 'great rush of sisterhood' with all of the women there. 'We *all* knew we were outsiders,' she wrote, 'in this vast and lame and very male institution.'[41]

Although of no legal significance, the resolution had a considerable influence on EC policy making in the eighties. Qualitatively different from the Manchester conclusions, it gave much more sense of the breadth and diversity of women's interests and introduced some important new emphases. In July 1981, the mandate of the Committee was extended. It became a permanent standing committee of the Parliament in 1984 – as the Committee on Women's Rights.

The origins of CREW

Ruth Wallsgrove's comments illustrate the distance which existed between the bulk of women's autonomous organisations and the kinds of developments discussed above. Despite the influence which, I have argued, feminism in general had had on the development of the EC women's policy up to this point, direct connections were noticeably lacking. By the early eighties, the women's movement had fragmented in most EC member states, unable on the whole to solve the contradictions involved in creating and sustaining broad-based or national organisations. Instead there was a proliferation of small and diverse activities concentrating on particular spheres and issues. While confrontational tactics and the resulting public shock had largely disappeared, a survey of available evidence would suggest that there was more rather than less activity taking place, creating a presence and an expertise across a broad swathe of society.[42]

It was hard, however, for women's organisations of this kind operating in one country to engage with the European arena – or indeed to know much about it. The only country where feminist groups did have this access was Belgium, where it was much easier to see Community institutions in their true role as extensions of local and national politics. What was needed to increase this kind of awareness were women's groups which were transnational in composition, and which could begin to take up issues emerging at the EC level, and spread information about them from a feminist point of view.

The group which sparked off a new initiative along these lines was the Women's Organization for Equality (WOE). WOE had been formed in 1971, and was made up of English-speaking women from a wide range of countries who found themselves for a variety of reasons living in Brussels. Initially this was a consciousness-raising (rap) group, concerned with mutual support, sexual politics and celebrating women's achievements across the world. By 1980 WOE had a membership of over 100, a continuing programme of events, and a lively newsletter. It operated alongside Belgian women's groups and French-speaking networks, but remained separate from them.[43]

WOE's activism showed no signs of diminishing towards the end of the seventies. And in 1978, because women were so clearly on the EC agenda, a special sub-group was set up called the Women's European Action Group, with the precise intention 'of finding out how the European institutions work, what they do (and don't do) for women, and how women get into politics'. Two years later WEAG turned into CREW – the Centre for Research on European Women. The aim of CREW was similar to WEAG but with more emphasis on 'closing the information gap' while keeping a 'definite feminist approach'.[44]

CREW was run as a cooperative but began from fairly early on to develop a rigorous attitude to work and information gathering. There were some who regretted this new emphasis and the loss of the more open and friendly WOE atmosphere. Some drifted away but in the end WOE itself dwindled. There was not enough energy to support two organisations and CREW seemed to represent the cutting edge. During the eighties, *CREW Reports*, (published from October 1981 in both English and French) provided a source of information and a focus for networking among feminist and grassroots women's organisations.[45] Its great achievement was to represent the EC as an exciting political arena. During this time, CREW was increasingly asked, despite its formal 'research only' role, to act as spokesperson for autonomous feminism at the European level. From 1981 on CREW began to plan, and to try to raise money for, a coordination of women's organisations to lobby the European institutions.

The Bonn conference

The big traditional women's organisations were better equipped to deal with Euro-lobbying than were the autonomous groups. The existence of the Standing Liaison Group and the stance taken by the Parliament alerted these groups to the fact that this might now be an appropriate time to set up a women's lobby across the EC. This move was encouraged by the Women's Information Service of the Commission, partly it would seem as a way of preempting any action by CREW. In May 1982 the Women's Information Service, in conjunction with the German Women's Council (*Deutscher Frauenrat*), sponsored a meeting of EC women's organisations in Bonn. The bulk of those invited were traditional women's organisations, with a few more feminist groups added in at the last moment. CREW was invited to the meeting together with members of the women's committee of the European Trade Union Confederation (ETUC).

Although no formal resolution was put forward, there was some discussion at the meeting of a proposal to establish a European women's lobby mainly on the basis of the big (traditional) women's councils. This suggestion was opposed by CREW, the trade union women and other feminist groups, on the grounds that as things were no such lobby could be truly representative of women.[46] The meeting was also given an indication that Ivor Richard (the Commissioner for Social Affairs) felt 'some scepticism' about a single organisation that would represent 'all the various and sometimes conflicting' interests of women.[47]

As a result of these direct and indirect oppositions, the development of a formal European women's lobby was postponed for a decade. Feminist women were strong enough at this stage to prevent a one-sided lobby being set up – they were not strong enough to create a more representative body. Soon after the Bonn conference, however, a grant was given to CREW by the Women's Bureau in DG V for the purpose of setting up a coordination of women's organisations, presumably to strengthen the feminist hand in any future negotiations. This led to a conference in Brussels in 1983 and to the creation of the European Network of Women (ENOW) – a loose association of grassroots, autonomous women's organisations.[48] Thus in the eighties no comprehensive, overarching women's representation existed at the European level. This left the way open for more diverse and fluid interventions by different groups of women on specific issues and at specific times.

The above accounts give some indication of the variety of women's activities developing at the European level in the early eighties. The contrasting priorities and style of the different strands is very marked and where they overlapped wariness as much as cooperation was the result. In the end, while there were clear advantages to be derived from avoiding permanent structures, the lack of cohesion was also damaging.

All of these developments took place as part of or in response to the process of implementation. Women came together to form new groups because increased awareness was seeping through about what had been adopted and to plan for new policy. Alongside this, but with few direct connections, the more focused process of judicial enforcement finally came into the picture. As a result, specific actions by the European Commission and rulings in the European Court began to play a part in fleshing out the detail of what had been negotiated. This affected the process of incorporation and application at national level and also provided a possible (but unreliable) tool for use by activist groups and agencies.

Judicial Enforcement – Some German Cases

Leaving judicial enforcement to the end of this chapter serves to emphasise that it is part of a political process. Nevertheless, it is an important part and one with its own dynamic, which has brought to the enforcement of the equal treatment policy techniques and a rigour primarily designed to break down barriers to trade and create the common market. Judicial enforcement at the level of the EC is authoritative, appears hierarchical and targets in an often unpredictable way particular aspects of policy and legislation. But because the European Court is responding to cases which, however distantly, represent genuine disputes, and because its rulings have to be applied right through the legal systems of the member states, complex interactions between the national and European levels are produced.

As discussed in chapter 4, two forms of enforcement are provided for in the Treaty – the so-called 'infringement actions' under Article 169, and the references from the national courts under Article 177. Under Article 169, the Commission can, if it considers that a member state has failed to fulfill an obligation under the Treaty, issue a 'reasoned opinion' and if necessary bring a case against the offending state before the Court.[49] Article 177 references from national courts to the ECJ, by contrast, involve no action by the Community administration and result from cases brought in national courts to enforce or interpret European measures. In the social field in particular, it is unlikely that individuals on their own will be able to argue for or support such a reference; they need to be advised and assisted by a larger body, an equality agency, for example, or a trade union.[50]

Four cases concerning Germany and the application of the Equal Treatment Directive, three references and an infringement action, all coming almost within the space of one year, illustrate some of the effects of such procedures. They relate back to issues raised in the first section of this chapter.

Germany and equal treatment

In the Commission's 1981 review of the implementation of the Equal Treatment Directive (ETD), Germany was faulted in a number of ways.[51] These included the limitation of the 1980 compliance law to the private sector, which according to the Commission left the self-employed and public employees inadequately protected. The Commission also objected to the fact that the additional maternity leave scheme (the *Mutterschutzgesetz*) was for mothers only, and to the fact that Germany had not listed or made any provision to review sex-specific occupations. The review in general adopted a broad view of equality, seeking to narrow as far as possible the exceptions and evasions that member states seemed prone to introduce.[52]

German officials may well have been irritated by the tone of the review, given their reluctance in the first place to implement the equal treatment measures. Despite the fact that the SPD government was again holding consultations on the possibility of introducing a full anti-discrimination law, the relevant government departments seem to have been unwilling to discuss with the Commission these more detailed complaints. As a result, a 'reasoned opinion' was finally issued by the Commission in October 1982, just as the SPD lost power. The new CDU-dominated government seemed happy to stonewall on the issues and let a case go to the European Court.

Before this happened, however, rulings were made in three cases referred to the ECJ by the German courts. The cases were all directly or indirectly the product of activity by the trade unions or equality units and of publicity surrounding the new compliance law. The first two of these cases concerned the same issue (incidentally, not one picked up in the Commission's review), namely, the inability of the German courts to award any real damages or apply an effective sanction even if employers were found guilty of discrimination in the hiring of workers.

In the first of these cases (*Von Colson and Kamann* v. *Land Nordrhein-Westfalen*) two women social workers had been refused employment in a male prison, although they seemed clearly the most competent applicants.[53] The Hamm Labour Court (*Arbeitsgericht*) found the discrimination blatant but could apply no effective sanctions against the employer. Unusually for a first level court, the Hamm officials took the initiative themselves to refer the case to the ECJ, asking if the ETD required stronger sanctions – either a requirement to hire the person or financial compensation. This case was joined with a similar case from Hamburg (*Harz* v. *Deutsche Tradex*) which involved the private rather than the public sector.[54]

In its ruling of 10 April 1984, the ECJ found against a requirement to hire but held that minimal compensation was not enough. Although member states had discretion as to what kind of sanctions they applied, these 'should ensure real and effective legal protection and have a genuine deterrent effect on the employer'. While not finding the ETD provisions either vertically or horizontally directly effective in this respect, the Court in effect urged the German courts themselves to construe national law to comply with this ruling. This both the Hamm and Hamburg Labour Courts subsequently did, granting each of the plaintiffs six months' pay plus interest by way of compensation.[55]

The third case (*Hofmann* v. *Barmer Ersatzkasse*) involved the disputed additional maternity leave scheme (*Mutterschutzgesetz*).[56] Ulrich Hofmann wished to take time off work to look after his baby so that the mother could return to work after the compulsory maternity leave period. He was not granted benefit because the additional leave was for the mother only. The issue before the ECJ was whether the granting of this additional leave came within the derogation allowed in the ETD for provisions 'concerning the protection of women, particularly as regards pregnancy and maternity' (Article 2(3)) or whether it was covered by the equality principle and should, as a result, be open to mothers and fathers equally. Hofmann and the Commission argued the latter, while the German government asserted that it came within their discretion and effectively concerned family rather than employment policy.

The ECJ, in a ruling which certainly surprised the Commission, supported the German government's case, arguing that the additional leave fell within the protection clause and could therefore quite properly be reserved to the mother only. In the course of the ruling, the Court stated, in a sentence which has been much quoted, that 'the Directive is not designed to settle questions concerning the organisation of the family, or to alter the division of responsibility between parents' (para. 24).

However, in a development which well illustrates the circularity of the implementation process, the German government, when making changes in 1986, replaced the mother's additional leave, as has already been described, with a parental leave scheme equally available to mother and father. Part of the reason seems to have been the adverse publicity generated by the Hofmann case, and the fact that a more 'progressive' woman minister, well in touch with both Catholic and feminist views of the family, was then in charge.[57]

Nevertheless, the Court's position was a restrictive one. Kirsten Scheiwe points out that the ruling in *Hofmann* was in marked contrast to the Court's usual 'generous and teleological mode of interpreting law', which often involved reading 'more into the law than what is written on its face'.[58] One cannot escape the feeling that the judges, while willing by this stage to make 'audacious' rulings concerning women in employment, were still wary about issues which involved motherhood, or the role of fathers in childcare.[59] They may also not have been willing, at this point and on this issue, to challenge what Ostner describes as the German authorities' 'understanding' that the EC's remit on social policy *only* covered issues to do with mobility of labour and employment.[60]

The infringement action then went ahead, but with the complaint about the *Mutterschutzgesetz* withdrawn. The main point at issue was whether the general provisions in the Federal Constitution, and more specific administrative provisions, provided equivalent guarantees in the public sector to those given by the amendments to the Civil Code in the private sector. In its ruling in May 1985, the ECJ rejected four out of five of the Commission's complaints, requiring the German government only to tighten up its procedures with regard to listing and reviewing sex-specific occupations. This ruling did not follow the main recommendations of the advocate general, Federico Mancini.[61]

There was surprise in the Commission and elsewhere at the ruling. Here again the decision may have been tactical, a desire not to confront the German government over issues involving a challenge to the Federal Constitution, and not to inflame a situation which was already contentious.

These examples demonstrate the complex processes and politics involved in judicial enforcement. The *Von Colson* and *Harz* cases were the starting point for a concern in the ECJ with sanctions in equal treatment which has had many ramifications; *Hofmann* marked the first but not the last attempt by the judges to set 'clear' boundaries between employment and family policy; and the infringement action demonstrated how unpredictable the outcomes of such cases can be. Three years earlier the British authorities had appeared equally obdurate over the work of equal value issue, but had been firmly put in their place by the Court.[62] In all of these cases valid legal arguments could have been made (and in some instances were made by the Advocate-General) to justify a different decision.

The attempts to implement the Directives thus set up a complex set of processes transcending the confines of the nation state. This chapter has demonstrated what some of these were, but only by way of examples. Similar reactions and interactions were occurring in respect of other member states and other actors. By this stage (the early eighties) the nature of women's politics as it developed around the EC policy had become more complex and its ramifications harder to follow. As will be evident from the discussion here, those involved in these developments quickly became concerned as much with devising new policy as with implementation. The next chapter will look at what happened to these aspirations in the EC of the eighties.

Notes

1 A rare exception is David Lewis and Helen Wallace, eds, *Policies into Practice – National and International Case Studies in Implementation*, Heinemann, London, 1984. For implementation in an EC context see Heinrich Siedentopf and Jacques Ziller, eds, *Making European Policies Work – The Implementation of Community Legislation in the Member States*, vol. 1: Comparative Syntheses, Sage, London, 1988.

2 For an early version of this section see Catherine Hoskyns, ' "Give us Equal Pay and We'll Open our Own Doors" – a Study of the Impact in the Federal Republic of Germany and in the Republic of Ireland of the European Community's Policy on Women's Rights', in M. Buckley and M. Anderson, eds, *Women, Equality and Europe*, Macmillan, Basingstoke, 1988.

3 Basic Law of the Federal Republic of Germany (*Grundgesetz*) Articles 3 (equality before the law), 6 (marriage, family, illegitimate children), and 9 (freedom of association).

4 Constitution of Ireland Articles 40(1) (personal rights), 41 (the family), 45 (2)(1) (social policy).

5 Garret Fitzgerald, *All in a Life – an Autobiography*, Macmillan, Basingstoke, 1991.

6 For insights into German and Irish feminism see Pauline Conroy Jackson, 'Managing the Mothers: the Case of Ireland' and Ilona Ostner, 'Slow Motion: Women, Work and the Family in Germany', both in Jane Lewis, ed., *Women and Social Policies in Europe*, Edward Elgar, Aldershot, 1993. See also discussion in chapter 2 this volume.

7 The material in this section is drawn from interviews conducted in Bonn in 1983 and in Dublin in 1985.

8 The full title is *Gesetz über die Gleichbehandlung von Männern und Frauen am Arbeitsplatz und über die Erhaltung von Ansprüchen bei Betriebsübergang* (*Arbeitsrechtliches EG – Anpassungsgesetz*) 13 August 1980. The sub-title means 'Labour Law to Comply with EC Provisions' and was added to make clear that the measures were being adopted under sufferance.

9 Anti-Discrimination (Pay) Act, 1974. This came into effect on 31 December 1975, just in time to meet the EPD deadline of 10 February 1976.

10 Employment Equality Act, 1977, Article 2.

11 See discussion in chapter 6 this volume. An account of German social security law in the light of the SSD is given in Klaus Bertelsman, Ursula Rust, 'Equal Opportunity Regulations for Employed Men and Women in the Federal Republic of Germany', in M. Verwilghen, ed., *Equality in Law Between Men and Women in the European Community*, Presses Universitaires de Louvain, Louvain-La-Neuve, 1986, vol. 2, pp. 106–14.

12 Information from interviews with officials in the *Arbeitsstab frauenpolitik*, Bonn, March 1988. The proposals were finally incorporated in the *Bundeserziehungsgeldgesetz* (BErzGG) of 6 December 1985.

13 The additional maternity leave scheme (*Mutterschutzgesetz*) followed the compulsory maternity leave period after the birth of the baby. The fact that it was restricted to mothers only was the subject in 1983 of a reference to the European Court (*Hofmann* v. *Barmer Ersatzkasse*). The *Hofmann* case and its implications are discussed in more detail at the end of this chapter.

14 The parental leave benefit is means-tested once the baby reaches seven months and is paid for out of federal taxes. Parents who give up work to take the benefit have the right to return to their employment, though not necessarily to the same job or status. For accounts in English of the benefit and its implications see Ostner, 'Slow Motion', pp. 101–3, and Karl Bieback, 'Family Benefits: New Legal Structures of Subsidizing the Family – a Comparison of Australian, British and German Social Security Systems', *Journal of European Social Policy*, vol. 2 (4), 1992, pp. 239–54.

15 The leave was first extended to 18 months, then 24 months. A further extension to 36 months is under discussion.

16 Ilona Ostner, 'The Women and Welfare Debate', in L. Hantrais, S. Mangen, eds, *Family Policy and the Welfare of Women*, Cross-National Research Group, Loughborough University, 1994, p. 46. Karl Biebeck also supports this view, see 'Family Benefits', p. 248.

17 This account is based on Rosheen Callender, 'Ireland and the Implementation of Directive 79/7/EEC: the Social, Legal and Political Issues', in G. Whyte, ed., *Sex Equality, Community Rights and Irish Social Welfare Law*, Irish Centre for European Law, Trinity College, Dublin, 1988.

18 This sort of situation was what the derogations in the SSD were intended to avoid. However, the Irish authorities, while aware of the implications of the Directive, seem to have been unable during the six years given for implementation to come up with a solution.

19 Callender, 'Ireland and the Implementation of Directive 79/7/EEC', pp. 12–13.

20 Deirdre Curtin, *Irish Employment Equality Law*, The Round Hall Press, Dublin, 1989, ch. 9.3.

21 A vivid account of popular involvement in this case is given in: *Wir wollen gleiche Löhne – Keiner schiebt uns weg!* (We want equal pay – Nobody can shove us aside!), Industriegewerkschaft Druck und Papier, Dortmund 1982. I am grateful to Gabriele Freidank for providing me with this information. For the Court judgment see *Bundesarbeitsgericht* AP 117 (Article 3 (2) *Grundgesetz*), 9 September 1981.

22 Conroy Jackson, 'Managing the Mothers', p. 42.

23 An account of how the referendum came about and its implications is given in Ailbhe Smyth, ed., *The Abortion Papers Ireland*, Attic Press, Dublin, 1992. For a governmental view, see Fitzgerald, *All in a Life*, pp. 440–46.

24 For information on the CTF see 'le travail des femmes', special issue *Revue française des affaires sociales*, December 1981. An assessment of the EOC in this period is given in Vera Sacks, 'The Equal Opportunities Commission – Ten Years On', *Modern Law Review*, vol. 49, 1986, pp. 560–92.

25 Catherine Barnard, *A European Litigation Strategy: the Case of the Equal Opportunities Commission*, LLM thesis, European University Institute, Florence 1990. Links with the EC fitted in well with the ethos of those in charge in the EOC in this period. Barnard describes them as preferring 'high level but low profile' consultation with opinion leaders, to generating 'a policy network at grassroots level', p. 32.

26 Interview, Dipak Nandy EOC, Manchester, February 1986. The EOC produced a full report of the conference proceedings under the title 'Equality for Women, Assessment – Problems – Perspectives, a European Project', EOC, Manchester, 1980. I have drawn widely on this report in the following account.

27 EOC, 'Equality for Women', p. 49.

28 Commission Decision of 9 December 1981 relating to the setting up of an Advisory Committee on Equal Opportunities for Women and Men (82/43/EEC).

29 Interview Nandy, February 1986.

30 Quintin's appointment established the tradition, continued ever since, that the head of the Bureau should be a French woman.

31 Elizabeth Vallance and Elizabeth Davies, *Women of Europe – Women MEPs and Equality Policy*, Cambridge University Press, Cambridge, 1986, p. 7. For the first time in this election the French Socialist Party (PSF) put a woman candidate at every third place on their list. This led to six women being elected out of twenty.

32 Interview, Yvette Roudy, Paris, July 1994.

33 Resolution on the setting up of an Ad Hoc Committee on Women's Rights, 26 October 1979, OJ C 289, 19 November 1979.

34 The full list of members is given in *Women of Europe*, Special European Parliament Issue, 19/81, pp. 93–4. Roudy gives an account of her background, the work of the Committee, and her approach to feminism in *A cause d'elles*, Albin Michel, Paris, 1985.

35 *Women of Europe*, 17/80, p. 3. A full transcript of the hearing was issued by the Parliament, document EP 68.457, 8 November 1980.

36 Roudy, interview, 1994.

37 She made this statement (but I thought with some affection) to a delegation from Rights of Women (UK) of which I was a member, in Strasbourg in June 1981.

38 The best source for these documents is European Parliament, *The Position of Women in the European Community – European Parliament Debates*, OOPEC, Luxembourg, 1981. This gives the draft and final texts of the resolution, and a full account of the debates,

amendments and voting. The full text of the report is given in European Parliament, *Working Documents 1980–1981*, Document 1–829/80–11, 29 January 1981.
39 EP, *Position of Women*, pp. 111–12.
40 Details of how the members voted is given in *Women of Europe*, 19/81, p. 91.
41 *Spare Rib*, April 1981, p. 13.
42 This is convincingly argued in Mary Katzenstein and Carol Mueller, eds, *The Women's Movements of the United States and Western Europe – Consciousness, Political Opportunity and Public Policy*, Temple University Press, Philadelphia, 1987.
43 I am grateful to Rebecca Franceskides and Marie-Françoise Stewart, both former members of WOE, for discussing this period with me.
44 *Women's Organization for Equality*, newsletters, March and April 1981.
45 *CREW Reports* existed alongside the more voluminous *Women of Europe* produced from 1977 to 1992 by the Women's Information Service in DG X of the European Commission. Together they provide a rich and varied women-centred account of the period.
46 The fullest account of the Bonn Conference is given in *Women of Europe*, 26/82, pp. 73–87. The issue of the lobby is only referred to obliquely, however.
47 *Women of Europe*, 26/82, p. 77. Richard's views, conveyed by a member of his cabinet, Karen Fogg, were particularly significant, since without financial support from DG V no such lobby could be set up. A difference of orientation was evident here between DG X (information) having good contacts with the traditional women's organisations and DG V (social affairs) with more links to CREW and autonomous feminism.
48 The UK delegation at the founding ENOW conference consisted of representatives from the Newcastle Tenants Project, Coventry Workshop, Southampton University Faculty of Law, the 300 Group, Welsh Women's Aid and the Northern Ireland Women's Rights Movement. This contrasts with the organisations representing the UK at the Bonn conference which were: the National Federation of Women's Institutes, the National Council of Women, the National Union of Townswomen's Guilds, and the UK Federation of Business and Professional Women.
49 For an account of the dialogue which went on with regard to equal treatment infringement actions see Gerassimos Zorbas, 'Some Examples of Commission Intervention on Equality', *Social Europe*, Supplement 2/86, pp. 127–53. In the period up to 1986 only six of these reached the stage of a case before the Court.
50 By 1987 (excluding the *Defrenne* cases) 22 references on equal treatment issues had been made to the European Court. Twelve of these cases came from the UK, five from Germany, four from the Netherlands and one from Ireland. It seems no accident that the early references all came from countries with active equality agencies or trade unions, and/or lawyers committed to fighting discrimination cases. For quick reference material on these cases, see Angela Byre, *Leading Cases and Materials on the Social Policy of the EEC*, Kluwer, Deventer, 1989.
51 Report from the Commission to the Council on the situation at 12 August 1980 with regard to the implementation of the principle of equal treatment for men and women as regards access to employment and promotion, access to vocational guidance and training, and working conditions, COM(80) 832 final, 11 February 1981.
52 The review was mainly the work of Camille Pichault, an experienced Belgian civil servant seconded to the Women's Bureau from 1979 to 1982. Pichault was both an active feminist and familiar with the ways of government.
53 *Von Colson and Kamann*, ECJ Case 14/83, 1984.
54 *Harz*, ECJ Case 79/83, 1984.
55 For a commentary on these two cases see Deirdre Curtin, 'Effective Sanctions and the Equal Treatment Directive: the Von Colson and Harz Cases', *Common Market Law Review*, vol. 22, no. 3, 1985, pp. 505–32.
56 *Hofmann*, ECJ Case 184/83, 1984.
57 This was Rita Süsmuth who became Minister for Youth, Family, Women and Health in 1985.
58 Kirsten Scheiwe, 'EC Law's Unequal Treatment of the Family: the Case Law of the European Court of Justice on Rules Prohibiting Discrimination on Grounds of Sex and Nationality', *Social and Legal Studies*, vol. 3, no. 2, 1994, pp. 252–3.

59 It is worth noting in this context that since its inception the Court has never had a woman judge. One advocate general has been a woman. A woman judge might well have agreed with this ruling, but it is unlikely that she would have been 'wary' about motherhood.
60 Personal communication with the author, May 1994.
61 *Commission* v. *Federal Republic of Germany*, ECJ Case 248/83, 1985.
62 ECJ Case 61/81, 1982. A good account of the 1982 infringement action against Britain is given in Jane Pillinger, *Feminising the Market – Women's Pay and Employment in the European Community*, Macmillan, Basingstoke, 1992, ch. 6.

8

Progress in a Cold Climate

By the early eighties the fragile conjuncture which had produced EC equal treatment legislation over the previous decade, had almost entirely vanished. In a situation of prolonged economic crisis, where recession and unemployment showed no signs of lifting, European governments whether of the right or left were struggling to restore competitiveness and negotiate new social and political deals. As nation state authorities lost control over economic management to the European or international level, they sought to corral popular opinion more closely and hold on tightly to the reins of social policy.[1]

In an increasingly fragmented world where the globalisation of communications and transnational awareness were creating diversity and dissonance, the EC provided a rare mix of coordinating structures which linked nation states and the elites within them. As a result, the EC became the main forum for debating the crucial problems facing Western Europe and for devising solutions. A 'women's presence' at this level thus gained a new significance.

It was in this context that a battle was fought out within the European institutions over the 'correct' labour market and social policies to be pursued both at EC and national level. The struggle was between those who were convinced of the need to cut costs and deregulate, whatever the social consequences, in order to compete more effectively, and those who conceded the need to improve competitiveness and restructure European business, but wished to do this by pursuing 'a European middle way', which would at the same time enforce a minimum set of rights for workers and encourage solidarity in European society as a whole.[2]

Gradually the deregulators began to predominate as it became clear how far the power balance between capital and labour had shifted. New technology was giving employers freedom to diversify and decentralise, and in many areas this made it possible for established industrial practices to be undercut and for trade unions to be outflanked or defeated.[3] Nowhere was this more evident than in Britain, where from 1979 the new Conservative Prime Minister, Margaret Thatcher, did everything possible to encourage employer freedom and curb societal controls and trade union power. In France, where the socialists came to power in 1981, the government was unable to pursue for long its plans for social reconstruction, though some important changes were made. The European Commission (with a weak president in the early eighties) could do little to counter these trends, and was forced to jettison proposals for reducing working time and protecting part-time workers in favour of programmes encouraging and monitoring 'flexibility' and deregulation.[4]

After a period of disarray at EC level, and near panic at the failure of the EC as a whole to compete with Japan and the USA, the underlying strength of the EC's coordinating structures became apparent. In 1985 a unanimous decision was reached by the member state governments to improve competitiveness by completing market liberalisation among the twelve, and by making important revisions to the Treaty of Rome through the Single European Act.[5] This involved introducing qualified majority voting in the Council of Ministers for most measures to complete the single market. The deadline for these developments was set at 1992, a date which quickly became an emotive symbol for the revitalised EC. Paradoxically, part of the success of this package was due to the appointment of Jacques Delors, the capable French finance minister, as Commission president from 1985. Delors was a convincing proponent of the 'European middle way', and it was largely as a result of his agency, and of ongoing tensions in the labour market, that social policy came onto the EC agenda again in the late eighties.[6]

It is against this backdrop of 'disorganised capitalism' that the position of women in the EC in the eighties, and the effects of the policies so far adopted, have to be evaluated. All women, whether paid or unpaid workers, whether indigenous or foreign, whether organising locally, nationally, or at EC level, were affected by these new circumstances. The willingness of women to continue to combine domestic work with part-time paid employment provided a highly 'suitable' labour force in this situation. As is shown in Appendix 6.2, two-thirds of the new jobs created between 1983 and 1989 in the EC (many of them part-time and/or temporary) went to women. Over the same period, unemployment among women throughout the EC remained higher than that of men. These two statistics taken together demonstrate the striking increase in women's labour market activity during this time.[7]

A key question for the eighties, therefore, as far as a women's employment policy was concerned, was what value would be put on this new congruence between women's working lives and the needs of industry, and whether an effective challenge could be mounted to continuing job segregation and stereotyping.[8] Since the EC and the single market programme were now setting the frame for such debates and struggles, the pre-existing concern with gender issues in employment at this level might provide an important lever. This would be doubly so if it enabled broader issues to be raised, going beyond the concerns of women in paid work, narrowly defined.

In these circumstances, the activism and policy development in the EC on women's issues during the seventies created some strengths for women. It was to prove hard for deregulatory zealots to dismantle the equal treatment legislation, particularly as the ECJ throughout the eighties continued to expand and enforce its provisions, at least as far as core employment rights were concerned. At the same time, transnational organisation among women and some international/regional infrastructures were developing. Very importantly these also involved the European Parliament, which after 1984 had a more progressive majority and at least some control over EC spending on social programmes, including those for women.

At the same time, and partly in response to these initiatives, a solid base of comparative and policy-oriented research was beginning to develop. This came from reviews and studies sponsored by the European institutions and also from less formal cross-cutting meetings of academics, activists and policy makers.[9] These kinds of developments represented a linking of organisational as well as national cultures and began to create a foundation for policy and action across the EC. This tied in with a continuing focus on women's issues in the international arena, as demonstrated by the OECD's high level conference on women in the labour market in April 1980, and the activity around the UN Decade for Women, which generated spectacular if controversial conferences in Copenhagen in 1980 and Nairobi in 1985.[10]

It is a measure of the strength of the women's presence at EC level that throughout the eighties a strong policy initiative on women's issues was maintained. The pathways and markers for this were provided by the three EC action programmes on equal opportunities for women which covered the period 1982–95. These action programmes were coordinated by the Women's Bureau (later renamed the Equal Opportunities Unit) in the European Commission, and funded through a budget line protected by a strong lobby in the Parliament, orchestrated by its Committee on Women's Rights. The programmes proposed new policy initiatives, monitored and developed old ones, and supported research and networking. Despite the impact of the recession and the compromises which had to be made, there was still a buzz around the policy during the eighties and the Women's Bureau remained an exciting place to work.[11]

The next two sections of this chapter will assess the first two of these action programmes against this background and in the light of three main questions: how far did these programmes stretch out beyond the elite and encourage networking and mobilisation among new layers of women; what new issues and emphases were developed during this period and what compromises had to be made; and to what extent were women because of this presence able to influence other strands of EC policy and get involved at a more general level of debate?

The chapter will end with an assessment of the jurisprudence of the European Court on equal treatment issues during this same period. The Court's rulings provided some legitimation for the policy and considerable publicity. Its agenda, however, was by no means women-centred and its rulings were at times at odds with what was being proposed elsewhere.

Parental Leave, Farm Women and the 1986 Directive

The New Community Action Programme on Equal Opportunities (Action Programme 1) was drafted in the interregnum period in the Women's Bureau, after Nonon had left and before Quintin took up her post.[12] It thus represented a direct follow up to the Commission's review of the Equal Treatment Directive, discussed in chapter 7. In essence, the text went back to the two-pronged approach pioneered in 1974 by Nonon's ad hoc committee, and involved a combination of equal treatment and special treatment. This was expressed as a continuation of individual rights through legislation (equal treatment) and equal opportunities in practice (special treatment).

According to one of those involved in the drafting, the intention was to sharpen up the analysis and presentation in the document by introducing some feminist terminology into the text. In the end this was considered impractical and the Women's Bureau was helped by Commissioner Ivor Richard's cabinet to put it into more 'acceptable' language. Thus in the interests of making progress some of the sparkle went from the text – a well-known dilemma for those seeking to negotiate in situations where the culture and power balance are alien.

Various new proposals for legislation were made in the equal treatment strand of the Programme. These included a Directive on occupational pensions (an attempt finally to tie up the anomalies and gaps created in this field by the *Defrenne* cases and the Social Security Directive), a Directive to extend equal treatment to the self-employed and to women in agriculture (an issue picked up from the Parliament's resolution) and a Directive on parental leave. This last proposal (Action 7) was seen as both helping to reconcile paid work with family responsibilities and as promoting the sharing of family responsibilities between men and women. It also fitted in with the Commission's concern with the reduction of working time.

In the special treatment strand of the Programme, the main emphasis was on positive action, which was seen as an essential complement to the equal treatment provisions. Most of the positive action proposals focused on cross-cutting issues which were seen as affecting all women – for example, vocational choices, desegregation of the labour market, and the impact of new technologies. The Programme took a bold step, however, in proposing a specific action on the needs of immigrant women in employment and training (Action 14). This was the only proposal, other than the Directive on the self-employed, to target a specific group of women.

The tone of the Programme was still strong despite its more 'correct' language. Its main thrust was that women should not bear the brunt of the economic crisis nor should this be seen as a reason for slowing down the application of equal treatment. The document contained a draft Resolution approving the Programme and committing member states 'to consider favourably' the provision of resources. This was passed to the Council of Ministers for discussion and adoption.

The Resolution then went through the same negotiating procedure as had the Directives and similar kinds of objections were raised. One of those who attended the meetings commented on the hostility of the working groups to the continuing emphasis on women's issues. The adoption of the Resolution by the Council (in a relatively intact form though with the resource commitment removed) seems to have owed a great deal to the presence of Yvette Roudy, by then attending as Minister for Women's Rights in France. According to Ivor Richard, 'she was good at convincing her colleagues' and her interventions were decisive.[13] This would seem to be the first occasion when the presence of a committed woman in the Council had a direct effect on policy. The adoption of the Resolution in July 1982 gave the Women's Bureau the go-ahead to begin work on implementation.[14]

Implementing the Action Programme

Odile Quintin took up her post as head of the Women's Bureau in April 1982 and stayed until 1990. A French career official in the Commission, she had previously been working in external affairs. As one colleague put it, she was 'coherent with the organisation'. On women's issues, she describes herself as being 'not militant but interested'.[15] When she came to the Bureau there were three permanent administrative level staff; when she left there were five, with another five on short-term contracts.[16]

One of Quintin's main concerns was to create support for the policy and expand its scope. To this end, she encouraged the creation of coordinating networks of experts, to provide additional sources of information and advice, produce comparative research and establish transnational links. The first of these (known as the 'law network') was concerned with the application of the three existing equality Directives, and was charged initially with the task of defining indirect discrimination and looking at examples of how this concept was applied in the different member states. The law network was particularly important in that it linked, and provided a forum for discussion between, the three different units in DG V which dealt with the implementation and progression of the three seventies Directives.[17]

The main thrust of activity initially was on the preparation of new legislation – concentrating on the three proposed Directives mentioned above, and on a legal instrument to give backing to the positive action measures. Thus under Action Programme 1 a package of four new proposals on women's rights was envisaged. Also of great interest to women were proposals on the reorganisation of working time and on the regulation of part-time work, which were being developed elsewhere in DG V. The adoption of these six measures in the early eighties would have meant a huge increase both in employment regulation coming from the EC, and in the promotion of women's rights.

However, the time was far from ripe for the adoption of new social policy legislation. Even as Action Programme 1 was being approved by the Council, Ivor Richard, the Commissioner responsible, was going through a bruising time in trying to progress the so-called Vredeling Directive, left to him by his predecessor.[18] This Directive, which aimed at giving workers in multi-national companies some rights to information, provoked great controversy, particularly among American companies operating in Europe, who saw their privileged (and largely unregulated) position under threat. An effective lobby was mounted, first in the Parliament and then in the Council, to weaken the text and delay adoption. The proposal was finally abandoned in 1986.[19] The whole episode demonstrated the power of transnational business when its position was under attack, the growing obduracy of the British government, and the inability of the weakened labour movement to generate effective countervailing pressure at the European level.[20] Since at this stage all measures in the Council still had to be adopted by unanimity, British opposition, by now directed on grounds of principle against almost all social policy legislation, was an extremely serious obstacle.

A similar fate, though orchestrated with less virulence, befell the Commission's measures on the reduction of working time and on part-time work, representing as they did a different view of how the state might intervene to reduce unemployment and encourage more flexible working.[21] No real mobilisation took place in support of these proposals and their very existence was little known beyond those directly involved. A moving speech on the implications for women of the likely defeat of these measures was made by Ivor Richard in an address to the Advisory Committee on Equal Opportunities in November 1982. Like Vredeling before him, he made a vigorous appeal to those present to mobilise at national level and take action in support of the Commission's initiatives.[22]

The four women's measures suffered a more varied fate, benefiting initially from a certain momentum deriving from past achievements and then being caught by the new polemics on social policy. Behind the apparently random nature of the decisions taken, a familiar rationale can be discerned. Thus the measures most closely related to equality in employment, namely the Directives on occupational pensions and the self-employed, were adopted, albeit in much weakened forms, while the positive action provisions, evoking as they did earlier concerns about special treatment, were demoted to a Recommendation. And once again provisions which stretched out from the employment arena to embrace and modify domestic and family relationships were in the end rejected. This affected the parental leave Directive and the bulk of the measures in the Directive on the self-employed which sought to improve the status of 'helper spouses'.

Parental leave

The precise reasons for the failure of the Parental Leave Directive are significant. The draft for this Directive, which was submitted in November 1983, concerned the period of additional leave allowed to parents after maternity leave was finished.[23] It thus attempted to regulate just that area of policy which the ECJ was considering in the *Hofmann* case, discussed in chapter 7. The justification for the Directive was given as the need to harmonise an area of working conditions in order to prevent disruption of the market, and to assist in the achievement of equal treatment by encouraging the sharing of family responsibilities between working parents. In order to encourage the involvement of fathers, the draft proposed that each parent should have a three-month *non-transferable* entitlement to leave. Thus, only if the father also took up his entitlement, would a couple acquire the right to the full six months of leave. Whether or not an allowance was paid was left to the discretion of national governments.

Resistance to the Directive gradually grew, fanned by the unremitting opposition of the British government. Françoise Rutherford attributes the resistance to the fact that the Directive was proposing to engineer a huge change in social attitudes before the base for this was adequately established in national practice.[24] Certainly, the attempt to target so directly the behaviour of men, and to prescribe this at the level of the EC, seems to have caused alarm. States were moving on this issue (as we have seen in the case of Germany) but because it was such a sensitive area preferred to keep control at the national level. The ruling in the Hofmann case, which was made in July 1984, suggested that this was also the view of the ECJ. In the end, the Directive was seen as too prescriptive and too controlling for the deregulatory eighties, and it was shelved in June 1986.

In November 1985, a formal review of the application of Action Programme 1 was issued by the Commission.[25] This assumed that the Commission and the member states were jointly responsible for implementation and listed the actions taken by the different parties. The tone of the review was unsure compared with earlier documents. Obstacles and defeats were noted and regretted but there was a hesitancy about how far and in what ways to push. A parallel exercise was carried out by the European Network of Women which, while still connected to and supported by CREW, was beginning to develop a more independent presence. The ENOW review was forceful and single-minded and was based for the most part on detailed information from grassroots organisations.[26] There is no evidence that the views of ENOW were listened to in the Commission, except at the most informal level, or that its information was taken into account; in a sense, however, that was not the prime purpose. The more important aim was to inform feminist and grassroots movements of the strategies being pursued at the European level, and of the actions of governments. The lack of resources available, and the narrow range of issues which could be taken up at EC level, made it difficult for ENOW to establish a functioning structure.

By this stage – the mid eighties – one can begin to discern the shape of a women's European policy network. Its strength can be adduced from the fact that at a very difficult time and when other related policies were not advancing, a certain expansion of remit and infrastructure took place in the women's policy. Its weakness can be seen in the failure to deliver visible and effective mobilisation on specific issues. The apparent contradiction between these two phenomena can be explained by the fragile links which existed, on the one hand to the grassroots movement and on the other to the centres of power.

One of the most interesting expansions of the women's network during this period came through the activities of the women, and particularly the farm women, who campaigned for the adoption of the Directive on self-employed women and women in agriculture. The characteristics of that campaign and its outcomes help to illustrate some of the points made above about political influence and the nature of lobbying.

Farm women and the Directive on equal treatment for the self-employed[27]

The Directive on equal treatment for the self-employed (SED), adopted in December 1986, applies to a broad range of women in different situations and performing different roles.[28] However, it is generally accepted that it was farm women who provided the locomotive force for the Directive, and it is their situation which is thus of particular interest.[29] The Directive broke new ground in that it focused in part on the overlap between domestic and productive work which takes place in the family business, and sought to create a new category of 'worker' out of this dynamic.

During the seventies, the focus of the EC women's policy, and indeed as far as employment was concerned of feminism generally, was on employees' wages and the situation of the urban workforce. However, gradually a perception grew that a counterweight was needed, on the one hand towards women in self-employed occupations, and on the other towards the rural areas. Women in agriculture (farm women) spanned the two. Though the ETD and the SSD in formal terms covered the self-employed, this aspect had not been stressed either in research or policy. Significantly, it was the traditional women's organisations and the women MEPs, both sensitive to the politics of the countryside, who first picked up and made visible these new concerns.

Liesbeth Klaver, examining the situation of farm women in the Netherlands, cites the increase in the capitalisation of the farm (which emphasised its business aspect) and the increase in divorce (which entangled the family in new legal arrangements) as creating the context in which farm women began to take action.[30] This effervescence resulted in follow-up to Christine Delphy's pioneering work in France in the early seventies, and led to new research which sought to analyse the connecting threads of inheritance, unpaid work and exclusion which made up patriarchy on the family farm.[31] In particular, such research helped to problematise the way in which the domestic work of the farmer's wife shaded into productive work, without acquiring the normal remuneration or status attached to the latter. The flight of young women from the land, particularly noticeable in France and Ireland, demonstrated the consequences of this patriarchal grip at a time when women's skills were badly needed to cushion crisis and transformation.

These factors, and increased awareness about their implications, led to greater activism in women's farming organisations. In the late seventies, COPA-cf, the women's committee of COPA, the powerful European farm lobby, began actively to campaign for better rights and status for farm women.[32] It was this activity and its repercussions which were picked up by women MEPs at their hearing in Milan in October 1980.[33] Soon afterwards the Women's Bureau in the European Commission commissioned Blanche Sousi, a French woman lawyer, to report on the legal and social status of self-employed women and women in agriculture.

In November 1982 COPA-cf, with funding from the European Commission, held a conference in Grado, Italy to rally support for legislation. The conference seems to have been effectively organised with national delegations discussing and reporting back on each proposal.[34] Sousi made her recommendations and it was agreed to press for an EC Directive. A draft embodying these recommendations was then drawn up in the Women's Bureau.[35]

The purpose of this draft Directive was to extend equal treatment specifically to the self-employed and to women in family businesses including agriculture. Its scope covered two different categories: the self-employed and 'spouses without professional status', the so-called 'helper spouses'. The provisions were designed to make it easier for women in the first group to undertake commercial activity on an equal basis with men. For the helper-spouses, the main aim was to encourage recognition for the productive work being done, and the award of appropriate entitlements, training and benefits (Article 7). Finally, the Directive moved out of the equal treatment sphere and into that of 'protection' by seeking to ensure that both self-employed women and female helper spouses had access to social security benefits and/or replacement services during pregnancy and motherhood (Article 8).

The Directive covered a broad scope and had implications for family, matrimonial, inheritance, employment and social security law. Its real innovation, however, was the attempt through law to draw a tighter boundary in the family business between domestic and productive work, and to prevent the seepage from the one to the other. As Prechal and Burrows have pointed out, in doing this the drafters sought to go behind the equal treatment principle and provide 'a legally defined occupational status' for workers who would previously have fallen outside its bounds.[36]

When the Directive was finally discussed at the beginning of 1986, it appeared that while the governments of France, Italy and the Netherlands were broadly in favour of the Commission's draft, other countries either had problems with specific points, or reservations about the whole project.[37] In particular, there was widespread unease about the implications of Article 7, which was seen as sanctioning state intervention in the 'private' relations between spouses. Strong opposition was expressed by Britain on the grounds that the measures went beyond the competence of the EC, and by Ireland on the helper spouses provisions, which were seen as an unjustified intervention in the affairs of the traditional rural family.[38]

Given this opposition, and the need for decisions to be taken by unanimity, it would seem that the Directive only survived because it connected with other concerns about the self-employed, and because it was seen as politically unacceptable at this point to drop completely measures for rural women. In the end, the Directive was adopted, but with the key articles on the measures for helper spouses and for maternity protection reduced to 'undertakings to examine' rather than requirements for action. This, as the Commission pointed out, was to use the language of a Recommendation rather than a Directive.

Although it was perhaps surprising that this Directive went through at all, at the end the pressure seemed to die away. It may well be, though there is no direct proof of this, that the big farmers' unions, and even COPA itself, although apparently supportive at the beginning, were not sorry to see the more radical measures weakened. It was also significant that the Directive was entirely drafted in DG V, and seems never to have involved DG VI, the powerful directorate general responsible for the CAP and for agricultural politics generally.

Nor were the women themselves in the end very forceful. Despite the urgency of the demands being made, activist farm women were a small minority of the total of women in farming. Sally Shortall, surveying the Irish scene, shows how difficult it is for farm women to break with tradition, and emphasises the extent to which subordinate roles have been internalised.[39] The fact that the struggle was taking place within the family unit meant that new tactics were needed and many women drew back from the implications of 'mixing business with emotions'. At the same time, there was a lack of knowledge about the EC and about how to bring pressure. The action was also limited to women farming their own land – the remit of COPA. Thus the campaign never involved women farm labourers, or sought to create solidarity among all women working on the farm. A combination of these factors helps to explain why in the end pressure for the Directive was muted.

Despite the hesitations set out above, and the weakness of the final version of the Directive, progress on some of its central issues were made at national level before, during and after the negotiations.[40] The issue also became more public as is demonstrated by the fact that in 1989 the National Farmers' Union in the UK was forced to defend its position before farm women in a series of programmes broadcast on the

BBC's Woman's Hour.[41] Klaver notes that in the Netherlands the issue of helper spouses is now on the agenda both of women's organisations and of the farmers' unions, and that 'the Directive has had a lot to do with that'. This sequence demonstrates once again the reciprocal interaction of national and EC political processes. Had Articles 7 and 8 been adopted in a stronger form this process would have been speeded up; it has continued, however, even with the weaker statement.

The example of the SED illustrates very well the dynamic of the eighties. Expansion of the women's policy was not ruled out but had become more difficult. Governments were showing increasing reluctance to enter into open-ended legal obligations in such complex and far-reaching policy areas, and were much less willing to compromise. Women (or groups of women) were in a position to put items on the agenda but not to exert decisive influence on the final outcome.

The Poverty Tribunal, the Social Dimension and Sexual Politics

Despite (or perhaps because of) the liveliness of the Women's Bureau and the continuing development of policy, there seems to have been considerable confusion within the different sections of the Commission as to how to treat the issue of women's equality. Undoubtedly great swathes of the Commission's bureaucracy were either ignorant of or indifferent to the developments taking place. The unwillingness of DG V1 (the agricultural DG) to involve itself in the issues raised by the SED is a case in point. When in 1986, a report on equal opportunities in the Commission was published, the in-depth interviews revealed both stereotypical attitudes on the part of men and procedural blocks to women's advancement. These undoubtedly affected attitudes to policy also.[42] Figures given in Appendix 5 of the numbers of women and men at different levels in the Commission provide the statistical backup for such views – both then and now.

Even those who knew about or were interested in the women's policy seem to have seen it as serving a discrete and specialised interest and not as something which had a broader purpose. In DG V itself the emphasis was still on the traditional aspects of EC social policy: free movement of labour, use of the European Social Fund, and health and safety at work. In industrial relations the main concern was with the social partners and with the encouragement of dialogue between management and labour. Although a line for women's projects had been included in the ESF, elsewhere there seems to have been little concern to incorporate women or women's interests into mainstream policy. As one EC official commented:

> People would have been more likely to say 'women are being dealt with elsewhere therefore we don't need to emphasise them here' than 'the emphasis on women is Community policy and therefore we must deal with it.'

The way the issue of gender was handled in the EC Poverty Programme is a good example of some of these points. The Poverty Programme (located in DG V in a neighbouring division to the Women's Bureau) was one of the most innovative offshoots of the 1974 Social Action Programme, with a brief which – unusually – reached beyond the employment nexus.[43] As such it was extremely vulnerable, and Poverty 2 (1985–89) was only approved with reluctance by the member states. Despite growing evidence of 'the feminisation of poverty' (the proposition that whatever definition of poverty is used more women than men will fall within it)[44] it was decided not to highlight this aspect of poverty in planning the themes for the Programme. Although there may have been good arguments for this decision, it is significant that when it was taken all six of the senior administrators for Poverty 2 were men. As a result of this initial stance, nothing was done in the final report to draw together and analyse the evidence which emerged from the projects about the links between gender and poverty.[45]

Little attempt seems to have been made by either the Women's Bureau, or the EP Women's Committee or traditional women's organisations to lobby on this issue, and it may well have been that those responsible did not see it as being in their interests to identify 'women' so centrally with the issue of poverty. In the end it was the European Network of Women which highlighted the issue and began to campaign. For ENOW, the issues raised in the analysis of poverty and its gendered foundations were of direct concern to its grassroots women members.

Unable to convince Poverty 2 to take these issues on board directly, ENOW put most of its efforts from 1986 onwards into organising a Tribunal in Brussels 'as a response to the marginalisation of women's poverty at EC level'.[46] The Tribunal, which was held in November 1988, brought poor women from the different member states to Brussels, to bear witness to their situation. The sessions were moving for those who attended and demonstrated the links between vulnerability, male violence, low pay and female poverty across the EC. The women came over as militants rather than victims: they appeared to be elated at being in Brussels but realistic about what they might expect from the experience.[47]

The Tribunal had a twofold objective: to bring women together to share their experiences and to influence policy in Brussels. It succeeded in the first but seems to have had little impact on the latter. In the harsh atmosphere of the eighties, the last thing most Brussels bureaucrats and member state officials wanted to know was the extent of the hardship being caused to women by the current economic conjuncture and their failure (or unwillingness) to mitigate its consequences. The Tribunal received little publicity, the press maintaining 'there was no story'.[48] Despite their bold efforts, the Tribunal organisers had neither the resources nor the contacts to break these barriers down.

The social dimension[49]

For all these reasons, there seems to have been insufficient pressure at this point to ensure that the gender perspective was taken centrally on board in other EC policy areas. Both DG V, and the Women's Bureau within it, were left on the sidelines during the planning for the single market and in the negotiations for the Single European Act (SEA). The nature of this exclusion was made particularly clear in the composition of and brief for the prestigious Cecchini group which was set up in 1986 by Jacques Delors to consider what the effects would be of *not* completing the internal market.[50] The final report said nothing about the advantages or disadvantages for particular social groups, and very little about the effects on employment. There were no women members of the core Cecchini group and few women, if any, seem to have been involved in the deliberations. As one of the members of the group said when questioned: 'the issue of the representation of women or of women as a separate category in our work was never raised. That wasn't really our purpose.'

In May 1988 in an influential speech to the ETUC annual conference in Stockholm, Jacques Delors revealed his strategy for reintroducing social policy into the newly invigorated EC.[51] In an eloquent plea, he urged the labour movement to make use of the opportunities opened up by the SEA,[52] and then go on with him to establish a platform of guaranteed social rights in the new single market. He stated his own firmly held view, 'the middle way' discussed earlier, that competition created a need for cooperation and that liberalisation and harmonisation went together. This was a remarkable speech for a Commission President to make, and evidence of how strong Delors felt himself to be at that point in time. The speech, however, was quite traditional in its view of social policy and industrial relations and completely ungendered in its formulations.

Thus Delors made no mention of the EC's equal treatment policy or of the experience of the Commission in working with and for women. Nor did he make any appeal to social movements or to any group outside organised labour. The emphasis was still on dialogue with the social partners although the need for alternative strategies was becoming clear.

The ambiguous attitude to the equal treatment policy was further demonstrated in a document produced during 1988 by an interdepartmental group in the Commission. In this it was argued, following Delors, that the social dimension was essential to the proper functioning of the single market, and that a middle way was required between what were referred to as 'normative' and 'decentralised' versions of social policy. The document cited the equal treatment policy, which was seen as 'on the whole, positive', as an example of a policy which involved a 'doctrinaire recourse to regulation' which was now inappropriate.[53]

This combination of statements in 1988 (and there are others which could be cited) suggest that both in the top echelons of the Commission and in DG V the women's policy was regarded as marginal and was certainly not seen as providing useful experience which could be applied elsewhere. During this same period, however, certain elements within the women's network began to react to this marginalisation. Thus from August 1988 onwards the EP Women's Committee began to prepare an 'own initiative' report on the consequences of the completion of the internal market for women, with the aim of filling some of the gaps left by Cecchini. This was supplemented in 1990 by a detailed study drawn up for the Equal Opportunities Unit (as the Commission Women's Bureau was now being called) by an economist, Pauline Conroy Jackson.[54]

Both of these documents looked at the impact of the single market on those sectors of the economy of particular importance to women and on the implications of the increasing concern with the mobility of the labour force. Both emphasised the need for enhanced infrastructures, especially in the area of childcare, if anything like a level playing field was to exist between men and women. These concerns were already being taken up by groups of women within the member states, resulting in a cascade of local initiatives, and a much enhanced demand for information and explanation.

The effects of this resurgent activity were made clear in the final text of the Social Charter, which was drawn up by the Commission at the end of 1989.[55] The section on equal treatment for men and women (para. 16), though brief, was weighty and related clearly to past policy and future needs. In it a distinction was made between 'equal treatment . . . which must be assured' and 'equal opportunities . . . which must be developed', a new formulation of the old difference between equal and special treatment. At a fairly late date, this was supplemented by a reiteration of the commitment to enable 'men and women to reconcile occupational and family obligations'. Thus the text of the Charter combined three perspectives on women's subordination which neatly summed up the focus of EC policy so far: equality, positive action and the family/paid work divide.

The Charter itself, in a considerably weakened version, was adopted as a non-binding declaration at a European Council meeting on 7 December 1989 by eleven out of the twelve member states. The British government refused to sign the Charter, thus marking its obdurate opposition to the Delors 'middle way'.

Sexual politics

A big increase in women's networking at international level occurred in the early eighties, between the UN Conferences in 1980 and 1985 which marked the middle and end of the UN Decade for Women.[56] This involved a sustained attempt to link women's activism in different parts of the world, particularly on issues to do with development, economic rights and sexual politics. One strand of this was a campaign to make more visible the international traffic in women, as 'entertainers' and prostitutes, and to examine both the modalities which made the trade possible and its spinoffs into other areas of gender relations. This work highlighted the inadequacy of international regulation in these areas and the unwillingness of governments to target the traffickers.

Some of these issues were raised at a ten-day workshop held in Rotterdam in April 1983 on the sexual slavery of women. Women who were active against or escaping from international trafficking and cross-border prostitution attended from all over the world. A bold attempt was made to cut through the secrecy surrounding these trades, and evidence was accumulated which put the spotlight on the indifference and/or complicity of many authorities, not least in Europe.[57]

European feminists were involved in these developments, and a follow through can be seen at EC level in the decision of the European Parliament's Women's Committee in December 1984 to produce an 'own initiative' report on all aspects of violence against women.[58] The rapporteur for this was the Dutch socialist and feminist, Hedy d'Ancona, then an MEP and both before and after a minister in the Dutch government. The report was unusual both in its subject matter and in its grassroots feminist perspective. After surveying the evidence across the board for child abuse, wife-battering, rape, sexual harassment at work, forced prostitution, and cross-border trade in women, the report urged those with responsibility to see these phenomena, not as 'accidental distortions' but as the causes and consequences of 'the unequal division of power between men and women'. The implication was that no policy in the employment field could produce advantages for women unless it took account of these conditions.[59]

In July 1986, just after the debate on the report, the EC Council of Ministers adopted the second action programme for women (Action

Programme 2, 1985–90).[60] This was a solid and realistic document, intended to build on the achievements of Action Programme 1 and develop new initiatives. It was implemented during the period when Jacques Delors was attempting to revive EC social policy, and was thus subject to the possibilities and difficulties already discussed. Action Programme 2 maintained the two-pronged approach already developed but placed less reliance on the legal route. Great emphasis was placed on the 'sharing of family and occupational responsibilities' and on measures to achieve this. Migrant women were mentioned as a group with special needs in the employment field, in the context of a paragraph which dealt with 'the problems of the most disadvantaged'.

This shift in the balance of priorities seems to have made it easier, as the various strands were implemented, for policy to move towards the crossover points between the public and the private and to take more account of the reproductive and sexual identities of women. It is significant that the main initiatives in this field, even if they started off as investigations or practical actions, came in the end to be embodied in law, though often of a non-binding kind. This was true in three important policy areas developed during this period, namely, childcare provision, the protection of pregnancy, and sexual harassment at work. It is striking that all of these involved either protection or special treatment, thus dealing with the preconditions for equality rather than equality itself.

A focus on the link between the availability of childcare and women's ability to take up paid work was one of the main new initiatives of Action Programme 2. Childcare was viewed in a broad sense including leave arrangements, infrastructure developments and different kinds of provision. In 1986 a network was set up by the Women's Bureau to develop policy on these issues, following the pattern of the law network.

This network seems to have functioned well and in 1988 produced a comprehensive report, comparing primary childcare provision across the EC, and making a preliminary analysis of the reasons for and the consequences of the differences.[61] The report sought to demonstrate the extent to which such differences disadvantaged certain groups of women and prevented the emergence of a fair labour market in the EC. Significantly (and not without controversy) the network then began to investigate, as one strand in its activities, the barriers to a greater involvement of men in childcare.[62]

The logical outcome of their work, the members of the network believed, was to campaign for a Directive to establish minimum standards in this field. A Directive on such an issue, which went so far towards the family and which involved considerable cost, was never likely. However, to the surprise of many, a Council Recommendation was adopted in March 1992 which represented a degree of commitment on the part of member states.[63] The Recommendation was somewhat blurred in the process of negotiation but it remained an important standard-setting document. It contained a commitment 'to encourage increased participation by men' in childcare (Article 6) and was thus the first EC equality measure actively to target male behaviour.

Parallel with this move on childcare went a concern with the protection of pregnant women at work. The ETD and SSD had given a derogation for measures to do with pregnancy, but very little was done until the early eighties at EC level to monitor the effects of this. However, in 1983–84 reports were published both by the EP Women's Committee and by the Women's Bureau.[64] These combined with an increasing case law at national and later EC level on issues surrounding dismissals for pregnancy. As with childcare, the logic of the evidence suggested the need for an EC Directive establishing minimum levels of protection and setting out the criteria to be applied in a variety of situations involving the pregnant worker.

This concern coincided with the priority being given to health and safety at work under the SEA, and led to a proposal for a new Directive on the protection of pregnancy, which combined the equal treatment and the health and safety approaches. As such, the Commission argued, it could be adopted under Article 118a using qualified majority voting. This adventurous gesture by the Commission, which in the end paid off, provided a good example of the strategy Delors was proposing in 1988. The Directive was adopted in October 1992 and, though considerably weakened in the negotiating process, it did provide for certain minimum entitlements for pregnant women in paid work. It thus contributed to the 'platform of guaranteed rights' proposed in the Social Charter.[65] It also suggested a new degree of integration between equal opportunities and mainstream social policy development.

The last of this trio of measures related to sexual harassment at work. Concern about this as an equal opportunities issue had been raised very strongly in the EP report on violence. Because of the clear link to employment, it was, of all the issues contained in that report, the one which was easiest for the Commission to take up. In 1987 a UK legal expert, Michael Rubenstein, was commissioned to survey practice on this issue in the member states, and make recommendations. A Council Resolution in 1991 supported further action. The Commission took the view that sexual harassment fell within the scope of the ETD, although it was not mentioned specifically. A Commission Recommendation spelling this out and providing definitions was adopted with accompanying guidelines in November 1991.[66] The Recommendation appears to have had some effect, with a number of the member states developing case law and legislation on this issue both before and after its adoption.[67]

As a result of the adoption of these three measures a somewhat different look had been given to the EC policy by the early nineties. Although it by no means yet dealt with the total situation of women, and although the focus on employment still remained, women's reproductive and sexual identities were being taken much more into account. This may in some part at least be attributed to the work of the women's network. Although generally positive in each individual case, the combination of these measures at this particular point raised some queries. These related to concerns about the double-edged nature of legal provisions which emphasise women's separate sex/gender identity in situations where the surrounding circumstances remain virtually unaltered, and men's lifestyles and control of power have hardly been challenged.[68]

In perhaps a subliminal recognition of some of these dangers, and certainly in response to the ghettoisation discussed earlier, the third action programme on equal opportunities (Action Programme 3, 1991–95), in a major break with the employment theme, put great emphasis on the need to encourage women into decision-making, and on the 'mainstreaming' of equal opportunities issues.[69] Thus, as 1992 came to an end, some groups of women were homing in on issues of representation and democracy at the European level – soon to be a major focus of attention in the EU more generally.

The Role of the Court, 1980–92

All of the developments so far discussed were fragile, depending on odd conjunctions of forces and on the wide spread of women's interests. Over this same period, however, policy development was underpinned and given a continuing importance by a series of rulings from the European Court of Justice (ECJ) relating to the interpretation and enforcement of Article 119 and the three Directives adopted in the seventies. These rulings followed on from the German cases discussed in chapter 7, and were again made possible by the steady stream of references coming up from the national courts. They created a separate strand to the women's policy, interacting and sometimes dovetailing with the rest, but deriving in the main from the particular nature of the cases referred and from the ECJ's own distinctive agenda and priorities.

The judicial strand in the women's policy has been extensively analysed by legal experts and legal activists, so much so that it sometimes appears as an autonomous development, the result of a cranky affectation of judges and lawyers. Feminist analysts have on the whole been sceptical, suspecting a different agenda and noting the limits to the ECJ's understanding of the situation of women.[70] The recent trend of analysing the Court itself, using a 'law and politics' or sociological perspective, is helpful in situating the equal treatment case law, as are writings by the judges themselves.[71] Given the ready availability of all of this material, I shall here only highlight some significant trends, before going on to consider explanations for the ECJ's disparate practice in equal treatment cases, and how this judicial component affects the policy overall.[72]

The ECJ's now numerous rulings on equal treatment are a mixed bag from the point of view of improving the situation of women, even given the wide range of views that exist on what that might involve. I would argue, however, that improving the situation of women has never been a prime objective of the Court, and that its rulings only have that effect if the interests of women coincide with other objectives being pursued. Nevertheless, some of the rulings have been beneficial, and have certainly gone well beyond what governments might have expected; others, viewed from a feminist perspective, have been restrictive.

In examining the main trends in the ECJ's jurisprudence on equal treatment, a distinction can be made between the rulings on employment issues and those on social security. In the employment cases (mainly concerned with removing barriers to women's access to and integration in the labour market) the ECJ has been innovative in some important ways. In particular, it has shown a willingness in its rulings to expand the concept of a worker, and give recognition to more women-identified characteristics. Two examples of categories of workers given value by the ECJ, are part-time workers (mainly women) and pregnant workers (solely women).[73]

The ECJ, initially in the *Bilka* case and then in a string of others, has sought by using the indirect discrimination provisions in the ETD to establish the rights of part-time workers to the same benefits and conditions (pro-rata) as full timers.[74] In this it has had some success, despite the fact that the Council of Ministers has consistently failed to legislate in a similar direction. The significance of these rulings is that they begin to give a higher status in law to part-time work and to the women who do it.

As far as pregnant women are concerned, the ECJ in *Dekker* cut through a great deal of legal controversy and confusion by ruling that, because only women become pregnant, any kind of detriment in the work situation relating to pregnancy constitutes direct discrimination for which no justification can be argued.[75] As a result, the pregnant woman as worker has gained both protection and greater legitimacy. In this instance, the Council of Ministers took action parallel to the judgment by adopting the 1992 Pregnancy Directive.

The message from the Court in these rulings seems to have been that a new and more fragmented workforce is coming into being and that women are a part of it. In recognition of this, the provisions agreed to by the member states on equal treatment should be firmly enforced. At this point, it could be argued that the ECJ has been beginning to apply something close to the Bacchi concept of 'same difference' discussed in chapter 1. While applying equality legislation, it has recognised women's differences and has done this in a way that begins to shift traditional norms and alter the employment context.

However, as Sandra Fredman has pointed out, this is still 'equality within a market order'.[76] The ECJ, while ruling in this way, has at the same time shown itself very ready to listen to arguments about economic impact (as it did in *Defrenne 2*) and to allow pleas of objective justification to be made by employers and governments. Thus it accepts the possibility that the principle of equal treatment can be overridden for 'objective', i.e., economic reasons – and stands by to act as arbiter.

If the ECJ does on occasion match Bacchi's requirements for equality legislation, it certainly does not meet those of Titia Loenen, who insists that the equality standard should pay attention to the burden of caring and who is bearing it.[77] These were issues which came up, though they were not dealt with, during the negotiation of the SSD, and they have been coming up ever since in the references which have flowed from it.[78]

After some initial rulings which prevented states from wriggling out of their direct commitments under the SSD, the Court's practice in respect of this Directive has become steadily more minimalist. It is not hard to divine some of the reasons. As was discussed in chapter 6, this is a Directive which very easily crosses over from the employment sphere into the areas of family and dependency. It is also unclear in its objectives and part of an incomplete legislative sequence.

Though the ECJ in other policy areas has not been adverse to filling in legislative gaps through its own rulings, this has not been the case here. The rulings of the Court have on the whole had the effect of restricting the personal and the material scope of the SSD, of expanding its exclusions, and of safeguarding member state discretion in questions of social assistance, means-tested benefits and the relief of poverty. In addition, few obstacles have been placed in the way of levelling down as a means of achieving equal treatment, even if this means disadvantaging women.[79]

The ECJ has here attempted to draw firm lines and enforce boundaries, rather than use the references to begin to establish the economic value of unpaid work or caring as an insurable risk. When it did make a favourable (to women) judgment in the *Drake* case, the Court was at pains to justify its decision in ways that did not raise either of these issues.[80] This caution ties in with the Court's expressed attitude to the family in equal treatment cases (first demonstrated in *Hofmann* and repeated a number of times since) that intervening in personal or domestic matters is not the function of either EC law or the Court. Mel Cousins, after an examination of the Court's record in social security cases in 1992 and 1993, points out that this restrictive view means that:

> women with childcare or other family responsibilities who are living in poverty, who one might think most in need of equality of treatment, are in fact least likely to receive it under the directive.[81]

A separate agenda

What is the rationale for these distinctions in the Court's practice? Several writers suggest that, as in the sixties, the Court has in more recent times seen it as its role to attempt to rescue the EC enterprise and set it on a viable course for the future.[82] On this argument, the ECJ in the early eighties, building on its important ruling in the *Cassis de Dijon* case, used its powers in an attempt to push governments further down the path of market integration.[83]

It seems likely that some at least of the judges in the ECJ, as part of this project, also favoured the Delors 'middle way' with regard to social policy. Reports coming from the ECJ in the mid eighties suggested that the judges felt the Council was dragging its feet on social legislation. In such circumstances, the Court may well have sought to *direct* the member states, or present them with a fait accompli, by making bold judgments. Since equal treatment was virtually the only strand of existing social policy producing references, it was this that provided the vehicle, at least as far as employment cases were concerned.

To suggest this is not to argue that the judges took a conscious decision to act in this way, but to indicate what might have been the intellectual context for judgments like those in *Bilka* and *Dekker*. If this is a valid hypothesis, it also helps to explain the restraints over the application of the SSD. For individualising benefits, tackling dependency, and valuing domestic work played no part in the Delors view of the social dimension. Thus in tracking those ideas and attempting to support them, the judges may well have been reluctant to alarm governments, or incur costs for business, on issues which (to them) were not of the essence.

Here clearly the Court's practice parts company with a women-centred policy for which tackling the overlap between paid and unpaid work, the public and the private, is crucial. Titia Loenen writes: 'as long as emancipation consists of more women entering the labour market without a concomitant shift in the balance of care, women will lose out again'.[84] The policy of the ECJ so far has been to encourage the former without tackling the latter.

The EC women's policy in the eighties was made up of three strands, women's diverse desires and interests, bargaining within and between the institutions, and the separate agenda of the Court. The interplay produced an incoherent policy, advantaging some women over others but providing opportunities for change. The Court, in avoiding (except in the case of pregnancy) issues relating to the family, and in emphasising employment rights over social security, was tipping the policy in a particular direction. The women's network on the whole refused to accept such limitations and put pressure on the policy makers to develop a more diverse programme.

As this account shows, the most positive aspect of the Court's rulings in this period was its willingness to recognise a more diverse labour market and different kinds of workers within it, many of them female. It was also, in another strand of its policy, beginning to establish some rights in the market for migrant workers from outside the EC. This new emphasis on diversity, and the beginnings of a concern with 'visible minorities', came together at the end of the eighties as an issue for the women's policy and for women's organisation more generally. It connected with the concerns in feminist theory about diversity and the category 'women', which were discussed in chapter 1. The next chapter takes the example of black and migrant women, and their activity and treatment at the level of the EC, as a case study of what 'dealing with diversity' might mean in the EC context.

Notes

1 For an account of global change and its effects on types of regulation in the EU see Sol Picciotto, 'The Regulatory Criss-cross – Interaction between Jurisdictions and Global Regulatory Networks', in W. Bratton et al., eds, *International Regulatory Competition and Coordination*, Oxford University Press, Oxford, forthcoming 1996.

2 Paul Teague, *The European Community: the Social Dimension*, Kogan Page, London, 1989, pp. 64–8.

3 Martin Rhodes, 'Whither Regulation? "Disorganised Capitalism" and the West European Labour Market', in L. Hancher and M. Moran, eds, *Capitalism, Culture and Economic Regulation*, Clarendon Press, Oxford, 1989.

4 Interview, John Morley, Head of Division on Labour Market Policies, European Commission, Brussels, 10 July 1987.

5 By this stage the 'southern enlargement' of the EC, bringing the total membership to twelve, was almost complete. Greece joined in 1981 and Spain and Portugal in 1986.

6 Charles Grant, *Delors – Inside the House that Jacques Built*, Nicholas Brealey, London, 1994, especially pp. 83–7.

7 CEC, 'The Position of Women on the Labour Market', *Women of Europe* Supplement 36/92, ch. 1.

8 For a sophisticated analysis of what 'value' means in the context of women's part-time work see Caitriona Carter, *Economic and Social Dynamics of Part-time Employment: Law as Policy within the EC*, PhD, Edinburgh, 1994.

9 For the results of two such meetings see Ronnie Ratner, ed., *Equal Employment Policy*

for Women, Temple University Press, Philadelphia, 1980; and Kirsten Hvidtfeldt, ed., *Strategies for Integrating Women into the Labour Market*, European Women's Studies in Social Science, Copenhagen, 1982.
10 For a detailed account of the UN conferences and the networking around them see Arvonne S. Fraser, *The UN Decade for Women – Documents and Dialogue*, Westview, Boulder, Colorado, 1987.
11 Interview, Chris Docksey, Brussels, 6 July 1987. Docksey worked as a legal officer in the Women's Bureau from 1986 to 1990.
12 *A New Community Action Programme on the Promotion of Equal Opportunities for Women 1982–1985*, COM(81) 758 final.
13 Conference for voluntary organisations, Equal Opportunities Commission, London, 23 July 1982. In an unusual trajectory, Roudy went from being an MEP and chair of the European Parliament's Committee on Women's Rights to a cabinet position in the French government, entailing membership of the EC Council of Ministers.
14 For full reference see Appendix 2.
15 Interview, Odile Quintin, Brussels, 17 September 1990.
16 Interview, Docksey, 17 September 1990.
17 The law network was formed in 1983 and its first coordinator was Angela Byre from the UK.
18 'Proposal for a Council Directive on Procedures for Informing and Consulting the Employees of Undertakings with Complex Structures, in Particular Transnational Undertakings', *Bulletin of the ECs*, Supplement 3/80.
19 A detailed account of the campaign is given in Ton DeVos, *Multinational Corporations in Democratic Host Countries – US Multinationals and the Vredeling Proposal*, Dartmouth, Aldershot, 1989. The issue of information for workers in transnational companies has been revived in the nineties with the adoption of the European Works Council Directive (94/45/EC).
20 'Don't Tell the Workers', *Agenor*, May/June 1983, pp. 1–19.
21 For the drafts see *Proposal for a Council Directive on Voluntary Part-time Work*, COM(81) 775 final, and *Draft Council Recommendation on the Reduction and Reorganisation of Working Time*, COM(83) 543 final, 23 September 1983. Carter, *Economic and Social Dynamics*, pp. 201–9, gives a detailed account of the negotiations which took place on the part-time work Directive.
22 The full text of this speech (and many other documents of interest) can be found in the archives which the Equal Opportunities Commission Library in Manchester holds on the activities of the Advisory Committee.
23 *Proposal for a Council Directive on parental leave and leave for family reasons*, COM(83) 686 final, 22 November 1983. Small changes were made to this draft and it was reissued in November 1984.
24 Françoise Rutherford, 'The Proposal for a European Directive on Parental Leave: some reasons why it failed', *Policy and Politics*, vol. 17, no. 4, 1989, p. 305.
25 *Report from the Commission to the Council on the implementation of the new Community action programme on the promotion of equal opportunities for women (1982–1985)*, COM(85) 641 final.
26 European Network of Women, *Assessment of the Community Action Programme on the Promotion of Equal Opportunities for Women*, mimeo, Brussels, November 1985.
27 I am grateful to Eleanore Cowper of the UK Women's Farm and Garden Association, Liesbeth Klaver of the Wageningen Agricultural University in the Netherlands, and Anne Bandin of COPA-cf for help with this section. None of them is responsible for the opinions expressed.
28 *Council Directive of 11 December 1986 on the application of the principle of equal treatment between men and women engaged in an activity, including agriculture, in a self-employed capacity, and on the protection of self-employed women during pregnancy and motherhood* (86/613/EEC).
29 Farm women is used here as the term most current during the period in question. This was preferred by those involved to 'assisting spouses', 'helper spouses' or 'farmers' wives'. Helper spouses was the term used as a shorthand during the negotiation of the Directive

and is used in that context here. During a COPA-cf seminar in 1992 on images of women, representatives of farm women agreed to drop that term and call themselves simply 'women farmers'.

30 Personal communication with the author, August 1994.

31 Delphy's essay on patriarchy 'L'ennemi principal' (published in *Partisans* in 1970) was based on her study of inheritance in French family farms. More recent research on farm women is usefully summarised in two special issues: *Sociologia Ruralis*, vol. XXV111, no. 4, 1988, and *Journal of Rural Studies*, vol. 7, no. 1, 1991.

32 COPA-cf stands for the initials of its title in French: *Comité des Organisations Professionnelles Agricoles de la C.E. – Commission Féminine.*

33 A full transcript of the hearing is given in European Parliament, document PE 68.457, 6 November 1980. See especially pp. 12–30 and 42–50.

34 I am grateful to Sonia Kurta, one of the British representatives who attended Grado, for information about the meeting.

35 *Proposal for a Council Directive on the application of the principle of equal treatment as between men and women engaged in an activity, including agriculture, in a self-employed capacity, and on the protection of self-employed women during pregnancy and motherhood,* COM(84) 57 final/2, 3 April 1984.

36 Sacha Prechal and Noreen Burrows, *Gender Discrimination Law of the European Community*, Dartmouth, Aldershot, 1990, p. 293.

37 The account in this and the following paragraphs is based on semi-restricted material relating in particular to an informal Council meeting of ministers responsible for women's issues, held in the Hague on 10–11 March 1986. At this meeting the draft of the SED was discussed in detail.

38 What the Irish authorities were really objecting to was an intervention which would give some rights to farmers' wives. See Sally Shortall, 'Power Analysis and Farm Wives: an Empirical Study of the Power Relationships Affecting Women on Irish Farms', *Sociologia Ruralis*, vol. XXX11, no. 4, 1992, pp. 431–51.

39 Shortall, 'Power Analysis', pp. 446–9.

40 For example, France adopted laws on helper spouses in 1982, the Netherlands set up a committee to look at their situation in 1984, and in 1993 Ireland's Second Commission on the Status of Women strongly recommended the adoption at national level of many of the measures on helper spouses that had been rejected in 1986.

41 The radio programmes were broadcast on 15 March, 18 July and 1 August 1989. Listeners were astonished to hear the wife of a big estate farmer in Sussex referring to herself as a 'dogsbody'.

42 Monique Chalude, Robin Chater and Jacqueline Laufer, *Equal Opportunities in the Commission of the European Communities*, COPEC (87) 256, 1986. This report was commissioned by the Committee on Equal Opportunities for Women and Men (COPEC) of the European Commission. The report gives a detailed and highly revealing account of management and personnel procedures, and as a result of its findings a positive action plan for women employees was finally introduced in the Commission.

43 Jane Dennett et al., *Europe Against Poverty: the European Poverty Programme 1975–1980*, Bedford Square Press/NCVO, London, 1982.

44 Hilda Scott, *Working Your Way to the Bottom, the Feminization of Poverty*, Pandora Press, London, 1984.

45 Special Issue, 'The Fight Against Poverty', *Social Europe*, Supplement, 2/89.

46 *Network News*, no. 19, September 1988, p. 1. The European Commission gave funding for some preparatory seminars.

47 I am grateful to Barbara Smith of the Castleford Women's Centre who was a participant and Linda Luckhaus of Warwick University who was in the audience, for talking to me about their impressions of the Tribunal.

48 Even the *Guardian* (London) which was generally sympathetic printed only a few short paragraphs on the story in its issue of 12 November 1988.

49 An early version of parts of this section appeared in 'The European Community's Policy on Women in the Context of 1992', *Women's Studies International Forum*, vol. 15, no. 1, 1992, pp. 21–8.

50 The full report runs to sixteen volumes. For a summary of its conclusions see Paolo Cecchini, *The European Challenge – 1992 and the Benefits of a Single Market*, Wildwood House, Aldershot, 1988.
51 *Discours du President Delors devant le Congrès de la Confédération Européenne des Syndicats*, Stockholm, 12 May 1988.
52 In saying this he was referring to the fact that under the SEA two new paragraphs (Article 118a and 118b) had been added to the social policy section of the Treaty.
53 Special Edition, 'The Social Dimension of the Internal Market – Interim Report of the Interdepartmental Working Party', *Social Europe*, 1988, pp. 62–3.
54 European Parliament, *Report drawn up on behalf of the Committee on Women's Rights on the 1992 Single Market and its implications for women in the EC*, Session Documents, A3-0358/90/Parts A and B, 6 December 1990; Pauline Conroy Jackson, *The Impact of the Completion of the Internal Market on Women in the European Community*, CEC, V/506/90-EN, 1990.
55 *Community Charter of the Fundamental Social Rights of Workers*, CEC, Brussels, December 1989. This was an attempt by the Commission to establish in what areas minimum standards needed to be set at European level. An Action Programme to implement the Charter was issued in November 1989, before the text was finally adopted.
56 Fraser, *The UN Decade*, passim.
57 A full account of the workshop was published in a special issue of *Nouvelles Questions Féministes*, Paris, winter 1984.
58 European Parliament, *Report drawn up on behalf of the Committee on Women's Rights on Violence Against Women* (d'Ancona report) A2-44/86.
59 Male MEPs were conspicuous by their absence during the debate on the report which took place on 10 June 1986. Despite this, 116 amendments were tabled and 314 MEPs took part in the voting on the following day. The resolution, without in the end too much revision, was adopted by 198 to 66, with 50 abstentions. (OJ C 176, 1986, p. 58.)
60 For full reference see Appendix 2.
61 Peter Moss, *Childcare and Equality of Opportunity – Consolidated Report to the European Commission*, CEC, V/746/88, 1988.
62 Interview Peter Moss, chair of the European Childcare Network, London, 12 August 1991.
63 For full reference see Appendix 2.
64 European Parliament, *Maternity, Parental Leave and Pre-School Facilities* (Le Roux report) PE 83.064; Dagmar Coester-Waltjen, *Protection of working women during pregnancy and motherhood in the member states of the EC*, CEC, V/1829/84.
65 Directive 92/85/EEC. An account of the negotiations is given in Evelyn Ellis, 'Protection of Pregnancy and Maternity', *Industrial Law Journal*, vol. 22, no. 2, 1993, pp. 63–7. See also Linda Luckhaus, 'Pregnancy and the Single Market', ESRC paper, 1995.
66 For full reference see Appendix 2.
67 European Parliament, *Measures to Combat Sexual Harassment at the Workplace – Action Taken in the Member States of the EC*, Women's Rights Series, W-2 1994.
68 For an expression of such unease in respect of the pregnancy Directive see Noreen Burrows, 'Maternity Rights in Europe – an Embryonic Legal Regime', *Yearbook of European Law*, 1991, pp. 273–93.
69 *Equal Opportunities for Men and Women – the Third Medium-term Action Programme 1991–1995*, COM(90) 449 final.
70 See, for example, Sandra Fredman, 'European Community Discrimination Law: A Critique', *Industrial Law Journal*, vol. 21, no. 2, 1992, pp. 119–35, and Linda Luckhaus, 'Intentions and Avoidance of Community Law', *Industrial Law Journal*, vol. 21, no. 4, 1992, pp. 315–22.
71 See in particular Anne-Marie Burley and Walter Mattli, 'Europe Before the Court: a Political Theory of Legal Integration', *International Organisation*, vol. 47, no. 1, 1993, pp. 41–76; and G. Federico Mancini, 'The Making of a Constitution for Europe', *Common Market Law Review*, vol. 26, 1989, pp. 595–14.
72 For a comprehensive account of the ECJ's jurisprudence on equal treatment see Sacha Prechal, Noreen Burrows, *Gender Discrimination: Law of the European Community*, Dartmouth, Aldershot, 1990.

73 For a fuller discussion of the *Bilka* and *Dekker* cases referred to here, see Catherine Hoskyns, 'Gender Issues in International Relations: the Case of the European Community', *Review of International Studies*, vol. 20, 1994, pp. 225–39.
74 *Bilka-Kaufhaus GmbH* v. *Weber von Hartz*, ECJ Case 170/84, 1986.
75 *Dekker* v. *Stichting Vormingcentrum*, ECJ Case C-177/88, 1990.
76 Fredman, 'EC Discrimination Law', p. 130.
77 Titia Loenen, 'Different Perspectives in Different Legal Studies: a Contextual Approach to Feminist Jurisprudence in Europe and the USA'. Paper for conference on Feminist Approaches to Law and Cultural Diversity, EUI Florence, November 1993, p. 8.
78 According to the Court's computer, 41 references for a preliminary ruling had been made citing the SSD by October 1994. I am grateful to Michael Kenny for doing this search for me.
79 For useful analyses of the impact of the Court's rulings in social security cases see Deirdre Curtin, 'Equal Treatment and Social Welfare: the European Court's Emerging Case-Law on Directive 79/7/EEC', in G. Whyte, ed., *Sex Equality, Community Rights and Irish Social Welfare Law*, Trinity College, Dublin 1988; and Julia Adiba Sohrab, 'Women and Social Security: the Limits of EEC Equality Law', *Journal of Social Welfare and Family Law*, vol. 16, no. 1, 1994, pp. 5–17.
80 *Drake* v. *The Adjudication Officer*, ECJ case 150/85, 1986. The case involved the right of a married woman to receive Invalid Care Allowance.
81 Mel Cousins, 'Equal Treatment and Social Security', *European Law Review*, vol. 19, no. 2, 1994, p. 143.
82 This is implied in Mancini, 'A Constitution for Europe', p. 612, and by Lenaerts as cited in Burley and Mattli, 'Europe Before the Court', p. 48.
83 ECJ Case 120/78, 1979. For the importance of this case in the development of the single market see: Renaud Dehousse, '1992 and Beyond – the Institutional Dimension of the Internal Market Programme', *Legal Issues of European Integration*, vol. 1, 1989, pp. 112–13.
84 Loenen, 'Different Perspectives', p. 10.

9

Dealing with Diversity[1]

There is a twofold rationale for focusing on the situation of black and migrant women[2] in the European Union. In the first place, the fact of colour distinguishes certain women from other women in fixed and visible ways, and in the second place, this particular 'difference' has significance in other areas of EU policy. Thus, although this is by no means the only relevant division among women, it is a key one, and in the EU context puts the focus not only on gender, but also on policies relating to migrants, immigration and race relations. Equally important, giving visibility to the situation of black and migrant women, and a hearing to their voices, helps to break through some of the silences imposed on groups designated as 'inferior' or 'other'.

Listening to those voices suggests that being black, migrant and a woman in the EU means not an accumulation of discriminations but a particular experience of society, disadvantageous in some ways but rich in others, and with its own internal contradictions and diversities. Black and migrant women interact with other women and with society in general in a range of different contexts and circumstances, and these diverse experiences need to be recognised before meaningful cooperation between women can take place. The spread of these interactions is made clear by the fact that embarking on this case study involves looking centrally at areas of EU policy making only touched on before. This in turn casts a different light on the women's policy, and on networking among women.

Viewing EU policies from this perspective brings home the extent to which nationality (often defined in a narrow sense) is given priority in EU policy and research. Although the intention may be to break down national divisions and create equal treatment for products (or people) that very process has the effect of giving enhanced importance to the national as a category, thus excluding non-nationals and obscuring other cross-cutting divisions. I have shown how the women's policy managed to some extent to break through those barriers; that process has never taken place with regard to race. Yet such a 'cross-national' concern with discrimination on grounds of colour and race is the more needed since the EU demonstrates in an extreme form what Adrienne Rich has called the 'white solipsism', namely the tendency 'to think, imagine and speak as if whiteness described the world'[3].

It is impossible at the moment to estimate with any accuracy how many black and migrant women there are in the EU. This category, which prioritises the concerns of women of third world origin, includes women who are citizens of an EU member state, women with rights of residence, and those who are 'undocumented'.[4] No figures, EU or otherwise, give the raw material necessary to make this calculation. There is a widely accepted estimate that in 1990 approximately six million people with third world nationality had rights of residence in individual EU states (none at the moment can have a right of residence for the EU as a whole).[5] Adding on, as a very rough estimate, another four million for citizens and the 'undocumented', and assuming women are 45 per cent of the total, would give a figure of just under five million for black and migrant women, approximately 2 per cent of the total EU population. This is roughly equivalent to the population of Denmark.[6]

This chapter will examine EU policies towards this five million, showing how the already established parameters of the women's policy are inflected for black and migrant women by the EU's other policies on migrants, immigration, and race relations. The aim is to see how black and migrant women are constructed in these policies, what the role of other groups of women is in this construction, and what this suggests about common and divergent interests among women. At the same time, looking at two additional policy areas helps to illuminate some key political trends taking place in the EC in the mid eighties. As the single market measures began to come into effect, the instinct of governments was to block any expansion of the Community's political remit, restricting sensitive issues either to the national level or, if coordination was essential, to the intergovernmental. The struggles over where and how to develop policies on immigration and race relations clearly illustrate this process.

The final section of the chapter will deal with the implications that these new developments have for organisation, and will examine from the perspective of black and migrant women two new EU lobbies created in the early nineties, the European Women's Lobby and the Migrants Forum. The emphasis in this chapter will be on developments in the late eighties and early nineties. This period, which covers the negotiation of the Maastricht Treaty and the coming into force of the single market, the most recent period dealt with in detail in this book, will thus be viewed through the eyes of black and migrant women.

Migrants and Immigration

Migration and immigration policies[7] are always likely to be controversial in situations where nation states coexist in contexts of contrasting wealth and poverty. The European Union has proved to be no exception to this rule, and controversy over these issues has steadily increased since the seventies. This has been fuelled by growing levels of unemployment in the EU, by the prospect of the single market, and by poverty and instability in neighbouring regions. The situation has been exacerbated by the lack of a clear division of competence in these matters between the European and national levels, and by the fact that a functioning and integrated EU political system does not yet exist.

Given the breadth of the subjects involved, it is only possible here to indicate the issues at stake and give an interpretation of some developments. It is clear, however, that policies for migration and immigration have set precedents for other developments in the EU of the nineties. At the same time, the greater attention now being paid to women's issues and the greater involvement of black and migrant women, are helping to highlight some of the gendered assumptions and gender-specific effects which were built into the EU's policies as they developed.

The interaction between Community and national levels of regulation on issues to do with migration and immigration has always been complex. The Treaty of Rome envisaged a common market in labour and included strong measures (Articles 48–51) to promote free movement for workers (see chapter 3). Though the Treaty does not qualify the term 'worker', both the Court and member state governments assumed or imposed an interpretation which limited rights and benefits under the Treaty to workers who were nationals of an EC member state. Richard Plender concludes that this interpretation is now so embedded in law and practice that it is inconceivable that it could be reversed.[8]

The result was to leave the dual labour markets of the individual member states essentially autonomous, and to enable national authorities to continue to regulate the supply of immigrant labour from the sources traditional to each country. They were able to do this secure in the knowledge that, unless or until such workers became citizens, they and the communities which grew up around them would in effect be restricted to the national market and subject to national regulation only.

The European Commission, in the ten-year period between the adoption of the Social Action Programme in 1974 and the issuing of its guidelines on migration policy in 1985, sought to reduce the gap between these two levels of labour market policy.[9] In particular, it attempted to establish some Community competence, not only over EC internal migrants, but also over 'third country' migrants – the terminology used for migrants coming from outside the EC. The Commission also showed some concern for the social integration of migrant communities in the host country, whether these communities were from other EC member states or from third countries.[10] In the hope of establishing a more consistent policy overall, the Commission proposed various forms of consultation and cooperation with the member state governments, aware that in so doing, at least in respect of third country migrants, it was moving into a sensitive area. Throughout the ten years, member states agreed to and 'welcomed' such consultation – but never actually allowed it to be implemented.[11]

In the proposals on internal EC and third country migrants made under the Social Action Programme in the seventies very little was said about women directly, despite the fact that at the same time strong measures were being adopted on women's equality. The term 'migrants and their families' was used frequently, the presumption being that the migrant was a man. The link with the women's policy, also part of the Social Action Programme, was never made. By the time of the 1985 guidelines, a change in both attention and discourse was evident. The situation of women migrants was mentioned at various points, indicating some concern with their special position. Reference was also made to the provisions on immigrant women in Action Programme 1 of the women's policy.[12] This was the first time in EC policy that a specific link between the migrants' and women's policies was recognised, and that women migrants were seen as having a role beyond that of 'family members'. The recognition (however low key) that migrant women had a place in both policies, immediately gave them a more real presence.

The situation of black and migrant women

By the early eighties, the presence of black and migrant women was being established in other ways. The economic crisis and the tightening up of immigration procedures across Europe were making migrant and ethnic minority communities both more fearful and more assertive. Within this movement women were becoming more visibly active and the dispersed effects of second-wave feminism helped to create greater awareness.[13] New research attempted for the first time to deal in detail with the real experiences and circumstances of migrant women, taking account of their cultural background, their domestic roles and their position in the segregated labour markets of Western Europe.[14]

This kind of research showed how little accurate information was available to policy makers and how in many cases even the existence of women migrants had been repressed in official documentation. It was this new awareness, together with the continuing concern of the

Commission over issues relating to migration, that persuaded those responsible for drafting Action Programme 1 to include the specific provisions on immigrant women. Isabelle von Prondzynski, who came to work for the Women's Bureau in 1983, wrote that by the early eighties 'migrant women had emerged as a key group requiring Community support'.[15]

As a follow-up to the commitment in Action Programme 1, three important studies were initiated by the Women's Bureau on the situation of migrant women. These were on demography and labour market statistics, legal barriers to employment, and specific training needs.[16] In 1986 a further study was commissioned from Mirjana Morokvasic on migrant women entrepreneurs in five EC member states.[17] In the same period, the European Parliament's Committee on Women's Rights produced a controversial report (prepared by Brigitte Heinrich of the German Greens) on discrimination against women in immigration law.[18] As a result of these studies, a more revealing picture of the lives of immigrant women began to emerge. The overwhelming impression was of women in diverse situations and with varied resources, seeking improvement, but coming up against daunting societal and institutional barriers, erected against them both as women and as migrants. The Morokvasic and Heinrich studies in particular contained vivid and personal accounts of both success and pain.

The Heinrich study caused great controversy when it was discussed in the EP Women's Committee, and again when it was adopted in the full Parliament.[19] The report raised questions about what would constitute a 'fair' immigration policy, free of racism and sexism. Heinrich's achievement was to force MEPs to confront the consequences for individual migrant or ethnic minority women of the adoption of restrictive immigration policies, for example those intended to 'prevent' marriages of convenience. Some women in the Committee, and more in the Parliament as a whole, found it hard to accept that migrant women should also have equal rights, and made clear that they rated the need to preserve 'national identity' above any cross-cultural solidarity among women.[20]

Action Programme 2 gave less formal prominence to the issue of migrant women.[21] However, the fact that by 1985 the issue of migrants was once again on the EC agenda meant that there was a concern in the Women's Bureau to press on with a policy initiative, once the results of the studies became available. A seminar on 'Migrant Women and Employment' was therefore arranged for September 1987 to consider the first three of the reports and make recommendations, particularly in the area of training. According to the organiser of the seminar and author of the training study, Colette de Troy, the seminar was designed for policy makers and researchers, 'to give the issue more importance'.

It was not intended for migrant women themselves, though in the end some came.[22] Before it took place, however, the Commission's capacity to deal with issues relating to migration had been severely curtailed.

The Council and the Court

The Commission's 1985 guidelines on migration policy were 'noted' in a Resolution of the EC's Council of Ministers on 16 July 1985. The governments edited the Commission's concerns, and stated firmly that 'matters relating to the access, residence and employment of migrant workers from third countries fall under the jurisdiction of the governments of the member states'. However, just before this Council Resolution was adopted, the Commission issued a Decision, addressed to the member states, which announced the setting up under Article 118 of a 'prior communication and consultation procedure' on migration policies in relation to non-member countries.[23] In this it established some quite rigorous procedures to enable it to monitor the actions of member states in this field, and to propose areas for consultation. The tone of the Decision was peremptory, the result according to one commentator of 'ten years of policy statements unaccompanied by effective implementing action'.[24]

In a surprise move in September 1985, Germany, France, Britain, the Netherlands and Denmark challenged the Commission's competence to adopt such a Decision, and initiated a case on this issue before the European Court of Justice.[25] This case, a direct action not a reference, wound its way through the Court's procedures until it reached a hearing in the middle of 1987. By this time it had become an important test case, not only on the issue of migration and free movement, but also on the Commission's powers under Article 118. The case was eventually heard when the single market programme was well under way and the new Single European Act was about to come into force.

The case revealed not only considerable anger and frustration between the Commission and the governments concerned, but also a deep divergence on the issues. Advocate-General Mancini attributed the decision to bring the case partly to member states' 'surprise' that the Commission should take such firm action, but mainly to deep fears about national security and identity. It also seems clear that the main motive of the governments concerned was to prevent measures involving restrictive immigration practices from being brought within the Community system and thus becoming subject to scrutiny by the Commission and the Parliament. As Mancini pointed out, governments had tried to preempt just such a development by means of a Declaration attached to the Single European Act, preserving immigration as a national matter.[26]

The case hinged first on the issue of Commission competence and second on the minor and procedural matter of whether the Commission should have consulted the Economic and Social Committee (ESC) before issuing its Decision. In the event, Mancini, in an outspoken and informative Opinion, found for the Commission on the competence issue, but against it (reluctantly) on the question of procedure. The Court, however, reversed this, and ruled at least partially against the Commission on competence but for it on procedure. The result was that the Decision was voided.

In effect the Court was in agreement with a great deal of the Commission's case. However, because the Decision was voided, the judgment was interpreted as a victory for the member states and a justification of their view that policy towards third country migrants fell for the most part outside Community competence. In 1988 the Commission reissued an amended Decision but the procedure of consultation was never established. The Social Charter, drawn up in 1989, accords responsibility for 'workers from non-member countries' to the member states, but urges that they should receive 'treatment comparable' to that of workers who are nationals (preamble, para. 9).

The Court in ruling in this way may have wished to give the Commission a way forward while not confronting the member states too directly. Looking back one can see that in the fraught political situation nothing but a full endorsement by the Court would have enabled the crucial first step towards Community competence over third country migrants to be taken. Despite the favourable aspects of the judgment, Kenneth Simmonds rightly saw it as a 'massive setback'.[27] It is significant that despite the priority supposedly given at the EC level to economic factors, in the case of third country migrants, it is their lack of citizenship rather than their economic status which is considered decisive. The ECJ has so far endorsed rather than challenged this situation.[28]

The shift to intergovernmentalism

The setback to the plans of at least some within the Commission to coordinate migration policy through the use of Article 118 allowed the member states to deal with these issues through intergovernmental rather than Community mechanisms.[29] This was anyway the trend for immigration issues, as it became clear that a coordinated immigration policy, with attendant changes in a wide range of associated areas, would be required if the aim of the single market programme to remove all internal border controls was to be realised. In matters as sensitive as these, the member states preferred to work together outside the Community system and away from public scrutiny. The main bodies used for this purpose were the working committees set up by the Schengen group, the Trevi committees (dealing with police cooperation) and the Ad Hoc Immigration Group, set up in 1986.[30] The Commission was involved with all these groups but in a servicing rather than a co-ordinating role. Its main task was to provide studies and information and to set out the foundations upon which policy could be built.

The net result of these developments was that negotiation over a common immigration policy and a policy towards migration was lifted out of the domestic to the European arena, but without the full underpinnings provided by the European institutions. This resulted in a significant closing off from public scrutiny of an area of policy where individual liberties and human rights were clearly an issue. Dealing with policy in such a way shifted the balance sharply towards the tradition-oriented, nation state dominated version of European identity discussed in chapter 1, and away from more positive thinking about the future which could only emerge from public debate and dialogue.

The effects of this new orientation on the Commission's policy on women migrants were quickly apparent. The seminar on 'Migrant Women in Employment' was held in September 1987, two months after the ECJ ruling. Odile Quintin, the head of the Women's Bureau, stated in her opening address that the policy was now 'controversial', but that they still hoped to be able to pass 'from research to action'. Despite an interesting programme and moving interventions by immigrant women, the seminar tailed away, and ended without concrete proposals.[31]

In the debate on the Heinrich report in October 1987, Manuel Marin, the Commissioner for Social Affairs, gave a clear statement to the European Parliament of the Commission's new position. He pointed out that most of the matters complained of in the report were now the responsibility of the national governments, and that after the Court's ruling the Commission could have 'no jurisdiction in these matters'. He asked MEPs to try to persuade their governments nonetheless to develop co-ordination with the Commission on questions of migration.[32]

As a result of the Court's judgment, it seems that considerable pressure was put on the Women's Bureau by the Commission hierarchy to confine both its research and policy to the situation of women who were EC internal migrants. This faced the Bureau with a dilemma, since both its estimation of where the need lay, and the emphasis in its research, had been on the situation of women migrants from third countries. The Commission did in the end produce a communication on the 'social situation and employment of women migrants', which continued to include third country migrants, but its content was bland.[33] Significantly, there was little publicity and no follow-up. Such an intervention was out of step with the way Community policy was developing.

No direct reference was made to immigrant or migrant women in the Third Equal Opportunities Action Programme (Action Programme 3) drafted in 1989.[34] There was, however, an emphasis on disadvantage, on the heterogeneity of the labour market, and on local employment initiatives. The way these sections were formulated allowed certain low key actions and pieces of research on migrant women to continue to be funded. As one of those involved put it: 'disadvantage does not yet depend on citizenship'.

In response to all these events, a groundswell of opposition began to develop, involving campaigns for more open procedures and more attention to human rights in the development of EC policies on migration and immigration. This came partly from black and migrant communities themselves and partly from church groups, other anti-racist organisations and some Community-wide professional associations.[35] In this, the European Parliament, almost totally excluded from the European-level negotiations on immigration, began to play an important role. The influence of these various support groups was not great, but they provided information, a certain base of concern, and some resources. The main issue taken up by these groups concerned the position of third country migrants with rights of residence in one EC member state, once the single market came into effect. With no right to free movement, they would be the only category of permanently settled persons required to obtain visas to travel within the Community.[36]

It was noticeable, as these campaigns developed, that black and migrant women were more openly active. As a result, the gendered effects of immigration policy became more visible.[37] Attention was paid, for example, to the situation of 'family members' whose rights of residence depended upon a migrant worker/breadwinner (usually a man), and who were then open to exploitation by employers and the state, and at times by their own families and communities. Black and migrant women also made clear the effects on family life and personal development of the restrictive, and ever changing, immigration rules. As one black British woman put it:

> You don't know what your rights are or if you have rights. You don't know if you can travel, have family visit you, go on holiday, challenge unfair treatment. You can't get on with your own life.[38]

Thus the combination of disadvantage which surrounded black and migrant women as regards EC policy was beginning to become clear. Not only, as with other women, was their unpaid work unrecognised by EC policies, but unless they had citizenship (and not always even then) they were unable to benefit fully from the advantages European law gave to paid workers. At the same time, they suffered from the racism and sexism inherent in the developing policies on migration and immigration. These additional factors negated the benefit they might have received from the equal treatment policies. These were some of the issues that fuelled bitterness in the campaigning that followed, and for which black and migrant women required and requested support – from black and migrant organisations and from other women.

One of the issues raised most strongly by black and migrant women was the numbing effect on daily life of the growing tide of racism across Europe. The fall of the Berlin wall in 1989 engendered a new fear of migrants, which in turn sparked off waves of racial harassment and an increased presence in formal politics for groups from the extreme right. Nothing in the immigration saga just described had prepared a firm basis for dealing with these phenomena at the level of the EC, and a similar, though more low key, struggle about EC competence in the area of race relations then developed.

Racism – A Policy Vacuum

Racism is not just a matter of vicious attacks, although such incidents are normally all that is reported.[39] Racism includes daily minor harassment and rebuffs, what the Dutch anthropologist Philomena Essed has called 'everyday racism'.[40] It also includes institutionalised racism, where assumptions about the characteristics and acceptability of certain groups and of particular cultures are applied, often unconsciously, to deny opportunities and achievement. Both racism and anti-racism take different forms in the member states of the EU, and ideas about how different ethnicities should relate and how minorities should be protected also vary.[41]

Much present-day racism in Europe has its roots in colonialism and in deep-rooted assumptions about which cultures are inferior or constitute a threat. Margaret Thatcher tapped into this in 1988 in her Bruges speech, when she claimed that the common experience of colonialism and of its 'civilising' mission was one of the main ties binding the European states together.[42] Such deeply internalised ideas about inferiority and superiority become more overt in situations of hardship and insecurity, and when resources are scarce. In these circumstances, racism may appear as a populist phenomenon expressed most strongly by those with least resources whose needs are not being met. If the situation becomes acute, and is not checked from the top, sooner or later political groupings will emerge to exploit and encourage such responses. The question of action from the top and the response of 'authorities' raises very crucially the question of what on this issue is 'the top' in Europe.

The EC dimension

Racism of all these kinds was a growing phenomenon in the eighties in Western Europe.[43] The requirements of economic restructuring, the sense of crisis, the growth in unemployment, all combined to create a need for scapegoats and to set the context for inter-ethnic rivalries. The national controls on immigration exacerbated this by creating the sense that certain people were 'problems' and that Europe could not 'afford' immigrants. By the end of the eighties, the situation had worsened with the onset of recession, and instability to the East. The Gulf War in 1991 encouraged indigenous Europeans to see not only Islamic states but also Islamic culture as a threat.

The European Parliament was the first of the European institutions to respond directly to this situation, triggered into action by the election in 1984 of ten MEPs from the French extreme right party, the *Front National*. Soon after the election the Parliament, now with a socialist majority, set up a committee of inquiry into the rise of fascism and racism in Europe. The rapporteur for this was Dimitrios Evrigenis, a former Greek judge in the European Court of Human Rights.

This report, while mainly concerned with the rise of the extreme right and its links across Europe, also considered the roots of racism and its relation to economic and social conditions.[44] The committee conducted a number of hearings and began to create a Community dimension to the study of these issues. At one of these hearings, the veteran Belgian Marxist, Ernest Mandel, commented perceptively that it was necessary for democratic authorities to take action quickly, before extreme right parties passed the threshold beyond which they would start to attract financial support and cause the political system to adjust towards them.[45]

Evrigenis, when presenting his report to the Parliament, adopted a positive tone. There were plenty of elements, he said, in the European democratic 'credo' which helped identify 'correct responses' to 'crucial questions'.[46] The recommendations in the report were addressed to the European institutions and included proposals for a broader definition of Community powers and responsibilities in the area of race relations (using Article 235 of the Treaty of Rome) and the setting up 'under the aegis of the European Communities' of an intercommunity forum to assist debate and improve representation. There was a strong emphasis throughout on the need for openness and dialogue. The Evrigenis report was adopted in January 1986 after a debate which avoided rhetoric and indicated a fair degree of consensus on the issues.

As a follow up to this report, the Presidents of the Commission, the Parliament and the Council 'including representatives of the member states meeting within the Council' signed a joint Declaration against racism and xenophobia in Strasbourg on 11 June 1986.[47] This marked an unusual departure for the Community institutions and, though the text was toned down in the negotiating process, the preamble referred both to EC and third country migrants and recognised the 'positive contribution' which they had made 'and can continue to make' to the member states and to the Community. Despite the convoluted terminology, this was an unprecedented tribute, especially to third country migrants. It has not to my knowledge been repeated since. In a debate in the Parliament on the Declaration, although consensus was on the whole retained, a hint was given of divisions to come. On the one hand, Glyn Ford, the British Labour MEP, defended the position of third country nationals, whom he evocatively labelled 'the thirteenth member state'; on the other, Olivier D'Ormesson of the French FN talked beguilingly of what he termed 'Community preference and the establishment of a European identity'.[48]

Emboldened by these developments, the Commission, also in 1986, funded a report from the Runnymede Trust in Britain on 'the extent of racism and xenophobia in Europe, the existing means of legal protection, and recommendations for new approaches'. Though this report was completed in 1987, it was never accepted by the Commission or published in the usual EC format.[49] The reason for the cool reception seems to have been that the report was considered to have trespassed too far into areas of member state competence, both in the analysis and in the remedies suggested. Since this was just at the period when the Commission was having its knuckles rapped by the member states over migration policy, the Commission hierarchy seems to have been unwilling to risk a fresh confrontation.

In fact the Runnymede report, while pulling no punches, represented a relatively measured view of the situation from the perspective of black and migrant communities. It suggested that such communities were not opposed in principle to policies on immigration and accepted that some restrictions were necessary. What such communities wanted above all was for provisions to be 'fair' and not racist, and for an ending of uncertainty. They also wanted the state in Europe to 'lift itself above the nation' and seek to protect and represent all who were within its borders.

Thus by 1987, as on the issues of migration and immigration, efforts by the Commission and the Parliament to establish a Community level of policy in the area of race relations had received a setback. On immigration, however, member states needed to coordinate their policies by intergovernmental if not by Community means. On race relations there was no such compulsion. The clear preference of member state governments was to deal with racism at the national level and by national means, thus retaining flexibility in the face of evolving political circumstances. National authorities appeared to see no necessity to establish legally binding legislation on race discrimination at the level of the Community, as had been done on the issue of sex discrimination.

These realities were clearly demonstrated in May 1990 when a Commission proposal for a Resolution (a non-binding measure) condemning racism and xenophobia, and approving certain actions to combat it, came before the Social Affairs Council. In the negotiations, the measure was so weakened that in the end the Commission refused to approve it. In particular, all reference to what groups were covered by the Resolution was removed.[50]

Meanwhile, the Parliament had been working on a second inquiry, this time into racism and xenophobia, with Glyn Ford as rapporteur. The meat of this report lay in its annexes, consisting of submissions both from government officials and from representatives of associations and voluntary organisations working in the field. The difference in tone between the two was often startling, especially in the case of Germany. In general, the government officials, with the notable exception of the representative of the Netherlands, sought to minimise the occurrence of racism, attribute it to a small minority of untypical individuals, and emphasise that it was being dealt with in a satisfactory manner. The representatives of associations gave a different impression, illustrating often in vivid terms the way racism was boiling up from the grassroots, to be exploited, sometimes in quite cynical ways, for political advantage. Alarm was expressed at the way issues were being brushed under the carpet and the lack of any real dialogue.[51]

The Ford report made 77 recommendations, directed at the competence and responsibilities of the Parliament, the Commission and the Council. It repeated the demands for race relations legislation and for funding for an association to represent migrants. It also proposed a European Residents Charter to guarantee the rights of residents in the new single market.

Such issues were now much more contentious within the Parliament itself, and the hints of difference noted earlier swelled into a major conflict, so that the resolution on the report was adopted by only a bare majority.[52] The basic argument of those opposed to the recommendations was that many of the proposals of the report, if adopted, would actually worsen racism and xenophobia by increasing the insecurity of the indigenous population. Thus the polarisation between those concerned with the 'thirteenth state' and those supporting 'Community preference' was becoming absolute, and little dialogue or compromise seemed possible. As predicted by Mandel, the politics of the right were beginning to move centre stage.

Race and gender

All of the reports discussed above lacked an integrated gender perspective.[53] Although Philomena Essed gave telling evidence to Evrigenis, virtually nothing of her approach was incorporated into the main body of the report.[54] This despite the fact that the report was generally eclectic and made an otherwise insightful analysis of the social and cultural roots of racism. The Runnymede report, at least as far as can be judged from the summary, equally made no reference to women's experiences, and furthermore referred to foreigners and immigrants throughout as 'he'. The Ford report showed a somewhat greater awareness, and one of the vice-chairs of the committee was Djida Tazdait, a French woman MEP of Algerian origin. Nevertheless, only two of Ford's 77 recommendations specifically referred to women.[55] These reports reflected the fact that even in the eighties 'progressive' writing on race relations still to a very large extent ignored the distinct experiences of women, although evidence and writing setting out and analysing these was already available.[56]

Viewing racism and xenophobia from the perspective of black and migrant women provides new insights and approaches. Essed's evidence to Evrigenis made the point very clearly. In her brief account she emphasised two main points: firstly, the specific and concrete forms taken by racism, and secondly, the need to examine the dominant culture as well as the customs and practices of minorities. Although neither of these points was made specifically with reference to women, the arguments were quite clearly drawn from a women's perspective and the tone adopted was very different from that of the other contributors. Essed proposed legislation on race discrimination at the EC level, on the same lines as the EC's Directives on sex equality.

Research done (mainly in 1992) for *Confronting the Fortress* expanded these points.[57] It suggested that, despite variations across countries and communities and between individuals, the majority of black and migrant women faced restraints and restrictions not met by other women, and different from those met by black and migrant men. These acted to reinforce their gendered roles and make any struggle for autonomy more difficult. The beleaguered position of many black and migrant communities affected the women within, involved as they normally were with maintaining the family and 'keeping life going'. As one woman put it: 'women bear the brunt when communities are under threat'.[58]

A further insight is provided by feminist writing on the symbolic effects of racist violence against women in communities deemed inferior. In the eyes of the attackers, targeting women disables the producers of 'unwanted' children and demonstrates the vulnerability of their societies. This encourages a macho culture within which white and immigrant men compete over women's bodies, and where women are constructed as possessions with little chance of autonomy.[59] Something of this can be seen in the attacks on Turkish women in Germany in Mölln and Solingen in 1992–93 – and in the reactions to those attacks.[60]

The contrast between action taken at the EU level on sex discrimination and the non-action on race discrimination, whether in employment or elsewhere, is very marked. In 1992–93 I worked with Marina Orsini-Jones on a project which attempted to evaluate the effects of different strands of EU policy on immigrant women living in the Italian city of Bologna. We found that the EU's sex equality legislation, in existence for more than fifteen years, had created a policy framework and a legitimacy which extended to the local level. It remained relatively intact even in the turbulent nineties. The absence of comparable legislation on race relations or race discrimination left a vacuum which nationalism and racism were rushing to fill. Pious declarations by EC/EU leaders condemning racism carried no weight (and in fact were entirely unknown at this level) since they were not linked to local or regional policy making by either legislation or significant funding.[61]

Thus, black and migrant women in the EU, the five million, found themselves by the beginning of the nineties in an exposed situation, as did black and migrant communities in general. To those women who were active and aware, it was becoming increasingly clear that an important level of debate and action was taking place at European level, both inside and outside the EU. It was also clear that the voices of third country migrants, the 'thirteenth state', were hardly heard, and that those of EC citizens of third world origin were muted. The question of organisation thus became crucial. Where could black and migrant women go for help and support? To other women, to black and migrant men, or to neither?

Black and White Women Organising in Europe

One cannot consider the question of black, migrant and white women working together at the European level without taking account of the developments discussed above. For these histories both set out some of the issues of particular importance to black and migrant women and also give an idea of the political constraints and realities within which action has to be taken and arguments made. Women, whatever their colour, class or nationality, have multiple connections to these issues. Not all black women want to be associated with or work for poor black migrants; many white women, as was evident in the parliamentary debates, feel pulls of culture or nationality which transcend or are as strong as solidarity among women; few white women are or want to be aware of how their position and history has rested on the marginalising of other women, and how this affects their behaviour. All of these attitudes are complex and defy easy categorisation or moral judgment. As far as organisation is concerned, the main question is whether there is sufficient solidarity among women to talk these differences out, and what kind of structures best promote this. This goes back to the debate set out in chapter 1.

These questions were posed most strongly in the early nineties, at the start of the Maastricht process, when the governments were fumbling to achieve a new shape for the Community.[62] This it was hoped would help to meet some of the pressures and challenges developing both within and outside existing structures, while preserving 'national sovereignty' and keeping politics at bay. Because of the reluctance of governments to develop a real politics at the level of the EC, the discussion of new structures took place in intergovernmental conferences (IGCs). These represented in essence procedures very little changed from those adopted in the fifties to draw up the Treaty of Rome. The experience of the eighties of developing an immigration policy outside the Community system seems to have been influential in these deliberations.

In order to influence this developing policy, interest groups and activists had to work along parallel lines to the IGCs, hoping that the ideas and programmes they were promoting would be taken on board by some at least of the politicians and officials involved. It was an indication of the balance of power within the EC at that time that the Parliament itself was in a similar position. In all of this process, 'women's interests', in a totalising sense, were to some extent taken on board, assisted by the existence of the women's policy, the activities of the women's network and the presence of some women decision makers. The interests of black and migrant communities were much less directly represented.

The extent to which the concerns of these communities did now have a higher profile at EC level was demonstrated during 1991 by two very different initiatives. In the first of these, anti-racist organisations, co-ordinated by the British Commission for Racial Equality, began to draft a Directive for adoption under Article 235. This obliged member states to take coordinated measures to promote race equality and prohibit racial harassment, and was given the title 'The Starting Line'. A campaign was initiated, mainly at national level, to persuade governments to take the measure on board.[63] In the second initiative, more radical immigrant organisations organised a consultation and a picket at Maastricht in December 1991.[64] This was timed to coincide with the meeting of EC Heads of State which gave final approval to the text of the Maastricht Treaty, now officially called the Treaty on European Union (TEU). After the meeting, the Heads of State issued a new Declaration on racism and xenophobia. Although the language was strong, no binding obligations or Community-level actions were proposed.[65]

Some recognition of the need for representation which these political developments implied was given in the establishment (at EC level and with Community funding) of the European Women's Lobby in September 1990, and of the Migrants Forum in May 1991. Each of these lobbies created structures which in theory could provide black and migrant women with new opportunities for visibility and direct representation. In reality this did not happen, and at the beginning at least black and migrant women were virtually excluded from both organisations. In order to understand the reasons for this, we need to look first at the way in which black and migrant women were organising at this point and then at the role and structure of these two lobbies.

From the grassroots up

A large number of precarious and fluid migrant organisations exist at grassroots level across Europe.[66] These mostly provide support and protection for their members and act to preserve minority cultures in the face of marginalisation or outright hostility. The majority are based on one community and one locality and only rarely do they move into overt political action. Beyond this level, some more developed structures may exist which attempt to engage with the authorities and develop a multi-ethnic base. The extent and nature of these latter organisations varies very much from one EU member state to another.[67]

Women are disproportionately represented in the support networks, which vary in strength and function according to the particular community and the position of women within it.[68] They are less well represented in the more structured organisations, which are for the most part dominated by male traditional or political leaders. The increased representation of black and migrant women at both the national and the European level depends on predominantly women's organisations moving to develop political campaigning as well as support work and organising across as well as within communities. To the extent that this is already happening, a women's presence is being created in the overwhelmingly male migrant political organisations.

Some examples may help to clarify these points and illustrate the changes taking place. *La Voix des Femmes* is a training and support organisation in Brussels for Turkish and North African women and girls. Formed in 1985, it has gradually expanded its remit and become more 'political'. One of its objectives is to demonstrate to a broader public the effects that racism has on the women who come for support. It receives a small amount of EU money for certain projects. In Denmark, a new organisation, *Soldue*, ('sun dove' in Danish), is seeking to unite women from different ethnic minority groups, and make representations to the Danish authorities. It is working with Danish women from the refuge movement on issues to do with violence against women. It is now receiving a small grant from the Danish government.[69]

Turkish women in Europe have a variety of local networks and some have organised a European support group. These women feel excluded from the dominant cultures in Europe and forced back on their own resources. They are linked by a telephone tree and can share information quickly. They meet once a year. They have resisted any more formal organisation or more direct political involvement for fear of losing flexibility. The Commission for Filipino Migrant Workers is probably the most effective migrant organisation in Europe. In it women are well represented since they have for the most part come to Europe in their own right and not as dependants. In 1992 Filipino women in Europe held a conference in Barcelona to share experiences and draw up demands. They raised issues concerning traffic in women, de-skilling and the treatment of foreign domestic workers.[70]

All of these are precarious organisations run with dedication and few resources. It is from them, and other similar organisations, that some presence for black and migrant women is being constructed at the European level. As can be seen from this account, diversity is as much an issue between groups of black and migrant women as it is between them and other women. Thus common action needs careful negotiation. Nevertheless, as with women more generally in the seventies, the need for organisation is pressing. The issues discussed earlier in this chapter indicate why the European level is now seen as important.

One sign that the situation of black and migrant women was beginning to be taken more seriously came in September 1991 when the European Parliament's Women's Committee held a hearing on the subject. This followed demands from black and migrant women's organisations and from the two women MEPs of ethnic minority origin then in the Parliament. The hearing consisted of presentations by some prominent migrant women and by outside 'experts' including an effective representative from the ILO. The hearing gave 'presence' to black and migrant women but did not decide on any concrete action. The Green group in the Parliament followed this rather staid and cautious gesture by organising a more political conference for 'immigrant women from the third world'. The aim of this was to establish a network at European level. A number of women activists attended who in the end decided that any network must be independent and not established under the auspices of one political grouping, however well intentioned. This meeting laid the basis for the Black Women in Europe Network, which came into being in 1993.[71]

These different layers of organisation and activity suggest that black and migrant women should have had a strong position within both the Migrants Forum and the European Women's Lobby, as these organisations were set up. The fact that this was not the case demonstrated both the multiple exclusions which black and migrant women face, and the difficulties which occur when new social movements attempt to engage the mainstream. A brief look at both of these organisations helps to explain these points and brings us back to our main theme of the relationship between black and white women in political activity.

The Lobby and the Forum

Both the European Women's Lobby (EWL) and the Migrants Forum were set up with encouragement from the Commission and the Parliament; and they continue to receive yearly subventions from Community funds. This represents some recognition by the Community as a whole that support is needed if social and community as well as business and economic interests are to participate in any direct way at the European level. Although all organisations set up in this way are in formal terms autonomous, the receipt of Community funds and the role that they are expected to play as 'peak' organisations, able to be consulted and give opinions, inevitably creates restraints. In the case of complex and multiple constituencies like women or migrants, this role raises difficult questions about accountability and legitimacy.

The EWL might well have been formed earlier – the money would certainly have been available from the Commission.[72] However, as discussed in chapter 7, disagreement between traditional and feminist organisations was too strong when the idea was first mooted in 1982 for it to be possible to form an organisation at European level which could claim to represent all women. However, gradually during the eighties these gaps narrowed. Traditional organisations became somewhat more radical and feminist organisations more willing to compromise. As a result, at a seminar held in London in November 1987, in a context where traditional women outnumbered feminist women by perhaps two to one, a unanimous decision was taken to set up a Lobby and seek funding from the Commission. To carry out the preparatory work representatives of forty women's organisations were chosen, mainly it would seem by the two women's bureaux in the Commission and those 'in the know' at the London seminar. The emphasis on 'organised' women did not exclude feminist groups or networks which had some structure (the European Network of Women, for example, was among those chosen) but it did very clearly exclude any direct representation of poor women, or of black and migrant women, who although having as we have seen quite a high level of organisation, were not known in these milieux.

The basic structure and ethos of the EWL developed over the next two years. Europe-wide women's organisations would be represented directly and women's umbrella organisations in each country would have the right to four seats. The aim was to represent women 'including the least privileged and least organised' and to promote their interests at the level of the EC. In true Community style, little guidance was given in the statutes as to how the national delegates should be chosen. In Britain, the decision was made to elect them on a regional basis, with one delegate each from Scotland, Northern Ireland, Wales and England. The Dutch, by contrast, allocated their delegates to interest groups: one to the feminist network, one to traditional women's organisations, one to ethnic minority women and one to women's health groups. Other countries were less egalitarian. In Germany, for example, the *Deutscher Frauenrat*, the big traditional women's council, allocated all the delegates to its member organisations.

More than seventy women came to the inaugural meeting of the Lobby in September 1990. The vast majority were white, professional and middle aged but with diverse backgrounds, skills and politics. Trade-union women were present but not numerous. Only two out of the seventy were ethnic minority women: one came from the Netherlands, one from a feminist Europe-wide organisation. Thus the main lines of the Lobby were set. It was clear that though black and migrant women were not excluded, and indeed were minimally present, it would be hard for them to have a strong influence or see that issues of concern to them were taken up. The issue of balance and representation among the Lobby's members was not addressed. The leaving of these decisions to the national level represented a mirroring of EC practice.

The Migrants Forum had a similarly long gestation. First proposed in the Commission's 1985 guidelines and endorsed by Evrigenis in his report, it in fact took five years for disputes about composition to be settled, and for the process of identifying candidate organisations to be completed.[73] In the end, as the need for such a body became urgent, it was agreed that organisations representing third country migrants should be full members, and organisations representing EC internal migrants, associates. The Forum was finally set up in 1991 'as a consultative organisation to represent the interests of migrants to the Community institutions'.

As with the EWL, the choice of delegates to the preparatory committee was crucial. This was carried out by the relevant division in the Commission with the help of CIEMI, a French migration research centre. The initial meeting of 67 organisations was called by the Commission in November 1990. There were only two organisations primarily representing women among the original organisations selected, although two or three more women attended as representatives of mixed organisations. To Jan Niessen (who acted as a 'neutral' chair) and Glyn Ford (who spoke at the meeting) 'it seemed like an all male affair'.[74] This situation caused some disquiet, with the result that in the constitution as finally approved 'improving the status of migrant women' is one of the criteria for membership. The conference to approve the constitution was held in May 1991. Here four or five women-only organisations were represented, and a handful more women attended as delegates.

At this meeting, the constitution was approved and the officers and a Board of Management elected. All of the officers were men. Three woman were elected to the Board of nineteen, the members of which were chosen to represent migrants from each of the member states of the EC, and the main 'home' regions from which migrants came. The main early activities of the Forum were to strengthen links with the base and create support groups in each member state. At a meeting in Birmingham to set these up for the UK, the Forum panel was criticised for the general marginalisation of women in its proceedings.[75]

Protest and reaction

In both the Lobby and the Forum, black and migrant women found themselves with very low representation when the initial structures took shape. There is no evidence that in either case the issue was raised in the formative stage by Commission officials or by those involved. Once the membership became public, however, protests were made in both organisations, and some action, though of very different kinds, was undertaken in each to attempt to right the balance.

In the Lobby, the visible absence of black women and the lack of any remedy in the statutes, resulted in a proposal from feminist women that a report should be commissioned looking into this situation and making recommendations. This led eventually to the drawing up of the report, *Confronting the Fortress*, referred to earlier in this chapter. The report was put together by a mixed team of black and white women, working together often uneasily but in the end with some comprehension and common concern. It attempted on the one hand to give voice and visibility to black and migrant women, and on the other to suggest to the Lobby how such women might be better involved. Recommendations included the development of more open and democratic structures, and the initiation of debate, dialogue and action on issues to do with racism and immigration.[76]

The report was contentious within the Lobby and was only adopted by a narrow margin at its 1993 General Assembly. There was much discussion as to whether this was a correct issue for the Lobby to take up since some maintained 'it was supposed to deal with issues of concern to *all* women'. Though many women were supportive, others clearly felt antagonistic and resented criticisms made in the report of particular national measures and attitudes. These reactions gave a clear indication that within the Lobby solidarity among women could not be assumed, and that extensive dialogue would be needed to achieve it, at least on this issue. It was also clear that the kinds of hierarchical structures and expert lobbying expected of an EC peak organisation could easily lead to exclusions, and to a lack of concern with (and time for) debate and dialogue.

The Migrants Forum tackled the issue differently, faced by the irrefutable fact that approximately 45 per cent of the people it was supposed to represent were women, and by pressure in particular from the EP Women's Committee. Thus quite soon after the inaugural conference was held, a women's committee was set up, the chair of which was given automatic membership on the Board. The women's committee, drawing together women from vastly different backgrounds and with different views and strategies, now meets four times a year at the Forum's expense. Its main aim so far has been to work through the experiences of members and see where there is common ground, and to get through to the Forum leaders that 'women have something to contribute'. A conference on the situation of migrant women, organised by the women's committee, was held in Athens in November 1994. At the time of writing there are eight women (including the Commission's representative, Annette Bosscher) on the Management Board of twenty-eight.[77]

Both the Lobby and the Forum are organisations in evolution. Several years after their formation both are still attempting to establish appropriate structures and effective working methods. Neither has really solved the problem of how to represent diverse constituencies or establish legitimacy. Black and migrant women, at the hinge point between the two, can either be rendered invisible as happened at the beginning, or if they gain appropriate representation, can act as links and catalysts. It is evident already that taking their situation seriously breaks down the monolithic categories of 'women' and 'migrants' and helps to reveal some of the multiple identities that people share.

However, faced with these barriers, many black and migrant women have shown that belonging to the Lobby and the Forum is important but not enough. They have continued to create autonomous networks, seeking cooperation with the 'peak' organisations as and when appropriate. Both the Lobby and the Forum require such surrounding activity if they are to function effectively.

Structural issues

Over the period discussed, the visibility of black and migrant women at European level has considerably increased. This breaking down of some of the restrictions imposed by stereotyping and marginalisation has great significance. Not only does it allow black and migrant women to represent themselves, it also brings forward new information and new perspectives for the women's movement as a whole. These on the one hand suggest areas where low-key, supportive cooperation between black and white women is urgently needed, and on the other throw light on emerging structural issues in the relations between women.

Trafficking in women, the terms for family reunion and the legal status of family members of migrants are areas where such cooperation is badly needed. On trafficking, Thanh-Dam Truong and Virginia del Rosario argue that only civil society, in which women's organisations play an important role, can redress the balance against the arbitrary and bureaucratic power of states in the EU which separately and together treat the victims of trafficking as unwanted aliens. They show that in the Netherlands it was only cooperative action of this kind which was able to force the government to switch policy, and adopt provisions which offered protection to women, even if undocumented, who reported trafficking abuses. Such cooperative action, with third world women in the lead, is now urgent on this issue at EU level.[78]

The structural questions are equally important. Black and migrant women point out that as white women improve their situations, very often black and migrant women come in to fill the roles they are leaving behind.[79] Instead of such work being taken up by the state or shared with men, it is done by other women. This helps to explain the continuing demand in countries like Italy and Spain for undocumented migrant women as domestics. In northern Europe, poor women who work in private service as nannies, cleaners and maids perform the same function. These insights are important for revealing the nature of class and race relations between and among women. They also help to explain how it is that a certain degree of liberation has been achieved (on the whole by educated and professional women) with very little alteration so far in the behaviour and work patterns of the majority of men.

A consideration of such topics serves once again to problematise the category of 'women' and to raise new questions about how and by whom women can be represented within European and other institutions. They also illuminate some aspects of what is happening to women in the nineties. These insights demonstrate the importance of representation and speech. None of this material comes out, no truc accounts are placed on the table, when marginalised women are regarded with pity or met with charity. They are only revealed when groups or individuals are there to speak for themselves.

As stated at the beginning, the focus in this chapter on black and migrant women has had a twofold purpose. On the one hand, it has tried to demonstrate some of the complex relations which now exist among and between women. On the other, it has sought to say something further about the politics of the EU in the eighties and nineties. What is striking on the latter count is the combination of decisions in the mid eighties which, as the single-market measures began to be adopted, sought to prevent an equivalent expansion of the Community's political structures. The bringing of the 'migration' case to the ECJ and the refusal to allow racism to be tackled at the European level were important elements in this.

The Maastricht Treaty has rightly been accused of creating 'a Europe of bits and pieces'.[80] While embodying detailed plans for further economic integration, the main effect of its provisions is to fragment the Community enterprise, returning some issues to the national level while projecting others to intergovernmental bargaining. For the first time, the scope of the European Court has been limited so that it no longer has jurisdiction over the whole of what is now termed the European Union. Though the original intention was to include a considerable expansion of the Community's social role in the new Treaty, the obduracy of the British government has meant that here too fragmentation has taken place, with the Social Protocol standing outside the Treaty and applying only to eleven member states. At the same time, the Treaty creates a new category of 'European citizens', and thus in theory at least opens up possibilities for debate and action on a much broader range of human rights issues.

Despite these moves, this study of the activities of black and migrant women and of women in general suggests that 'politics' cannot be put back in the cupboard at the whim of governments, and that the European arena has now become a part of politics for many groups. In this situation, the Community institutions are themselves divided, with important elements in the Commission and Parliament still seeking to establish some kind of constituency at the EU level. To take advantage of this situation, women need to aggregate their strengths. Only organisations which both recognise women's diversity and seek to extend the common ground between women are likely to be able to achieve this.

Notes

1 Much of this chapter has been influenced by my experiences as a member of the project team which drew up for the European Women's Lobby the report *Confronting the Fortress – Black and Migrant Women in the European Community* (European Parliament, 1995), and by the work which I did for it. I am grateful to the other members of the team for their support and encouragement. They bear no responsibility for the opinions expressed here.

2 I have used the terms 'black and migrant' because these were the terms used (after much debate and consultation) in *Confronting the Fortress*. No terminology is satisfactory, certainly not across Europe, but this combines the term 'black', which for all its limitations has a political connotation, and 'migrant' which is the most frequently used EU term. When referring to EU documents which use a particular terminology (usually migrant or immigrant) I have followed this.

3 Adrienne Rich, *On Lies, Secrets and Silence*, Virago, London, 1980, p. 299.

4 The term 'undocumented' is used rather than 'illegal' or 'clandestine', because it has fewer pejorative connotations and is the term most generally used by organisations which speak for women in this situation.

5 Guiseppe Callovi, 'Immigration and the European Community', *Contemporary European Affairs*, vol. 3, no. 3, 1990, pp. 17–18.

6 If anything, this is an underestimate. A useful and up-to-date breakdown of figures is given in Ceri Peach's paper, 'Emerging Trends and Major Issues in Migration and Ethnic Relations in Western and Eastern Europe', seminar on Post-War Migration to Europe, University of Warwick, 1993.

7 At the level of the EU, the terms immigration policy and migration policy are often confused, as are the terms immigrant and migrant. Generally speaking, immigration policy covers all aspects of policy which determine rights and treatment at the point of entry, while migration policy includes in addition policies on employment, settlement and status, once entry has been granted.

8 Richard Plender, 'Competence, European Community Law and Nationals of Non-Member States', *International and Comparative Law Quarterly*, vol. 39, 1990, p. 605. A senior judge of the ECJ, now retired, whom I interviewed in 1993, expressed the view that it would have been 'out of the question' to interpret Article 48 as applying to all workers, even non-nationals. He conceded that in this respect people were treated differently (i.e., less favourably) than goods, since imports from outside the EU are subject to common trade rules, and free movement therefore applies to all goods, whatever their origin.

9 For policy in the seventies see Daniel Duyssens, 'Migrant Workers from Third Countries in the European Community', in P. Kapteyn, ed., *The Social Policy of the European Communities*, A.W. Sijthoff, Leyden, 1977, pp. 141–2; the full text of the Commission's 'Guidelines for a Community Policy on Migration' is given in *Bulletin of the ECs*, Supplement 9/85.

10 Integration is the term normally used in EU documentation for policies designed to improve the situation of migrant or ethnic minority communities and to assist them to adjust to life in Europe. All of these terms are value laden, and while the individual policies may be advantageous, the objective of 'integration' has been questioned by black and migrant communities. The campaigning slogan of 'not integration but rights' is now quite widely used.

11 For a detailed account of the struggle between the Commission and the member states on this issue see the Opinion of Advocate-General Mancini in ECJ Case 281/85, discussed later in this chapter.

12 CEC, 'Guidelines', p. 12, n. 1.

13 Colette de Troy found that despite the widespread indifference of women's organisations in Europe to the needs of migrant women, the authorities with the best general infrastructures for women were also those which were beginning to develop provision for migrant women. (Colette de Troy, *The Specific Training Needs of Immigrant Women*, CEC, V/1909/86, 1986, ch. 1.)
14 A good example is Annie Phizacklea, ed., *One Way Ticket – Migration and Female Labour*, Routledge, London, 1983. This contains an insightful essay by Mirjana Morokvasic on the way in which migrant women had been and were being constructed in both mainstream and more 'women-centred' research.
15 Isabelle Von Prondzynski, 'The Social Situation and Employment of Migrant Women in the European Community', *Policy and Politics*, vol. 17, no. 4, 1989, p. 348.
16 These three reports are usefully synthesised in Colette de Troy, *Migrant Women and Employment*, CEC, V/928/87, 1987.
17 Mirjana Morokvasic, *Minority and Immigrant Women in Self-Employment and Business*, CEC, V/1871/88, 1988.
18 Brigitte Heinrich, *On Discrimination Against Immigrant Women in Community Legislation and Regulations*, European Parliament, A2-133/87, 1987, parts A and B, plus Annex.
19 See 'Left-right clash in the Reichstag' *CREW Reports*, vol. 7, no. 6, June 1987, p. 10; and report on the debate in Parliament, OJ Annex no. 2–356, 13 October 1987.
20 I myself attended the meetings of the Women's Committee which discussed the final text of the report on 13–14 July 1987. A number of women MEPs were quite clearly struggling with contradictory emotions and pulls on their loyalties.
21 'Equal Opportunities for Women – Medium-term Community Programme 1986–90', *Bulletin of the ECs*, Supplement 3/86, para. 22 (d).
22 Interview, Colette de Troy, Brussels, 7 July 1987.
23 The texts of the Resolution and the Decision are given in *Bulletin of the ECs*, Supplement 9/85, pp. 17/20. According to Article 189 of the Treaty of Rome, a Decision is 'binding in its entirety upon those to whom it is addressed'. Both the Council and the Commission can adopt Decisions. Article 118 gives the Commission the task of 'promoting close cooperation' between member states in the social field. See chapter 3 this volume for a discussion of its origins.
24 Kenneth R. Simmonds, 'The concertation of Community migration policy', *Common Market Law Review*, vol. 25, 1988, pp. 177–200.
25 *Germany and Others* v. *the Commission*, joined ECJ cases 281, 283, 284, 285 and 287/85, judgment 9 July 1987.
26. General Declaration on Articles 13 to 19 of the Single European Act, *Bulletin of the ECs*, Supplement 2/86, p. 24.
27 Simmonds, 'Concertation', p. 200.
28 On the whole, when the ECJ has made judgments favourable to third country migrants, these have been on the basis either of a relationship which that third country migrant has had with an EU migrant, or as a result of intergovernmental or Union agreements with the home country of the migrant (e.g., the EU/Turkey association agreements). They have not been made to third country migrants in their own right, or on the basis of the economic contribution being made by such migrants to EU development.
29 The speed with which the governments began to coordinate their activities with regard to third country migrants, at least as far as immigration issues were concerned, shows that their objection was not to coordination as such, but to achieving it through the Community system.
30 France, Germany and the Benelux countries set up the Schengen group in 1985 outside the EC framework in an attempt to speed up the removal of border controls. They were soon joined by Italy and Spain. Increasingly this group has been used to pioneer joint immigration policies despite the fact that not all EU members belong.
31 An account of the seminar is given in Colette de Troy, *Migrant Women and Employment – Community Seminar, Final Report*, CEC, V/902/88, 1988. See chapter 10 this volume for further details.
32 OJ Annex No 2–356/71, 13 October 1987.

33 Communication from the Commission on *The Social Situation and Employment of Migrant Women*, COM(88) 743, 15 December 1988.
34 *Equal Opportunities for Men and Women – the Third Medium-term Action Programme 1991–1995*, CEC, COM(90) 449 final.
35 One example of the latter was the Immigration Law Practitioners Association (ILPA) which set up a European Network in 1991 and began to compile and distribute comparative and European information on immigration issues.
36 Joint Council for the Welfare of Immigrants, *Unequal Migrants: the European Community's Unequal Treatment of Migrants and Refugees*, Centre for Research in Ethnic Relations, University of Warwick, 1989.
37 For a telling account of these see Jane Goldsmith, 'The Effects on Women of the Creation of the European Internal Market in 1992, with particular reference to the Problems of Black and Ethnic Minority Women in the UK', unpublished paper written for Anita Pollack MEP, London, 1990.
38 *Confronting the Fortress*, p. 55.
39 Much has been written on racism and race relations over the last fifteen years. I have made particular use in this section of two books which develop a comparative and European perspective: John Solomos and John Wrench, eds, *Racism and Migration in Western Europe*, Berg, Oxford 1993; and Michel Wieviorka, ed., *Racisme et xénophobie en Europe – une comparaison internationale*, Editions La Découverte, Paris, 1994.
40 Philomena Essed, *Everyday Racism*, Hunter House, Claremont 1990; originally published in Dutch in 1984.
41 A sensitive account of the differences between Britain and France in these respects is given in Cathie Lloyd, 'Race Relations in Britain and France: Problems of Interpretation', Research Paper No. 17, Centre for Research in Ethnic Relations, University of Warwick, 1991.
42 Speech made to the College of Europe, Bruges, 20 September 1988.
43 For a close monitoring of racism, discrimination and official responses across Europe, see *Migration News Sheet*, produced in Brussels by church groups and the main anti-racist organisations in France, Britain and the Netherlands.
44 European Parliament, *Report drawn up on behalf of the Committee of Inquiry into the Rise of Fascism and Racism in Europe* (Evrigenis Report) A2–160/85/rev and Annexes 1–4, 1986.
45 Evrigenis Report, Annex 4, pp. K1–4.
46 OJ Annex No 2–334/95, 15 January 1986.
47 *Declaration Against Racism and Xenophobia*, OJ C 158/1–3, 25/6/86.
48 OJ Annex No 2–340/106-113, 11 June 1986.
49 A summary entitled *Combating Racism in Europe – A report to the European Communities* (October 1987) is available from The Runnymede Trust.
50 The Commission proposal included the following paragraph: '. . . any measure taken in this connection must protect all persons on Community territory, whether they are nationals of Member States or of non-member countries, foreigners in a Member State or nationals who are perceived or who perceive themselves as belonging to a foreign minority.' It was the deletion of this paragraph by the member state governments which caused the controversy. For the proposal and the text as adopted see OJ C 214/32–36, 16/8/88 and OJ C 157/1–3, 27/6/90.
51 European Parliament, *Report drawn up on behalf of the Committee of Inquiry into Racism and Xenophobia* (Ford report) A3–195/90 and Annex, 1990.
52 Voting was 188 in favour, 146 against with 18 abstentions, a low majority for an EP resolution of this kind. For an account of the running battle in the EP over this report, see issues of *Migration News Sheet*, June to December 1990.
53 For views of what this would involve see Haleh Afshar and Mary Maynard, eds, *The Dynamics of 'Race' and Gender – Some Feminist Interventions*, Taylor and Francis, London, 1994.
54 Evrigenis Report, Annex 4, pp. D1–7.
55 Recommendations 35 (on asylum policy) and 59 (on an independent right of residence for immigrant women).

56 In addition to the sources already cited in this section, see generally the work of Giovanna Campani (Italy), Mirjana Morokvasic (France) and Annie Phizacklea (Britain). *The Empire Strikes Back* (Hutchinson, London, 1982) contains forceful and gendered accounts of racism in Britain.
57 See above, note 1.
58 *Confronting the Fortress*, p. 54.
59 This dynamic is well described with regard to the US in bell hooks, *Yearning – Race, Gender, and Cultural Politics*, Turnaround, London, 1991, ch. 4.
60 Eight Turkish women and children were killed in firebomb attacks in Mölln in November 1992 and in Solingen in May 1993. For the reactions see the *Guardian* (UK) 1/6/92 and 15/4/94.
61 Catherine Hoskyns and Marina Orsini-Jones, 'Immigrant Women in Italy – Perspectives from Brussels and Bologna', *European Journal of Women's Studies*, vol 2, 1995, pp. 51–76.
62 For a detailed account of this process see Richard Corbett, *The Treaty of Maastricht – From Conception to Ratification*, Longman, London, 1994.
63 An account of the Starting Line project is given in *Combatting Racism in Europe*, Churches' Commission for Migrants in Europe, Briefing Paper no. 16, Brussels, 1994, pp. 16–19.
64 The main organisations involved were the British SCORE (Standing Committee on Racial Equality in Europe) and KMAN, an organisation of Moroccan workers in the Netherlands.
65 The full text of this Declaration is given in Annex 1V of the Conclusions of the Maastricht European Council (9 and 10 December 1991).
66 Some indication of the numbers and spread is given in *Ethnic Minority and Migrant Organisations: European Directory 1991*, Joint Council for the Welfare of Immigrants, London, 1991.
67 A comparative and analytical account of these developments is given in J. Rex and B. Drury, eds, *Ethnic Mobilisation in a Multicultural Europe*, Avebury, Aldershot, 1994. The chapter by Giovanna Campani on Italy is the only one to pay substantial attention to the activities of women.
68 Giovanna Campani, 'Immigrant Women in Labour Market and Family Networks – Philippino, Chinese and Maroccan Women in Italy', Transitions Conference, Berlin, May 1991.
69 I am grateful to Hayriye Balci and Chandra Jayamanne for information respectively on *La Voix des Femmes* and *Soldue*.
70 For an account of the Turkish women's network see *Confronting the Fortress*, pp. 45–7. A full report of the Barcelona Conference has been produced by the Women's Programme, Commission for Filipino Migrant Workers, Amsterdam.
71 Information from Jyostna Patel and Umran Beler, who attended these meetings.
72 Some of this material on the Lobby appeared originally in a note in *Feminist Review*, no. 38, 1991, pp. 67–70.
73 Some account of the origins of the Migrants Forum (although it ignores entirely the issue of the representation of women) is given in John King, 'Ethnic Minorities and Multilateral European Institutions' in J. Leaman and A. Hargreaves, eds, *Racism, Ethnicity and Politics in Contemporary Europe*, Edward Elgar Press, London, 1995. I have drawn on this source in the section that follows.
74 *Confronting the Fortress*, ch. 3.
75 Information from Emma Franks and Sumita Dutta, who attended the Birmingham meeting in April 1992.
76 This account of the writing of the report and the reactions to it is drawn from my own experiences as a member of the project team, and from discussions with others in and around the Lobby during this period.
77 I am grateful to Hansa Patel and Martha Osamor for talking to me about the work of the women's committee and for providing me with documentation.
78 Thanh-Dam Truong, Virginia del Rosario, 'Captive Outsiders: Trafficked Sex Workers and Mail-Order Brides in the European Union', in J. Wiersma, ed., *Insiders and Outsiders:*

on the Making of Europe 11, Pharos, Kampen 1994. See also Chris De Stoop, *Elles sont si gentilles, Monsieur – Les trafiquants de femmes en Europe*, La Longue Vue, Brussels, 1993.
79 *Confronting the Fortress*, passim. See also Patricia Weinert, *Foreign Female Domestic Workers: Help Wanted!*, ILO, Geneva, 1991.
80 Deirdre Curtin, 'The Constitutional Structure of the Union: A Europe of Bits and Pieces', *Common Market Law Review*, vol. 30, no. 1, 1993, pp. 17–69.

10

Unity, Diversity, Solidarity

In this final chapter, I want to pick up the threads identified in the introduction and examine some of the issues raised in the light of the detailed material set out in the book. My contention is that a European perspective helps to illuminate some of the situations women face in the nineties, and that a women-centred approach throws fresh light on international politics in general and the EU in particular. The three threads are: the nature of the women's policy and its effects; organisation and mobilisation among women; and the structure and ethos of the EU.

The Women's Policy

An important and intriguing question, which people often ask, is why the women's policy has developed so strongly in comparison with other strands in the EU's social programme. The account in this book suggests some explanations. The policy, I would argue, owes its existence to the coincidence in the early seventies of three conditions: the material need to open up the market to new forms of labour, widespread mobilisation among women across the EC, and the presence of Article 119 on equal pay in the Treaty of Rome. It should be emphasised, as argued in chapter 3, that Article 119 was included not just for economic reasons, but as an indirect result of women's activism before, during and after the war.

These conditions laid the basis for the strong development of the policy during the seventies. This was helped by the feeling among politicians that women were not a threat, and that to 'assist' them would not affect the general conduct of industrial relations. Subsequently, the presence of women at all levels in society and the growing importance of equality to middle-class women were significant factors in maintaining momentum. By the eighties, the degree of infrastructure around the policy made it hard to dismantle or downgrade directly. It is significant that the strong policy on equality in employment has enabled some spillover to take place towards sexual politics and the political representation of women.

The trajectory of the women's policy provides an illuminating case study of how bureaucrats, law-makers and popular movements interact in the EU framework. The fact that this material has hardly been taken up either in studies of policy making in the EU or in detailed studies of EU social policy, is a telling illustration of the way in which knowledge and experience can be filtered.[1] In the context of debates about 'the social dimension', however, more attention is being paid to these issues. Thus Wolfgang Streeck in a recent text refers to the equal opportunities policy (along with measures on health and safety at work) as representing in the EU context a federalism which is 'encapsulated'.[2] By this he seems to mean that although the policy has developed some (weak) federal characteristics, these are confined to a single area and have few repercussions. This designation appears to accord the women's policy importance, but also in a more subtle way continues its marginalisation. The purpose of this chapter is to suggest an alternative analysis.

The equality principle

The main effect of the women's policy has been to establish a complex and on the whole broadly defined principle of equality between women and men as one strand in the law of the European Union. Since European law is a powerful tool this has some significance. The evidence from Bologna, discussed in chapter 9, of the impact of EC equality laws at local level, suggests that in a normative sense at least the effect of this legal principle has been far-reaching. The vacuum created by the absence of a similar EU commitment on race equality emphasises the point. Achieving this at the level of the EU makes equality between men and women part of the overarching system of regulation which is shaping economic and to some extent social development. The result has been to open up space for gendered debate and for the handling of 'gender conflict'.

If, as this would suggest, it is useful to have a principle about the situation of women endorsed at the level of the EU, is this the right principle to have? Many people, myself included, have been critical of the emphasis in the EU policy on equality, and its restriction until quite recently to women in paid work. However, this may not have been as disadvantageous as was at first thought. Evidence would suggest that in countries where traditional culture (defining women primarily as homemakers) is strong, Germany and Belgium, for example, the emphasis on equality in paid work has been significant. Without

EU prompting, it is unlikely that strong equality legislation in the employment field would have been adopted, certainly not at such an early stage. In particular, in a time of recession and unemployment it has been important to emphasise the formal right of women to do paid work on equal terms with men.

Equality can be a harsh principle, however, especially in the short term, as is made clear by the European Court's 1994 judgment in *Avdel*, accepting a levelling down of rights.[3] It needs both to be interpreted with an eye to difference, as was argued in chapter 8, and flanked with provisions which alleviate disadvantages and encourage positive action. But except in the relatively narrow areas of pregnancy and maternity rights, it is hard to see how special treatment can be strongly endorsed in law without running the risk of reinforcing stereotypes of women's situation. The recent addition to Article 119, adopted during the Maastricht negotiations and now forming part of the Social Agreement (see Appendix 1 for text) illustrates this point. Apparently favourable to women, it could well in the future be used to undermine the principle of equality, and damage women's position in the longer term.[4]

The equality principle can also, if the derogations are narrowly drawn, itself be used to limit positive action for women. This was the issue in the *Kalanke* case on which the European Court ruled in October 1995.[5] The case concerned a 1990 law from the German state of Bremen on equal treatment in the public service. This provides that if women and men candidates have equal qualifications, and the post is in a sector where women are under-represented, then a woman should be appointed. The point at issue was whether the derogation for positive action in the Equal Treatment Directive (which as was shown in chapter 6 was considerably narrowed down during the negotiations) permitted such a measure. The Advocate-General's Opinion, delivered on 6 April 1995, was that it did not. He argued that while remedial action for women could be allowed, the derogation did not cover preferential treatment for women 'at the point of selection' which could create direct discrimination against men.

The Court's judgment, which agreed with these arguments, is controversial, particularly in the light of the rapidly developing 'quota' movement to encourage the representation of women, discussed in chapter 1. As Appendix 4.3 shows there is a big difference in the measures EU member states are taking in this respect. The British government, for example, does very little to increase the participation of women in political decision making and Britain has a correspondingly low number of women in Parliament. The Court's judgment begins to harmonise provisions, significantly by encouraging a levelling down rather than by sanctioning preferential treatment.

It is becoming clear, however, that what would make most difference to the situation of women is not more measures based on equality or special treatment, but new measures which address particular aspects of women's situations. Two key issues in this respect are: the individualisation of benefits (which would reduce dependency and increase women's direct income), and greater public responsibility for and recognition of caring. The current climate at EU and national level is not conducive to either of these developments, especially as they would involve a substantial redirection of resources. They are, however, beginning to be forcefully argued at both an academic and a political level.[6]

Equality between men and women is a somewhat lonely principle in EU law. It is the only one which transcends the principle of reciprocal national rights, and one of the few which directly affects social relations. It is not yet supported by any other human rights provisions, for example on race equality, disablement or freedom of speech. To assert those rights, individuals or groups must still rely on either national or international provisions.

This privileged position in my view has distorted the impact of the sex equality measures and made them less effective than they might otherwise have been. The fact that the sex/gender division is recognised at EU level, while other group identities are not, means that the equality principle is not easily carried over to or applied in contexts of greater diversity and complexity. As was shown in chapter 9, it has been hard for the Women's Bureau in the European Commission to develop a policy on black and migrant women or on poor women because these categories are hardly recognised as a concern of the EU. Thus the women who chiefly benefit from the European policy are those whose main or only disadvantages stem from sex and gender. Women with additional or other needs cannot reliably look to the EU for support.

Implementation and scope

So far, the women's policy has mainly been discussed in terms of the principles it seems to project and the provisions adopted. However, once the detailed implementation of these measures is examined, rather different issues are raised. A recent study undertaken for the European Commission shows that while harmonisation of equal treatment law is virtually complete, in practice these laws have significantly different effects, because they are inserted into very different systems and traditions.[7] No one system is necessarily better than any other for women; what is more important is the ethos that surrounds the measures, and in particular the status and attitudes of the trade unions. Mobilisation among women at the grassroots on employment issues is not at present strong, given the economic climate, and the emphasis in the Community system on the individual litigant reduces effectiveness. As was pointed out in chapter 7, those most in need of equal treatment under European law are least likely to receive it. Thus, as feminist legal analysis would predict, while European law can act as a destabiliser and sometimes as a catalyst, it cannot be relied on to improve the situation of women.

Data on the current situation of women in the EU (see Appendices 6.1–6.7) supports these conclusions. As Appendix 6.1 shows, the most striking fact about the labour market participation of women since the sixties has been the increasing employment of married women and women in their child-bearing years. But much of this new work is part-time and, as Appendix 6.5 demonstrates graphically, the overall occupational pattern of men and women is still markedly different. The average earnings gap between men and women across the EU is between 20 and 30 per cent, smallest in Denmark and Italy, and greatest in Ireland and the UK (Appendix 6.4). The fact that during the eighties the gap has not substantially increased, given the fragmentation of jobs and the levels of unemployment, may be in part the result of equal pay policies, and also of the (very gradual) move of some women into higher paid jobs.

Outside the employment sphere, Appendix 6.6 shows how extensive the variations are between EU member states on the level of childcare provision and the length of the school day, both factors which have a strong effect on the kinds of jobs women can take. No EU harmonisation has taken place here. By contrast the birthrate and the numbers of children per woman show a convergence, with the levels in the EU southern member states dropping to match those of the north.

These data suggest that the main effect so far of the EU women's policy has been to legitimate and facilitate the entry of more women into certain jobs in the labour market, and to this end to eliminate some of the most extreme cases of unequal treatment. The statistics show that women still predominate in part-time work and in particular occupations, suggesting that so far the policy has had little effect on the social constraints which affect women's employment patterns. The German and Irish case studies, discussed in chapter 7, show how skilfully governments have manoeuvred to maintain the essence of this situation. It is significant that the ECJ judgments in equal treatment cases, as analysed in chapter 8, reinforce rather than challenge these effects.

This quantitative evidence goes some way to explain the pressure which there has been and still is from women to expand the scope of the policy. The market-making requirements may have been met but the needs of women for autonomy and equality have not. Appendix 2 which lists the provisions adopted by the EU in the area of women's rights over twenty years shows some significant shifts taking place. Very slowly, the domestic and the sexual are creeping up on the EU, and the barrier between the public and private is becoming harder to maintain. Not only are pregnancy, childcare and sexual harassment all now to some extent regulated at EU level, but abortion rights and homosexuality are also coming onto the agenda.[8]

Male behaviour

One important test of a policy for women is the extent to which male behaviour is either targeted or affected. Here the largely male bureaucracies in the Commission, Court and Council have proved not only resistant to change themselves but reluctant to promulgate measures which have this direct aim. The Parliament, more fluid and politically responsive, has been more progressive in these respects. Nevertheless, it remains the case in the period covered that, of all the measures adopted, only the Recommendation on Sexual Harassment and one article in the Childcare Recommendation have the direct purpose of changing men's behaviour.

Indirectly, however, the effect on men is growing. The new emphasis on women in decision making in the third Action Programme (continued in the fourth Action Programme now in draft) can be seen to a large extent as a response to this male inertia. Though the 'politics of presence' raises many problems, as discussed in chapter 1, this is an issue which can mobilise a wide range of women. The Parliament's pressure for more women Commissioners, and its accusation of sexism against Padraig Flynn, the Social Affairs Commissioner, at its hearings in January 1995, illustrate this. The argument increasingly being made is that unless women are present in the decision-making bodies, any policy for women will be distorted and few new measures will be adopted. This is compelling talk, although it assumes a unity among women which, as has been argued in chapter 9, does not necessarily exist in practice.

These are two examples of the way the scope of the policy has expanded over twenty years. However, over the same period, the willingness of the Council to pass strong, binding law on equal treatment issues has diminished, and there are signs (the *Avdel* case is one) that the Court is also entering a more restrictive phase. Although law is an unreliable instrument, without its cutting edge the women's policy is in danger of becoming hortatory rather than authoritative. The judgment in *Kalanke* seems to confirm a significant pull-back by the Court in these areas.

In seeking to push the policy beyond market-making, and towards state-building or society-creating measures which would create greater autonomy and power for women, the way women organise is a crucial factor. In the seventies, market-making and feminist demands were to some extent pushing in the same direction. To create the same impetus at a time of cutbacks, and when neo-liberal ideology is in the ascendant, demands different tactics.

Organisation

How women organise, and for what, is one of the main themes of this book, and some of the underlying issues were discussed in chapter 1. Looking at the EU level suggests certain stages or patterns in women's organisation which can be identified in a very general and schematic way under the headings unity, diversity and solidarity.

Events in the late sixties and early seventies in Belgium, which I have called 'the founding moment' of the EU women's policy, illustrate very well the unity mode. Here working-class women (the Herstal strikers), lower-middle-class women becoming attached to careers (the air hostesses) and professional women (the lawyers) together contributed to a series of actions which in the end forced both the Belgian authorities and the European Court to respond. The actions were spontaneous, but they resonated across classes because a common level of subordination *as women* was deeply felt. The fact that similar, if not so precisely targeted actions, were taking place across Western Europe, created a backdrop which had its effect on political developments.

It was this buzz outside, together with women's increasing entry into the labour market, which enabled 'lone' women and others to argue more successfully within the European institutions for equal treatment measures. The process of negotiation and adoption, as examined in chapters 5 and 6, illustrated very clearly the extent and nature of bureaucratic and male control, and the methods used to filter both people and issues. Here again connections were made and influence felt between women inside and outside the institutions, not because formal channels existed, but because of common experiences of subordination as women.

Diversity

What I have called the women's European policy network began to take shape as a result of these achievements. This network, in comparison with the more usual forms discussed in chapter 1, was based on an assumed commonality of interest rather than on formal (or even informal) structures. During the eighties, the effects of second-wave feminism enabled a more diverse range of women's interests to emerge, necessitating not an assumption of commonality but a reassessment of where it lay.

The women's network as it began to develop contained five main strands discussed in more detail in chapters 7 and 8. These were: the Advisory Committee on Equal Opportunities (consisting of representatives of the equality agencies in the different countries), the expert committees set up by the Women's Bureau in the Commission to undertake research and generate policy proposals, the European Parliament's Women's Committee, the traditional women's organisations, and the feminist groupings, centred on and to some extent coordinated by CREW and ENOW. The last two strands were uneasily brought together in 1990 with the formation of the European Women's Lobby.

These different strands stimulated, but by no means controlled, a variety of contacts made on an individual basis with the Commission and the Parliament by researchers, organisations, training agencies and others, all seeking to contribute to or profit from the growing infrastructure around the women's policy. At the same time, different groups of women began to emerge with distinct and separate interests. Farm women and black and migrant women have been discussed earlier as examples of this trend. Despite these involvements, European networking only touched a fraction of women's activity throughout the EC. Distance, lack of resources and the abstraction of EC processes put many women off. Perhaps more important, the EC was seen as having little to offer women concerned with sexual politics, violence against women, and unpaid work.[9]

The network as it developed was biased towards educated and professional women. Such women had the skills the Commission needed in developing policy and the resources to operate at the European level. The Advisory Committee, consisting mainly of women already overburdened with work at the national level, never had the capacity to represent or mobilise the collectivity of women. The 'high level but low profile' policy style of the British EOC was not designed to create a constituency at the European level. Nevertheless, some more populist and egalitarian influences were felt through the EP Women's Committee, some elements in the European Commission, and CREW/ENOW.

Where were the trade unions in all this? Clearly the bias towards professional women in the networking would have been considerably mitigated had there been a strong seam of trade union women with links back to the labour movements in the member states taking up women's issues at the European level. Although there were active trade union women (Emilienne Brunfaut and Maria Weber, for example), they were as much engaged with struggle inside the trade unions as with action outside.

At various points in my narrative, I have shown that the trade unions opposed autonomous organisations and activities for women at the European level on the grounds that these would be dominated by professional women. This prediction became a self-fulfilling prophecy as trade unionists neither became substantially involved in these activities nor established a strong parallel action for women workers. Recent work by Cynthia Cockburn has shown how deeply rooted sexism is in European trade unions. It is only now in the nineties that attempts are being made to improve the representation of women and give more power to women's committees.[10] Gradually, however, trade union women are becoming more involved in European women's activities. When this happens, a better balance can be struck. It remains the case that trade unions are not well suited to networking. Their structures are on the whole hierarchical and rigid and, contrary to what one might suppose, not geared to action.

One of the questions asked about networks is to what extent they include decision makers. In the case of the women's network, women in the European institutions or in national delegations have frequently, either spontaneously or working with others, used their position to support demands for women-centred policies. Usually such women have been at a relatively low level in the hierarchy, but there are some examples where women with links to the women's movement or to feminism have moved into higher positions, while maintaining and attempting to act upon these commitments.

Yvette Roudy and Hedy d'Ancona, who were both MEPs and then became ministers respectively in French and Dutch socialist governments, are two such examples. 'Supported' women of this kind begin to make slight dents in the power hierarchies. At the same time, the new openness to women has brought into politics more 'system' women and, sometimes, women with militantly right-wing opinions. The Italian debate over the 'feminists of the right' who came to power with the Berlusconi government in April/May 1994 is significant in this respect.[11]

Networking in Brussels takes place at a highly professional level. One offshoot of this has been the development of 'feminist consultants'. CREW began to move in this direction during the eighties, gradually abandoning its status as a cooperative and operating on a more commercial basis. This professional image enabled it to win contracts from the Commission, including the important one of managing the EU IRIS network for women's training programmes.[12] Though some have seen this as giving away too much of what feminism stands for, it can also be seen as inserting feminist ideas in new contexts and at new levels.

Since then other feminist women, active in research and policy development, have set themselves up around the Commission, acting as consultants and taking up some of the work now contracted out from Commission DGs. This enables them to introduce a gender dimension and ask questions about the situation of women in contexts which go beyond the women's policy. This status, though often precarious, gives relative autonomy and some escape from the controls and sexism inherent in big bureaucracies.

Looking at positions within, and absences from, this kind of networking illustrates both the fragmenting of the women's collectivity and the diversity of roles which women are taking. Do women in these circumstances still share common interests? If so, how can these be identified and a politics constructed which takes account of difference and builds up solidarity?

Solidarity

Fragmentation was not surprising, given the unwillingness of women on the whole to force hierarchies on each other, and the fragmenting mode of the eighties. It has become clear, however, that a considerable gulf now lies between women who have been able to profit or at least snatch advantages from this fragmentation, and those who have found themselves marginalised by its causes and consequences. Johanna Brenner (writing about American feminism) suggests that since the seventies there has been in most Western countries a 'selective incorporation of feminist demands'. This in effect prioritises equality over equality/difference and, by assigning certain advantages, tends to cut middle-class and professional (mainly white) women off from grassroots mobilisation. This process helps to explain the apparent contradiction between the advances women seem to be making overall and the steady deterioration in the situation of those women with fewest privileges and least access to resources.[13]

These tendencies are also visible at the European level. Despite the women's policy and the women's network, links to grassroots women's organisations are few, and issues of disadvantage hard to raise. The EU women's policy remains largely 'horizontal', geared to promoting access to the labour market and removing barriers for (undifferentiated) women. The policy has not on the whole developed a vertical dimension designed to tackle class differences and disadvantage. The contrast here with ILO policies for women (which prioritise disadvantage) and those of the UN (which are now primarily concerned with violence against women) is marked.[14]

I would suggest that the predominantly elitist view of women's issues taken by the EU reflects the elitism inherent in the integration project as a whole, as discussed in chapter 1. The view is very prevalent in

Brussels circles that issues of poverty and disadvantage are not the concern of the EU and should be dealt with at national or local level.[15] This horizontal focus has two effects. First, it means that little sense of responsibility for society as a whole is generated at the European level, and second, it perpetuates a framework where decisions about economic integration can be taken without real consideration of their social costs.

There are groups and individuals, particularly in the European Commission, who instinctively or consciously oppose such views. They are, however, normally on the defensive and can generally be reined in by superiors or colleagues or by the disapproval of governments. This was certainly the case over policies on migration and anti-racism, discussed in chapter 9. A minor but nonetheless significant example of the political effects of such uncertainty of direction concerns the outcomes of the 1987 seminar on Migrant Women in Employment, held by the Commission's Women's Bureau (see chapter 9, p. 171). At the end of a well-prepared and challenging seminar, participants were considering objectives and planning to draw up a programme of action. They were taken aback by the behind-the-scenes discouragement for such a course being given by previously enthusiastic Commission staff. The impression was given that if campaigning were to take place, it would be better done at the national level.[16]

The Commission's role in this instance was to prepare materials and make cross-national comparisons, but not to encourage transnational political activity. The result was that the development of a European political process was truncated and activists forced back to the national. Something similar seems to happen with the support which the Commission gives in its programmes to the self-organisation of grassroots groups. Groups involved with the Poverty Programme, for example, were encouraged to 'participate' – but clear limits were set on how far this could go and in what directions.

There is a great temptation for women's organisations operating at the EU level to mirror this kind of politics rather than challenge it. Pressure is strong for women to demand rights without rocking boats. However, women are better placed than perhaps any other group to pursue an alternative political strategy. Not only have many women had the experience of achieving results in collective action, mobilising across class, ethnic and national divides, but some structure already exists for carrying such concerns into the EU. It is clear, however, that such a politics can no longer be constructed only on the basis of unity or sisterhood. The seventies model, attractive as it may seem, is not in the nineties likely to lead to effective action. Assuming that the unity of the seventies still exists, or can be reconstructed, means in effect that many women go unrepresented.

That is not to say that there is no need for collective action by women. The hurts imposed on 'female-sexed bodies' and the restrictions involved in 'living as female' still exist, although their effects may now be more differentiated.[17] However, to create effective action in the current circumstances in Europe needs awareness and sensitivity and above all the right base for organisation and action. Rosi Braidotti, searching for a perspective which can encompass women both as diverse individuals and as a community, identifies two elements. First, the need to see all women as 'locally situated' and as developing 'situated perspectives'; and second, the 'conjugation' of this with what she calls 'the responsibility for and accountability to our sex.' Thus difference is accommodated through the responsibility of women to each other.[18]

Although these principles are formulated in an abstract way, they seem to me to provide a workable base for organisation among women in the nineties; organisation based not on simple unity, but on a recognition of diversity, which may, among certain groups and on certain issues, lead to solidarity and common action – in the EU as elsewhere.

The Politics of the EU

In the introduction, I undertook to examine the implications for EU theory and practice of the experiences of the women's policy. I intend to do this here by looking first at the relation of the economic and the social in the development of the EU, then at neo-functionalist theory, and finally at the political dilemmas which the EU faces in the nineties.

The relation of the social to the economic in the EU has been one of the themes of this book. I have shown how from the beginning the social has been subsumed within the economic and only given a separate focus when this appeared functional or necessary to economic integration.[19] Streeck's formulations, cited in chapter 1, suggest a permanent imbalance of forces at the European level, which will keep social policy marginal.[20] Martin Rhodes, after surveying all the possibilities, sees a 'European' social policy as most likely to be achieved by harmonisation in a downwards direction.[21]

Giandomenico Majone, in an earlier analysis, distinguishes between traditional social policy, which he sees as almost impossible to achieve at European level, because of the entrenched nature of national processes, and what he calls 'social regulation' which he sees as steadily developing a European focus in areas like consumer protection and environmental law. Interestingly, he includes equal treatment for men and women in the labour market within this latter category.[22]

One could, however, view developments differently from any of these positions, and argue that it is surprising, given the way conditions are stacked against the adoption of social measures at the European level, that the issue of a European social policy keeps appearing on the agenda. Far from disappearing, the question of what to do about the social, and to what extent people should be regulated and protected, by whom and at what cost, has become one of the key questions for the nineties. That the social implications of European integration form part of this debate was made clear by the British Government's vetoing in 1991 of the social provisions proposed at Maastricht. And what is being debated in the mid nineties at the level of the EU is what I called in chapter 3 society-creating social policy, that is social policy which binds society together and serves as both a protection and a control.

So far there has not been enough muscle behind the labour and social movements in the EU to produce substantial egalitarian or redistributive policies. However, as I have argued earlier, the system has been artificially weighted against such a development, because of the priority given in both practice and theory to elite coordination and elite control. As Altiero Spinelli put it:

> Monnet had the great merit of having built Europe and the great responsibility to have built it badly . . . we are still paying for his false departure.[23]

The example of the women's policy contributes to these arguments in significant ways. For the reasons already discussed, there *was* some muscle behind the demand for women's rights in the seventies, with the untypical results which are the subject of this book. However, the outcomes have not been as substantial as might have been expected, partly at least because of the nature of the EU policy process. Despite incremental changes in the powers of the European Parliament and a considerable expansion in the scope of EU policy, the political process has changed very little. Interest groups form networks, make gains or lose influence, but the political process is not transformed.

This brings us back to neo-functionalism, and helps explain why the processes identified by that theory have not brought about the changes Haas predicted. The development of the women's policy validates Haas's findings to some extent, showing that the existence of law and policy at the supranational level does alter the behaviour of interest groups, and brings about, if not a shift of loyalties to the centre, at least a shift of attention. However, because there is no participatory political system into which this can feed, instead of being reinforced and becoming genuinely transnational, the impetus is redirected back to the national. Thus people are discouraged from feeling 'European' and the political base of the nation state is in formal terms at least preserved.

Many of the events discussed in detail in this book reflect that pattern, despite the fact that women have a privileged position in the EU spectrum. On the whole, expectations that a genuine European dimension is being created are dashed and impetus lost. It is likely that this pattern is particularly pronounced where the Commission's competence is unclear or where popular movements are concerned. As a result elite control continues. Milward's thesis that European integration was always intended by the politicians to bolster the nation state rather than create a supranational alternative, is borne out by this experience.

A multi-layered politics

The elites and politicians of the European Union now face a dilemma. There are good reasons for continuing with economic integration, even to the extent of EMU and a single currency. In an increasingly uncertain world, Europe may well need that kind of coordination. However, the 'permissive public opinion', which both neo-functionalists and neo-realists agreed was necessary for integration to continue, appears no longer to exist. The publicity given to 1992 focused people's attention on the EU and many, for a great variety of reasons, did not like what they saw. The 'Maastricht process' compounded their disillusion.

As this book has shown, little support has been given at EU level for the development of transnational popular politics. Yet, without this, the project of an 'ever closer union' for the EU will have inadequate support. Elites cannot produce popular approval and indeed are widely mistrusted. Dominique Wolton's vigorous account of the current situation of the EU expresses this mistrust in strong terms, and urges Europe's populations to exert more control. 'Constructed yesterday by 50,000 bureaucrats and politicians,' he writes, 'Europe has become, with the ratification of Maastricht, suddenly the concern of its 350m inhabitants.'[24]

However, this dissonance between politics and economics can also open up space for more radical strategies. Despite myths and images about the nation state, its sovereignty and functions are already fragmenting. What is needed is a multi-layered politics which follows suit, recognising people's diversity and different identities, and building appropriate and fluid political structures to match.

The experience of the women's policy, the only EU policy which has travelled even partially along this route, is important here. Far from being marginalised and encapsulated, what is remarkable is the seepage and spillage which has taken place, despite the obstacles discussed above, with the result that 'the fathers' have been unable to keep the women's policy under control and confined to the economic sphere. The reason for this seepage is that women have raised their voices and used legal channels and policy instruments creatively to generate social change in ways undreamed of by the pragmatists who drafted the Treaty of Rome. This example suggests that the distinction Majone makes between social policy (national) and social regulation (European) may be difficult to maintain. As the history of the women's policy shows, labour market policy quickly spills over into the private and the personal, and the very existence of the EU is undermining the ability of nation states to deal adequately with social policy issues.

Where does this leave integrating gender? As we have seen, some space has now been carved out in the EU arena for 'gender conflicts', and the issue has entered at least partly into bureaucratic consciousness. However, confrontation and deadlock continues together with some small gains. What is becoming clear is that 'gender' cannot be 'integrated' without far more change taking place in society than is at present acceptable to the majority of its male elites.[25] The EU experience, however, as described in this book, shows that cracks in the edifice exist and that these can be exploited, given an undoctrinaire approach, a willingness to act inside and outside the formal system, and political will. In demonstrating that the EU system can be politicised in the interests of its democratic majority, women in all their complex and varying identities have marked an important trail. It remains to be seen whether other social groups and actors will follow suit.

Notes

1 Honourable exceptions to this are Doreen Collins who dealt substantially with equal pay in *The European Communities: the Social Policy of the First Phase*, Martin Robertson, London, 1975; and Jane Pillinger, who broke new ground in *Feminising the Market – Women's Pay and Employment in the European Community*, Macmillan, Basingstoke, 1992.

2 Wolfgang Streeck, 'Neo-Voluntarism: A New European Social Policy Regime?', *European Law Journal*, vol. 1, no. 1, 1995, p. 44. For a more positive treatment see Stephan Leibfried and Paul Pierson, 'Prospects for Social Europe', *Politics and Society*, vol. 20, no. 3, 1992, pp. 338–9.

3 In *Smith* v. *Avdel Systems Ltd* (ECJ Case C-408/92, 1994) and in other cases heard alongside it, the ECJ applied the equality principle strictly, allowing equal treatment in pension age to be complied with by levelling down and prohibiting transitional arrangements that would favour women. For a commentary on these cases see *Equal Opportunities Review*, no. 58, November/December 1994.

4 For an assessment of the possible implications of the amendment see Sacha Prechal and Linda Senden, *Equal Treatment After Maastricht*, CEC, V/653bis/94.

5 *Kalanke* v. *Freie Hansestadt Bremen*, ECJ Case C-450/93.

6 See for example Linda Luckhaus, 'Individualisation of Social Security Benefits', in C. McCrudden, ed., *Equality of Treatment between Men and Women in Social Security*, Butterworth, London, 1994, pp. 147–62; and Riki Holtmaat, *Met zorg een recht*? (To care for a right?) dissertation, University of Leiden, 1992.

7 Barry Fitzpatrick, Jeanne Gregory and Erika Szyszczak, *Sex Equality Litigation in the*

Member States of the EC, CEC, V/407/94. I am grateful to Jeanne Gregory for additional information.

8 In these last two areas, the creation of the single market and free movement within it are giving rise to 'rights' issues which focus on the EU; see Elizabeth Spalin, 'Abortion, Speech and the European Community', *Journal of Social Welfare and Family Law*, 1992, pp. 17–32, and Kees Waaldjik and Andrew Clapham, eds, *Homosexuality: a European Community Issue*, Martinus Nijhoff, Dordrecht, 1993.

9 The degree of involvement with the EU of women's associations and women's officers in the UK is usefully surveyed in Charlotte Bretherton and Liz Sperling, 'Women's Networks and the European Union – Towards an Inclusive Approach?', *Journal of Common Market Studies*, forthcoming 1996. Their findings support these conclusions.

10 Cynthia Cockburn, *Women and the European Social Dialogue*, CEC, V/5465/95.

11 'Feminists of the right' was a term used in the media. There was a sharp debate in Italy as to whether women such as Irene Pivetti, the chic and austere speaker of the lower chamber, could in any sense be called feminist. See articles in *Epoca*, 17 May 1994; and *L'Espresso*, 27 May 1994. I am grateful to Marina Orsini-Jones for providing me with this material.

12 The IRIS network was set up in 1988 by the European Commission. It consists of originally 71 and now more than 300 training programmes for women which exchange experience and develop links across the EU. As a result of this work, CREW is now able to some extent to act as a 'voice' for women's training needs at the EU level.

13 Johanna Brenner, 'US Feminism in the Nineties', *New Left Review*, no. 200, 1993, pp. 101–59.

14 For ILO policy see Sandra Whitworth, 'Gender, International Relations and the Case of the ILO', *Review of International Studies*, vol. 20, no. 4, 1994, pp. 389–405.

15 This argument, strengthened by the new emphasis on subsidiarity, has been used by the German government to block the continuation of the EU Poverty Programme.

16 I attended this seminar and recall the deflation I felt. I have subsequently checked these impressions with others who were there.

17 The phraseology is from Teresa de Lauretis, see chapter 1 this volume, n. 9.

18 Rosi Braidotti, 'The Exile, the Nomad and the Migrant – Reflections on International Feminism', *Women's Studies International Forum*, vol. 15, no. 1, 1992, p. 9.

19 The arguments are well set out in Linda Luckhaus, 'The Role of the "Economic" and the "Social" in Social Security and Community Law', in G. Weick, ed., *National and European Law on the Threshold to the Single Market*, Peter Lang, Frankfurt, 1993.

20 Wolfgang Streeck, 'From Market-Making to State-Building? Reflections on the Political Economy of European Social Policy', in S. Leibfried and P. Pierson, eds, *Prospects for Social Europe: the European Community's Social Dimension in Comparative Perspective*, The Brookings Institution, Washington DC, 1995.

21 Martin Rhodes, 'Subversive Liberalism', Market Integration, Globalisation and the European Welfare State, *European Consortium for Political Research*, Madrid, April 1994.

22 Giandomenico Majone, 'The European Community Between Social Policy and Social Regulation', *Journal of Common Market Studies*, vol. 31, no. 2, 1993, pp.153–70.

23 Cited in Kevin Featherstone, 'Jean Monnet and the "Democratic Deficit" in the EU', *Journal of Common Market Studies*, vol. 32, no. 2, 1994, p. 150.

24 Dominique Wolton, *La dernière utopie – Naissance de l'Europe démocratique*, Flammarion, Paris, 1993, p. 11.

25 Advocate-General Tesauro implicitly recognised this in his Opinion in the *Kalanke* case, when he remarked that ending the disparity between men and women would involve 'a substantial change in the economic, social and cultural model which is at the root of the inequalities'. He showed in his arguments that he was not about to facilitate this.

Appendices

Appendix 1

Article 119

The text as adopted in 1957

Each member state shall during the first stage ensure and subsequently maintain the application of the principle that men and women should receive equal pay for equal work.

For the purpose of the Article 'pay' means the ordinary basic or minimum wage or salary and any other consideration, whether in cash or in kind, which the worker receives, directly or indirectly, in respect of his employment from his employer.

Equal pay without discrimination based on sex means:

a) that pay for the same work at piece rates shall be calculated on the basis of the same unit of measurement:

b) that pay for work at time rates shall be the same for the same job.

New third paragraph adopted in 1992 under the Social Protocol of the Treaty on European Union (Maastricht Treaty)

This Article shall not prevent any Member State from maintaining or adopting measures providing for specific advantages in order to make it easier for women to pursue a vocational activity or prevent or compensate for disadvantages in their professional careers.

(Note: because of the British veto on new social policy provisions, this paragraph was not adopted as an amendment to the Treaty of Rome, but is included in the Social Agreement which was adopted by the other eleven member states.)

Appendix 2

EU Legislation and Policy Development on Women's Rights

The Seventies Directives

Council Directive 75/117/EEC of 10 February 1975 on the approximation of the laws of the Member States relating to the application of the principle of equal pay for men and women. (Equal Pay Directive – EPD)
Official Journal L 45, 19.2.75, p. 19.

Council Directive 76/207/EEC of 9 February 1976 on the implementation of the principle of equal treatment for men and women as regards access to employment, vocational training and promotion, and working conditions. (Equal Treatment Directive – ETD)
Official Journal L 39, 14.2.76, p. 40.

Council Decision 77/804/EEC of 20 December 1977 on action by the European Social Fund for women
Official Journal L 337, 27.12.77, p. 14.

Council Directive 79/7/EEC of 19 December 1978 on the progressive implementation of the principle of equal treatment for men and women in matters of social security. (Social Security Directive – SSD)
Official Journal L 6, 10.1.79, p. 24.

Proposals, Resolutions and Recommendations, 1981–86

Commission Proposal for a Council Directive on part-time work
COM (81) 775, 22 December 1981.

Council Resolution of 12 July 1982 on the promotion of equal opportunities for women (approval of Action Programme 1)
Official Journal C 186, 21.7.82, p. 3.

Commission Proposal for a Council Directive on parental leave and leave for family reasons
COM (83) 686, 22 November 1983.

Council Resolution of 7 June 1984 on action to combat unemployment among women
Official Journal C 161, 21.6.84, p. 14.

Council Recommendation 84/635/EEC of 13 December 1984 on the promotion of positive action for women
Offical Journal L 331, 19.12.84, p. 34.

Council Resolution of 3 June 1985 on equal opportunities for girls and boys in education
Official Journal C 166, 5.7.85, p. 1.

Second Council Resolution of 24 July 1986 on the promotion of equal opportunities for women (approval of Action Programme 2)
Official Journal C 203, 12.8.86, p. 2.

More Directives

Council Directive 86/378/EEC of 24 July 1986 on the implementation of the principle of equal treatment for men and women in occupational social security schemes
Official Journal L 225, 12.8.86, p. 40.

Council Directive 86/613/EEC of 11 December 1986 on the application of the principle of equal treatment between men and women engaged in an activity including agriculture, in a self-employed capacity, and on the protection of self-employed women during pregnancy and motherhood. (Self-Employed Directive – SED)
Official Journal L 359, 19.12.86, p. 56.

'Soft Law' and Proposals, 1987–91

Commission Proposal for a Council Directive on completing the implementation of equal treatment for men and women in statutory and occupational social security schemes
COM (87) 494 final, 23 October 1987.

Commission Recommendation 87/567/EEC of 24 November 1987 on vocational training for women
Official Journal L 342, 4.12.87, p. 35.

Commission Proposal for a Council Directive on the burden of proof in the area of equal pay and equal treatment for women and men
COM (88) 269 final, 27 May 1988.

Communication from the Commission on the social situation and employment of migrant women
COM (88) 743, 15 December 1988.

Council Resolution of 16 December 1988 on the reintegration and late integration of women into working life
Official Journal C 333, 28.12.88, p. 1.

Proposal for Council Resolution on the sharing of family and occupational responsibilities 8 June 1989 (blocked by UK 12.6.89)
Not published.

Council Resolution of 21 May 1991 on the third medium-term Community action programme on equal opportunities for women and men (1991–95)
Official Journal C 142, 31.5.91, p. 1.

New Issues and Areas

Commission Recommendation of 27 November 1991 on the protection of the dignity of women and men at work (tackling sexual harassment)
Official Journal C 27, 24.2.92, p. 1.

Council Recommendation 92/241/EEC of 31 March 1992 on childcare
Official Journal L 123, 8.5.92, p. 16.

Council Directive 92/85/EEC of 19 October 1992 on the introduction of measures to encourage improvements in the safety and health at work of pregnant workers and workers who have recently given birth or are breastfeeding
Official Journal L 348, 28.11.92, p. 1.

Council Resolution of 22 June 1994 on the promotion of equal opportunities for men and women through action by the European Structural Funds
Official Journal C 231, 20. 8.94, p. 1.

Council Resolution of 6 December 1994 on equal participation by women in an employment-intensive economic growth strategy within the EU
Official Journal C 368, 23.12.94, p. 3.

Commission Proposal for the fourth medium-term action programme on equal opportunities for women and men (1996–2000)
COM (95) 381, 19 July 1995.

(Note: Directives are addressed to member states and are binding as to the results to be achieved but leave to national authorities the choice of form and methods. Recommendations and Resolutions are termed 'soft law' and are non-binding. They can, however, be cited to demonstrate the intentions of the Community legislator.)

Appendix 3

Sex Equality Provisions in Eight Member States 1970–95

Belgium

Constitution – Articles 10 and 11

1975 Royal decree of 9 December made national collective agreement on equal pay binding on all employers

1978 Title V of Law on economic restructuring included detailed provisions on equal treatment in working conditions, training and promotion

1987 Royal decree of 14 July provided for positive action in the private sector (similar measures for public services adopted in February 1990)

1992 Royal decree of 18 September defined sexual harassment and required private employers to establish appropriate procedures (similar protection extended in March 1995 to the federal public services)

1994 Law of 20 July made it an offence for any party list in political elections to include more than two-thirds from one sex

1995 Law of 3 April amended maternity provisions in line with the EC Directive 92/85

A number of modifications have been made to social security provisions to remove instances of direct discrimination against women.

Denmark

All collective agreements in Denmark are interpreted as embodying an equal pay clause.

1975 Equal Status Council (ESC) set up by administrative act

1976 Act on equal remuneration for men and women clarified the right to equal pay and extended it to all workers not covered by collective agreements

1978 Act on equal treatment in working conditions gave ESC formal powers. The Act was amended in 1989 to include new maternity leave provisions. Under this act positive action for women is illegal unless specifically authorised.

1985 Act on equality in public bodies sought to ensure a more balanced composition by providing that where possible equal numbers of men and women should be proposed for vacancies (similar measures for state subsidised bodies adopted in 1990; extension to the private sector remains controversial)

1986 Equal pay act amended to include equal pay for work of equal value

1988 Act on equal opportunities required all public authorities to work to promote gender equality and increased the powers of the ESC

1994 Act on employment leave included arrangements for childcare leave, educational leave and sabbaticals

France

Constitution – preamble

Code du travail Articles L 122 (35) and (45)

Code pénal Articles 416 and 416 (1)

1972 Law 1143 of 22 December on equal pay set out definitions and procedures and required the labour inspectorate to enforce its provisions

1975 Equal treatment law provided for equal treatment in hiring and dismissal and protection for pregnant workers. Justification could be argued (*motif légitime*).

1980 Rape defined as a criminal offence

1982 Law 596 established new rights for helper spouses

1982 Provisions which set a minimum 25 per cent quota for women on municipal electoral lists were ruled unconstitutional by the Constitutional Council

1983 Law 635 of 13 July on equal opportunities in employment (*égalité professionnelle*) prohibited all forms of unequal treatment no matter what the circumstances. It also provided for positive action plans to be established in major companies.

1984 Decree 69 of 30 January granted state aid to companies which implemented equality plans for staff

1992 Law 1179 of 2 November inserted a (somewhat narrow) definition of sexual harassment into the labour code and empowered the labour inspectorate and workplace health committees to enforce it

A number of amendments and instruments have attempted to apply equal treatment in statutory social security schemes.

Germany

Constitution – Article 3

1975 Judgment of the Federal Constitutional Court to the effect that the pension position of women must be improved over the next ten years

1980 'Compliance law' covered discrimination in hiring, promotion and dismissal, and measures to promote equal pay

1982 Equalisation of actuarial data for men and women

1983 Law (revised 1986) on 'pension-splitting' designed to improve the pension position of non-employed women

1985 Law on parental leave and on pension rights for child-rearing years

1994 'Second statute on equality' covered equal opportunities in the judiciary, the federal civil service and federal agencies; set levels of compensation to be awarded in hiring and promotion cases involving discriminations; and established principles and procedures to be followed in cases of sexual harassment

1994 November. The following sentence was added to Article 3 of the Constitution: 'The state must promote the effective enforcement of the equality of women and men and must work towards the abolition of existing disadvantages'.

1995 Law regulating 'crisis pregnancy' set new (and strict) conditions for the availability of legal abortion

A considerable effort has gone into positive action for women in decision making, particularly at the level of the Länder. Some of these measures are now being challenged in the courts.

Ireland

Constitution – Articles 9, 40 and 41

1974 Anti-Discrimination (Pay) Act set up system of Equality Officers of the Labour Court to investigate disputes about equal pay and issue recommendations

1977 Employment Equality Act covered equal treatment in relation to recruitment, promotion and training, and set up the Employment Equality Agency to assist with enforcement and review

1981 Maternity (Protection of Employees) Act provided for paid maternity leave and the right to return to work

1985 Social Welfare (No.2) Act sought to implement equal treatment in statutory social security

1991 Worker Protection Act extended to part-time workers the protection of employment laws

1994 Introduction of new 'survivors pension', equalising provision for widows and widowers, along with a scheme providing pensions for home-makers

1994 Code of Practice launched on sexual harassment

1995 Abortion Information Act established right of doctors and health clinics to give information on abortion services abroad

Italy

Constitution – Articles 3 and 37

1977 Law 903 9 December on equal treatment in employment

1984 Law 863 19 December providing for equality advisors at regional level

1991 Law 125 10 April on equal opportunities and positive action covered amendments to the 1977 law and support and funding for positive action programmes

1992 Law 215 28 February on the promotion of women in business

1993 Act 277 4 August modified the electoral system for the Chamber of Deputies providing that 75 per cent of the seats would be elected on a 'first past the post' system and 25 per cent by proportional representation. In the latter case, lists bearing more than one name must be composed alternately of male and female candidates. In municipal elections neither sex must comprise more than 75 per cent of the candidates on lists presented.

1995 The above electoral measures were ruled unconstitutional by the Constitutional Court

A comprehensive law on violence against women, under discussion since the 1980s, was approved by the lower Chamber of Parliament.

The Netherlands

Constitution – Article 1

1975 Equal pay act

1980 Equal treatment acts for both the public and private sectors

1989 Amendment to the above improving definitions and procedures and for the first time allowing group actions in sex discrimination cases

1994 General equal treatment act providing for protection at work, and in other areas, against discrimination across a broad range of factors including sex, race, religion and political preference

Numerous complex (and often controversial) changes have been made to Dutch social security law to comply with equal treatment provisions.

The equal treatment acts allow positive action for women to combat inequalities and improve representation. Measures must be temporary and proportionate to the objectives being sought.

United Kingdom

1970	Equal Pay Act adopted to come into force in 1975
1975	Sex Discrimination Act (SDA) covered direct and indirect discrimination in cmployment, the provision of services and education; and set up the Equal Opportunities Commission (EOC)
1986	Sex Discrimination Act provided for equal retirement ages and repealed some protective legislation for women
1989	Employment Act repealed some exceptions to the SDA and made provision for certain kinds of positive action
1993/94	New provisions for pregnant workers included in the Trade Union Reform and Employment Rights Act (TURER) and in other social security and health and safety regulations.

Social security legislation has been amended to remove (mainly direct forms of) discrimination in a variety of benefits.

Note: During the last twenty years protective legislation for women in most of the above countries has gradually been repealed. In some cases, but by no means all, this has been replaced with new regulations for both women and men. Provisions over night work remain controversial.

Appendix 4

Women and Parliamentary Representation

4.1 Participation of Women in National Parliamentary Assemblies in the EU Member States

State	*Date Elections*	*Lower Chamber percentage (Women/Total)*	*Upper Chamber percentage (Women/Total)*	*Total National Parliament percentage (Women/Total)*
Belgium	1995	11.3 (17/150)	23.6 (17/72)	15.3 (34/222)
Denmark	1994	33.0 (59/179)	*	33.0 (59/179)
Germany	1994	26.3 (177/672)	19.1 (13/68)	25.6 (190/740)
Greece	1993	5.3 (16/300)	*	5.3 (16/300)
Spain	1993	16.0 (56/350)	12.6 (32/254)	14.6 (88/604)
France	1993/92	6.0 (35/577)	4.9 (16/321)	5.6 (51/898)
Ireland	1992	12.0 (20/166)	13.3 (8/60)	12.4 (28/226)
Italy	1994	13.9 (88/632)	8.3 (26/315)	12.0 (114/947)
Luxembourg	1994	16.6 (10/60)	*	16.6 (10/60)
Netherlands	1994/91	31.3 (47/150)	28.0 (21/75)	30.2 (68/225)
Portugal	1991	8.7 (20/230)	*	8.7 (20/230)
United Kingdom	1992	9.2 (60/651)	6.5 (79/1207)	7.4 (139/1858)
TOTAL		14.5 (608/4179)	8.6 (215/2484)	12.3 (823/6663)
EUROPEAN PARLIAMENT	1994	25.7 (146/567)	*	25.7 (146/567)

* No Upper Chamber

Source: *Women in Decision-Making*, Brussels, 1994 and 1995.

4.2 Women in the European Parliament by Member State, 1989 and 1994

State	*No. of Women in 1989*	*Total MEPs in 1989*	*Women percentage in 1989*	*No. of Women in 1994*	*Total MEPs in 1994*	*Women percentage in 1994*
Belgium	6	24	16.7	8	25	32
Denmark	6	16	37.5	7	16	43.8
Germany	26	81	32	35	99	35.4
Greece	1	24	4.2	4	25	16
Spain	9	60	15	21	64	32.8
France	19	81	22.2	26	87	29.8
Ireland	1	15	6.7	4	15	26.7
Italy	10	81	12.3	9	87	10.3
Luxembourg	3	6	50	2	6	33.3
Netherlands	7	25	28	10	31	32.2
Portugal	3	24	12.5	2	25	8
United Kingdom	12	81	14.8	16	87	18.4
TOTAL	103	518	19	144*	567	25.3

* The discrepancy between the figure here for the total of women MEPs and that in 4.1 derives from differences between those elected (4.1) and those taking up seats (4.2).

Source: European Parliament/*Crew Reports.*

4.3 Actions by Governments to Increase the Participation of Women in Political Decision-Making

Country	*Statistics*	*Support NGOs*	*Scientific Research*	*Information and Awareness Raising*	*Positive Action*	*Legal Frame-Work*
Belgium	X	X	X	X	X	X
Denmark	X			X	X	X
Germany	X	X	X	X	X	X
Greece	X		X	X		
Spain	X	X	X	X		
France	X					
Ireland		X		X	X	
Italy				X		X
Luxembourg						
Netherlands	X	X	X	X	X	
Portugal	X	X	X	X		
United Kingdom	X				X	

Source: Women in Decision-Making Network, *Panorama*, Brussels, 1994, p. 41.

Appendix 5

Equal Opportunities in the European Commission

5.1 The Percentage of Female Staff in the Commission by Category, 1977–94*

Category	Date		
	Dec. '77	*Jan. '84*	*Jan. '94*
A	6.9	9.3	13.5
LA	44.1	45.5	50.1
B	42.1	39.1	37.4
C	79.9	80.7	80.4
D	2.7	11.2	22.1
ALL	44.5	45.4	45.4
Numbers of Women	3359	4177	6075
Total Staff	7546	9206	13386

Key to categories

A administrative and management
LA language services
B executive and technical
C secretarial
D manual and service

* Temporary and auxiliary staff are excluded from these figures.

5.2 Women Commissioners

1958–88 – none
1989–92 – 2 out of 17
1992–94 – 1 out of 17
1995–99 – 5 out of 20

5.3 Women and Men in the A Grades of the Commission, 1994*

Grade	*Women*	%	*Men*	%	*Total*
A1	1	1.9	51	98.1	52
A2	4	2.5	153	97.5	157
A3	29	7.0	387	93.0	416
A4	90	9.2	889	90.8	979
A5	118	14.4	703	85.6	821
A6	96	16.3	494	83.7	590
A7	139	19.4	579	80.6	718
A8	44	31.9	94	68.1	138
Total	521	13.5	3350	86.5	3871

* Each category in the Commission is divided into between four and eight grades

Sources for all these tables: *Equal Opportunities in the Commission of the European Communities*, 1986; *Women at the European Commission, 1984–1994*, 1995; Personnel Directorate, European Commission.

Appendix 6

Data on Women in the EU – Comparative Statistics

6.1 Labour Market Participation of Women by Age Group in the Community, 1960–92

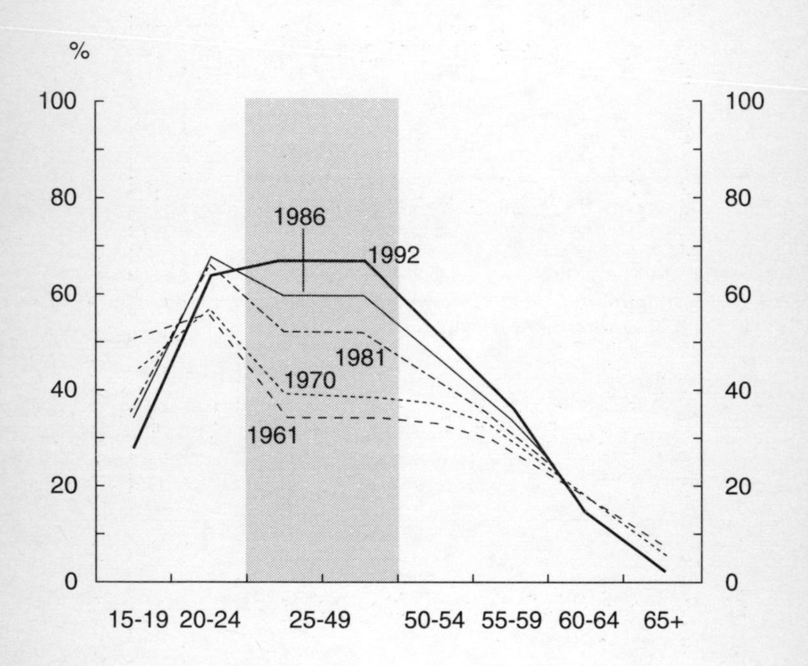

Note: Figures shown are for twelve member states.

Source: *Employment in Europe*, 1994, p. 48.

6.2 Women's Full-time and Part-time Employment, 1983–89

	Increase in women's employment between 1983 and 1989 (%)			*Share of part-time working in the increase in women's employment (%)*	*Women's share in part-time working (%)*		
	Total	*Contribution of part-time*	*Contribution of full-time*		*1983*	*1989*	*Developments*
Belgium	12.6	8.4	4.3	66.2	84	89.6	↑
Denmark	10.1	0.5	9.7	4.5	84.7	78	↓
Germany	6.8	2.8	4.0	40.8	91.9	89.6	↓
Greece	12.1	–3.1	15.3	–25.9	61.2	64.4	↑
Spain	na	na	na	na	na	77.2	na
France	5.8	5.0	0.8	86.8	84.4	83.3	↓
Ireland	5.0	2.0	2.9	41.2	71.6	73.2	↑
Italy	7.7	2.4	5.3	31.0	64.8	64.7	=
Luxembourg	10.4	2.1	8.3	20.0	88.9	81.8	↓
Netherlands	36.3	32.0	4.3	88.1	77.3	70.2	↓
Portugal	na	na	na	na	65.9 (86)	69.8	↑
United Kingdom	20.2	10.3	10.0	50.7	89.8	87.0	↓
Europe 10	11.6	6.1	5.5	52.7	85.7	82.8	↓
Europe 12	nd	nd	nd	nd	nd	82.4	

Source: EC Labour Force Survey in *Women of Europe*, Supplement no. 36, 1992, p. 43.

6.3 Employment Indicators in the Community, 1965–93

	Millions unless otherwise specified					
	1965	*1975*	*1985*	*1990*	*1992*	*1993*
Total						
Total population	293.2	312.4	322.0	327.7	331.0	331.6
Population of working age (15–64)	188.0	197.9	215.2	219.7	221.7	223.3
Total employment	122.6	124.3	122.7	132.8	132.0	128.8
Ratio of employment to working-age population (%)	65.2	62.8	57.0	60.5	59.5	58.0
Total unemployment	2.6	5.3	15.0	12.2	13.9	15.8
Unemployment rate (%)	2.1	4.1	10.8	8.3	9.4	10.5
Youth (<25) unemployment rate (%)			23.3	16.8	18.4	20.1
Employment in agriculture	20.1	13.9	10.4	8.6	7.6	7.1
Employment in industry	49.5	48.3	41.3	43.0	41.0	39.3
Employment in services	53.1	62.2	71.1	81.2	85.0	82.3
Share of employment in agriculture (%)	16.4	11.2	8.4	6.5	5.8	5.5
Share of employment in industry (%)	40.4	38.8	33.6	32.4	31.1	30.5
Share of employment in services (%)	43.3	50.0	57.9	61.2	62.9	63.9
Men						
Total population	142.3	152.0	156.6	159.7	161.3	161.8
Population of working age (15–64)			107.3	109.5	110.7	111.0
Total employment	83.0	81.9	75.8	79.6	77.8	76.0
Ratio of employment to working-age population (%)			70.6	72.7	70.3	68.4
Total employment		3.3	8.0	5.8	7.2	8.3
Unemployment rate (%)		3.9	9.4	6.6	8.1	9.3
Youth (< 25) unemployment rate (%)			21.6	14.7	17.4	19.5

Employment in agriculture	13.3	9.1	6.7	5.6	5.0	4.8
Employment in industry	38.0	37.1	31.7	32.8	31.3	29.7
Employment in services	31.6	35.7	37.3	41.2	41.5	41.4
Share of employment in agriculture (%)	16.0	11.1	8.9	7.0	6.4	6.3
Share of employment in industry (%)	45.8	45.3	41.9	41.2	40.2	39.2
Share of employment in services (%)	38.0	43.6	49.2	51.8	53.2	54.5
Women						
Total population	150.9	160.4	165.4	168.0	169.7	169.8
Population of working age (15–64)			107.9	110.2	111.0	111.2
Total employment	39.6	42.5	46.9	53.2	53.9	53.5
Ratio of employment to working-age population (%)			43.5	48.3	48.5	48.1
Total unemployment		2.3	7.0	6.4	6.8	7.5
Unemployment rate (%)		5.1	13.0	10.8	11.3	12.3
Youth (< 25) unemployment rate (%)			25.0	19.1	19.5	21.0
Employment in agriculture	6.8	4.8	3.6	3.0	2.6	2.4
Employment in industry	11.5	11.2	9.6	10.2	9.7	9.4
Employment in services	21.5	26.5	33.8	40.0	41.5	41.7
Share of employment in agriculture (%)	17.2	11.3	7.7	5.7	4.8	4.6
Share of employment in industry (%)	29.0	26.4	20.4	19.1	18.1	17.5
Share of employment in services (%)	54.2	62.4	71.9	75.2	77.1	78.0

Note: Figures shown are for twelve member states, but exclude the German new Länder.

Source: *Employment in Europe*, 1994, p. 42. (Original sources: Eurostat national estimates of population and employment and unemployment rates for comparison between member states: 1993 figures are provisional: 1965 figures from OECD.)

6.4 Women's Average Earnings as Percentage of Male Earnings, 1980–91

A. Trends in gender pay ratios for manual workers 1980–91

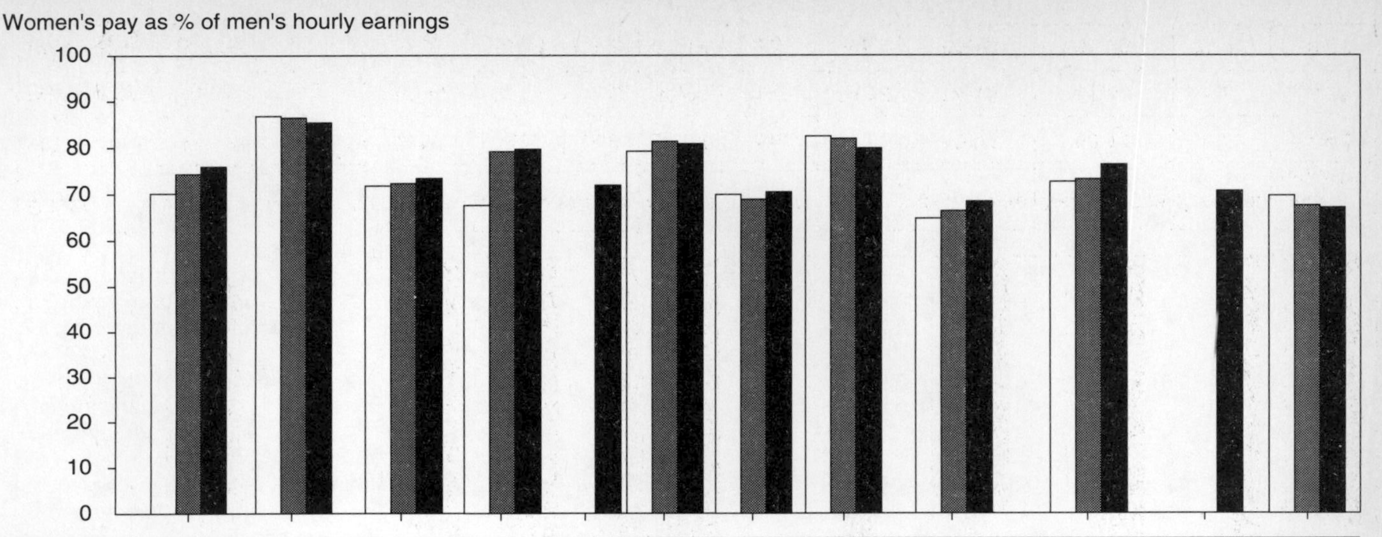

Country	Belgium	Denmark	Germany	Greece	Spain	France	Ireland	Italy	Luxembourg	Netherlands	Portugal	United Kingdom
1980	70.25	86.05	72.37	67.46	n.a.	78.28	68.70	83.22	64.71	73.05	n.a.	69.77
1985	74.29	85.83	72.84	78.79	n.a.	80.76	67.30	82.74	65.92	73.56	n.a.	67.09
1991	75.59	84.47	73.79	79.18	72.22	80.25	69.51	79.30	67.95	76.17	70.78	67.15

Note: The most recent data for the Netherlands and Luxembourg is 1990, and for Italy the pay gap is estimated from information for 1989.

Source: Eurostat, 'Earnings: Industry and Services', 1992

B. Trends in gender pay ratios for non-manual workers 1980–91

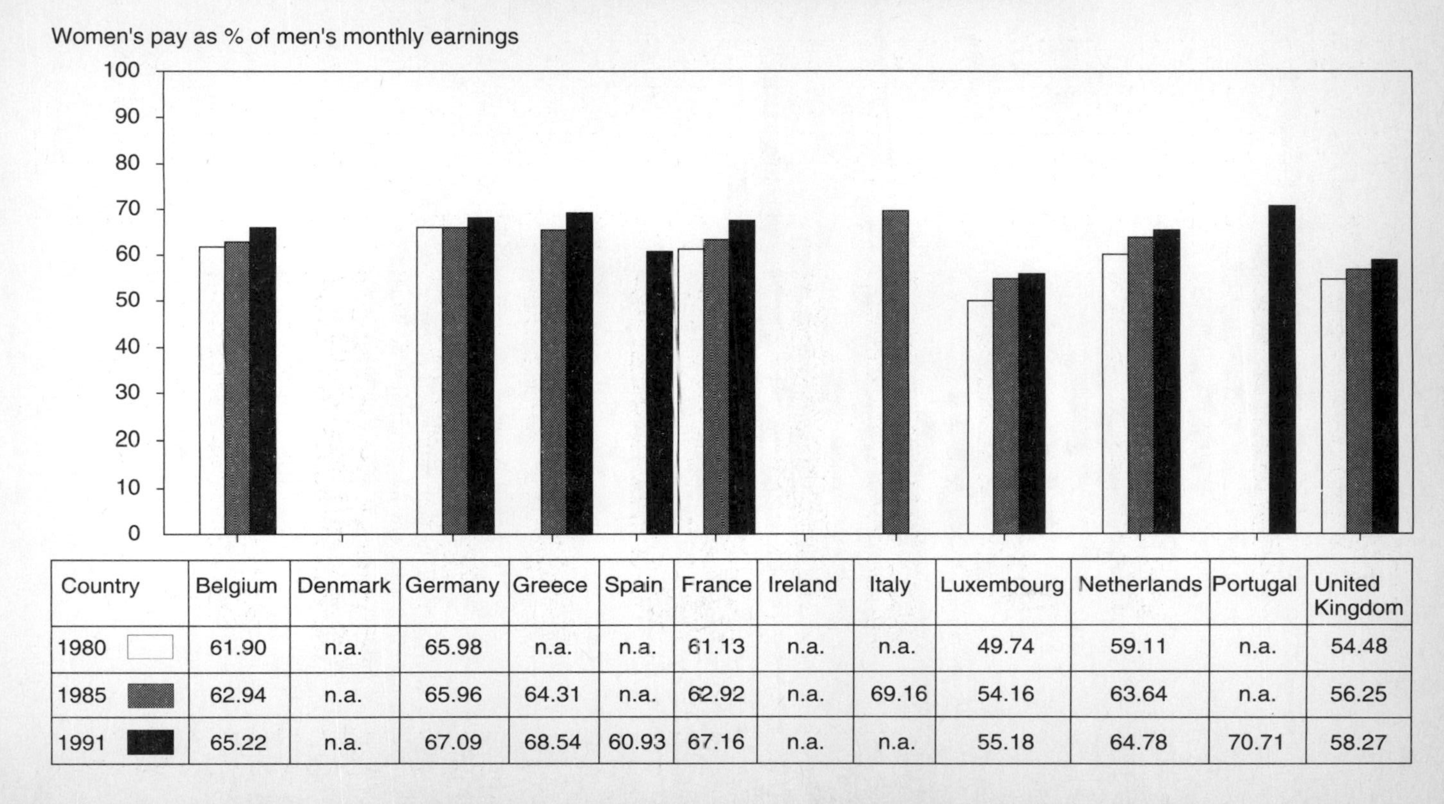

Country	Belgium	Denmark	Germany	Greece	Spain	France	Ireland	Italy	Luxembourg	Netherlands	Portugal	United Kingdom
1980	61.90	n.a.	65.98	n.a.	n.a.	61.13	n.a.	n.a.	49.74	59.11	n.a.	54.48
1985	62.94	n.a.	65.96	64.31	n.a.	62.92	n.a.	69.16	54.16	63.64	n.a.	56.25
1991	65.22	n.a.	67.09	68.54	60.93	67.16	n.a.	n.a.	55.18	64.78	70.71	58.27

Note: The most recent data for the Netherlands and Luxembourg is 1990. Data for Denmark and Ireland is missing.

6.5 Occupations of Men and Women in the Community, 1992

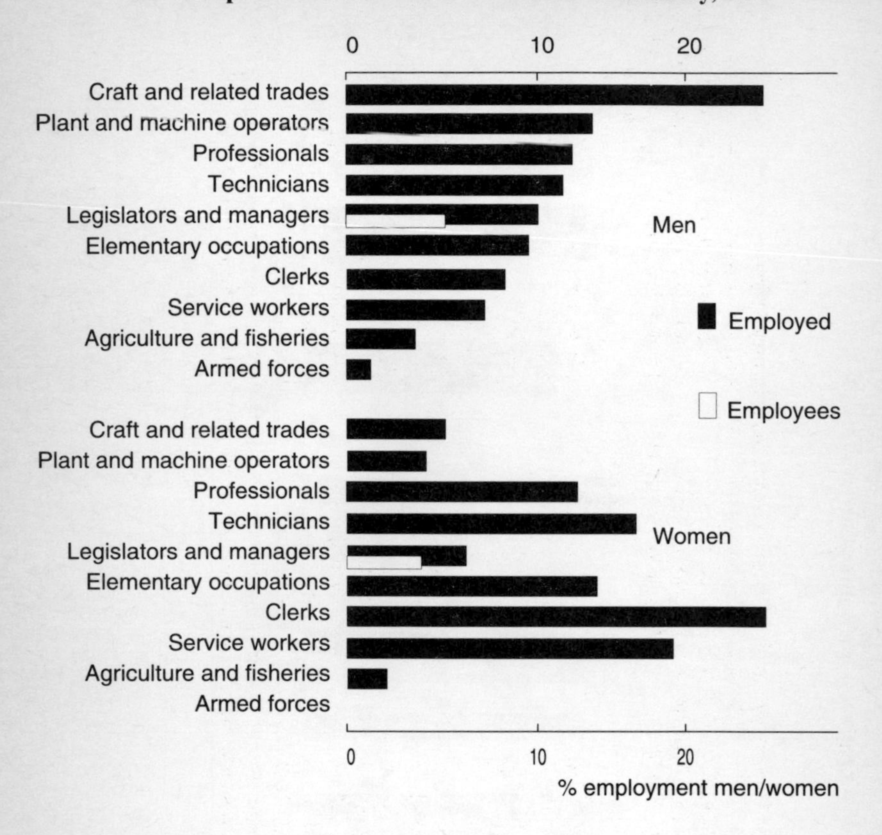

Notes: 1. Figures shown are for ten member states, Belgium, Denmark, Germany, Spain, France, Italy, Luxembourg, Netherlands, Portugal, United Kingdom

2. Virtually all the self-employed, irrespective of occupation, are included in the category 'legislators and managers'. This accounts for the distinction between 'employed' and 'employees' being made in this category only.

Source: *Employment in Europe*, 1994, p. 179.

6.6 Places in Publicly Funded Childcare Services as Percentage of All Children in the Age Group 1986–89

	Year	*For children under 3*	*For children from 3 to compulsory school age*	*Age when compulsory schooling begins*	*Length of school day (including midday break)*	*Outside schools hours care for primary school children*
Germany	1987	3%	65–70%	6–7 years	4–5 hours (a)	4%
France	1988	20%	95%+	6 years	8 hours	?
Italy	1986	5%	85%+	6 years	4 hours	?
Netherlands	1989	2%	50–55%	5 years	6–7 hours	1%
Belgium	1988	20%	95%+	6 years	7 hours	?
Luxembourg	1989	2%	55–60%	5 years	4–8 hours (a)	1%
United Kingdom	1988	2%	35–40%	5 years	6½ hours	(–)
Ireland	1988	2%	55%	6 years	4½–6½ hours (b)	(–)
Denmark	1989	48%	85%	7 years	3–5½ hours (a,b)	29%
Greece	1988	4%	65–70%	5½ years	4–5 hours (b)	(–)
Portugal	1988	6%	35%	6 years	6½ hours	6%
Spain	1988	?	65–70%	6 years	8 hours	(–)

Key: ? = no information; (–) = less than 0.5%; (a) = school hours vary from day to day; (b) = school hours increase as children get older.

Source: *Women of Europe*, Supplement no. 31, 1990, p. 10.

6.7 Demographic and Social Indicators, 1988–90

A Total populations and female populations in thousands (1 January 1990)

	Belgium	*Denmark*	*Germany*	*Greece*	*Spain*	*France*	*Ireland*	*Italy*	*Luxembourg*	*Netherlands*	*Portugal*	*United Kingdom*	*EUR 12*
Total population	9 948	5 135	62 679	10 046	38 925	56 304	3 507	57 576	378	14 893	10 337	57 309	327 037
Females	5 088	2 605	32 443	5 103	19 821	28 866	1 755	29 608	194	7 534	5 343	29 356	167 715
% females	*51.1*	*50.7*	*51.8*	*50.8*	*50.9*	*51.3*	*50.1*	*51.4*	*51.2*	*50.6*	*51.7*	*51.2*	*51.3*

B Birth rate indices and population trends (1989)

	Belgium	*Denmark*	*Germany*	*Greece*	*Spain*	*France*	*Ireland*	*Italy*	*Luxembourg*	*Netherlands*	*Portugal*	*United Kingdom*	*EUR 12*
Percentage of EU:													
population	3.05	1.57	19.04	3.08	11.93	17.22	1.08	17.65	0.12	4.55	3.16	17.55	100.0
births	3.14	1.60	17.73	2.64	10.53	19.92	1.34	14.76	0.12	4.92	3.08	20.22	100.0
Average number of children per woman: 1977	1.71	1.66	1.40	2.27	2.65	1.86	3.27	1.98	1.45	1.58	2.45	1.69	1.96
1989	1.58	1.62	1.39	1.50	1.39	1.81	2.11	1.29	1.52	1.55	1.50	1.81	1.58

C. Women living alone or as single parents per 100 women (1988)

	Belgium	*Denmark*	*Germany*	*Greece*	*Spain*	*France*	*Ireland*	*Italy*	*Luxembourg*	*Netherlands*	*Portugal*	*United Kingdom*	*EUR 12*
Total	25.1	48.6	32.7	18.0	13.9	26.1	21.4	22.9	23.0	26.6	16.9	25.4	25.5
Without child	20.6	39.7	27.0	13.3	8.2	20.3	13.5	17.1	17.7	20.8	10.9	18.8	19.6
With child(ren)	4.5	8.9	5.7	4.7	5.7	5.8	7.9	5.8	5.3	5.8	6.0	6.6	5.9

D. Percentages of GDP allocated to social protection and maternity and family allowances (1988)

	Belgium	*Denmark*	*Germany*	*Greece*	*Spain*	*France*	*Ireland*	*Italy*	*Luxembourg*	*Netherlands*	*Portugal*	*United Kingdom*	*EUR 12*
Social protection	28.7	28.5	28.1	:	18.1	28.3	22.6	22.9	26.6	30.7	17.0	23.6	25.6
of which													
maternity/family	2.18	3.47	1.91	:	0.28	2.86	2.69	1.11	2.36	2.35	1.15	2.23	1.96
– maternity	0.08	0.43	0.21	:	0.16	0.47	0.44	0.11	0.38	0.12	0.14	0.18	0.23
– family	2.10	3.04	1.70	:	0.12	2.39	2.25	1.00	1.98	2.23	1.01	2.05	1.73

Source: Eurostat, *Women in the European Community,* 1992, pp. 10, 23, 32, 46.

Select Bibliography

All sources discussed or referred to in the text are listed here, but not all the material in the notes. Reports or documents of the European Commission are listed under the abbreviation CEC – Commission of the European Communities. However, where a Commission report has a clear author it is listed under that author. Legislation of the EU and references for cases in the European Court of Justice are not included in this bibliography. Full references to these are given in the notes. The main provisions of the EU women's policy with full references are listed in Appendix 2; they are not included here.

Acklesberg, M. and Diamond, I., 'Gender and Political Life – New Directions in Political Science', in B. Hess and M. Ferree, eds., *Analysing Gender*, Sage, London, 1987.

Afshar, Haleh and Maynard, Mary, eds, *The Dynamics of Race and Gender*, Taylor and Francis, London, 1994.

Atkins, Susan and Luckhaus, Linda, 'The Social Security Directive and UK Law', in C. McCrudden, ed., *Women, Employment and European Equality Law*, Eclipse Publications, London, 1987.

Bacchi, Carol, *Same Difference – Feminism and Sexual Difference*, Allen & Unwin, Sydney, 1990.

Barnard, Catherine, *A European Litigation Strategy: the Case of the Equal Opportunities Commission*, LLM thesis, European University Institute, Florence, 1990.

Bercusson, Brian, *Human Rights and the European Community: Towards 1992 and Beyond*, European University Institute, Florence, 1989.

Black Women's Collective, 'Many Voices One Chant – Black Feminist Perspectives', *Feminist Review*, no. 17, 1984.

Bono, Paola and Kemp, Sandra, eds, *Italian Feminist Thought – a Reader*, Blackwell, Oxford, 1991.

Braidotti, Rosi, 'The Exile, the Nomad and the Migrant – Reflections on International Feminism', *Women's Studies International Forum*, vol. 15, no. 1, 1992, pp. 7–10 .

Brenner, Johanna, 'US Feminism in the Nineties', *New Left Review*, no. 200, 1993, pp. 101–59.

Brocas, Anne-Marie, Cailloux, Anne-Marie and Oget, Virginie, *Women and Social Security*, International Labour Office, Geneva, 1990.

Brunfaut, Emilienne and Vogel, Eliane, 'Le droit à l'égalité des rémunérations', *Revue du Travail*, Brussels, 1968, pp. 1505–55.

Buckley, Mary and Anderson, Malcolm, eds, *Women, Equality and Europe*, Macmillan, Basingstoke, 1988.

Burley, Anne-Marie and Mattli, Walter, 'Europe Before the Court: a Political Theory of Legal Integration', *International Organisation*, vol. 47, no. 1, 1993, pp. 41–76.

Burrows, Noreen, 'Maternity Rights in Europe – an Embryonic Legal Regime', *Yearbook of European Law*, 1991, pp. 273–93.

Byre, Angela, *Leading Cases and Materials on the Social Policy of the EEC*, Kluwer, Deventer, 1989.

Caldwell, Lesley, 'Italian Feminism – Some Considerations', in Z. Baranski, S. Vinall, eds, *Women and Italy*, Macmillan, Basingstoke, 1991.
Callender, Rosheen, 'Ireland and the Implementation of Directive 79/7/EEC: the Social, Legal and Political Issues', in G. Whyte, eds, *Sex Equality, Community Rights and Irish Social Welfare Law*, Irish Centre for European Law, Trinity College, Dublin, 1988.
Campani, Giovanna, 'Immigrant Women in Labour Market and Family Networks – Philippino, Chinese and Maroccan Women in Italy', *Transitions Conference*, Berlin, May 1991.
Carter, Caitriona, *Economic and Social Dynamics of Part-time Employment: Law as Policy within the European Community*, PhD thesis, Edinburgh University, 1994.
Castle, Barbara, *The Castle Diaries 1974–76*, Weidenfeld, London, 1980.
CEC, *A New Community Action Programme on the Promotion of Equal Opportunities for Women 1982–1985*, COM(81) 758 final, 1981.
CEC, *Equality of Treatment Between Men and Women* (Communication of the Commission to the Council) COM(75) 36, Brussels, 12 February 1975.
CEC, 'Equal Opportunities for Women – Medium-term Community Programme 1986–90', *Bulletin of the ECs*, Supplement 3/86, 1986.
CEC, *Equal Opportunities for Men and Women – the Third Medium-term Action Programme 1991–1995*, COM(90) 449 final, 1990.
CEC, Report from the Commission to the Council on the situation at 12 August 1980 with regard to the implementation of the principle of equal treatment for men and women as regards access to employment and promotion, access to vocational guidance and training, and working conditions COM(80) 832 final, 1981.
CEC, 'The Position of Women on the Labour Market – Trends and developments in the twelve member states of the European Community 1983–1990', *Women of Europe*, Supplement No. 36, 1992.
CEC, 'Guidelines for a Community Policy on Migration', *Bulletin of the ECs*, Supplement 9/85.
CEC, *Premier programme de politique économique à moyen terme* (1966–70) Medium Term Economic Programme, Luxembourg, 1967.
Cecchini, Paolo, *The European Challenge – 1992 and the Benefits of a Single Market*, Wildwood House, Aldershot, 1988.
Cépède, D., 'Les aspects sociaux du Traité de Rome', *Informations Sociales*, Paris, September 1958.
Clarke, Wendy, 'The Dyke, The Feminist and The Devil', *Feminist Review*, no. 11, 1982, pp. 30–39.
Cockburn, Cynthia, *Women and the European Social Dialogue – Strategies for Gender Democracy*, CEC, V/5465/95.
Coenen, Marie-Thérèse, *La grève des femmes de la F.N. en 1966*, Pol-His, Brussels, 1991.
Collins, Doreen, *The European Communities: the Social Policy of the First Phase*, Martin Robertson, London, 1975, vol. 2: The European Economic Community 1958–72.
Cousins, Mel, 'Equal Treatment and Social Security', *European Law Review*, vol. 19, no. 2, 1994, pp. 123–45.
CRISP, 'Les grèves féminines de la construction métallique et la revendication pour l'egalité de rémunération', *Courrier Hebdomadaire (Centre de Recherche et d'Information Socio-Politiques – CRISP)*, nos 325–6, 24 June 1966, pp. 1–52 .
Curtin, Deirdre, 'Equal Treatment and Social Welfare: the European Court's Emerging Case-Law on Directive 79/7/EEC', in G. Whyte, ed., *Sex Equality, Community Rights and Irish Social Welfare Law*, Trinity College, Dublin, 1987.
Cuvelliez, Marie-Thérèse, 'Les femmes ont intérêt à être emmerdeuses' (Women ought to be bloody minded), *Bulletin, Maison des Femmes*, Brussels, February 1978.
Dahlerup, Drude, ed., *The New Women's Movement – Feminism and Political Power in Europe and the USA*, Sage, London, 1986.
Delphy, Christine, *Close to Home*, Hutchinson, London, 1984.
Docksey, Christopher, 'The European Community and the Promotion of Equality', in C. McCrudden, ed., *Women, Employment and European Equality Law*, Eclipse Publications, London, 1987.

Doeuff, Michéle le, *L'Etude et le rouet*, Seuil, Paris, 1989.
Ellis, Evelyn, 'Protection of Pregnancy and Maternity', *Industrial Law Journal*, vol. 22, no. 2, 1993, pp. 63–7.
Essed, Philomena, 'Black Women in White Women's Organizations: Ethnic Differentiation and Problems of Racism in the Netherlands', *New Feminist Research*, vol. 18, no. 4, 1989, pp. 10–15.
European Parliament, *Report drawn up on behalf of the Committee on Women's Rights on Violence Against Women (d'Ancona Report)*, A2–44/86, 1986.
European Parliament, *The Position of Women in the European Community – European Parliament Debates*, Luxembourg, 1981.
European Parliament, *Report drawn up on behalf of the Committee of Inquiry into the Rise of Fascism and Racism in Europe (Evrigenis Report)*, A2–160/85/rev and Annexes 1–4, 1986.
European Parliament, *Report drawn up on behalf of the Committee of Inquiry into Racism and Xenophobia (Ford report)*, A3–195/90 and Annex, 1990.
European Parliament, *On Discrimination Against Immigrant Women in Community Legislation and Regulations (Heinrich Report)* A2–133/87, 1987.
European Parliament, *Report drawn up on behalf of the Ad Hoc Committee on Women's Rights on the position of women in the European Community (Maij-Weggen Report)*, Part I – Motion for a Resolution/Part II – Explanatory Statement, Document 1–829/80–1 and 2, 1981.
European Women's Lobby, *Confronting the Fortress – Black and Migrant Women in the European Union*, European Parliament, Luxembourg, 1995.
Eurostat, *Women in the European Community*, Luxembourg, 1992.
Featherstone, Kevin, 'Jean Monnet and the "Democratic Deficit" in the EU', *Journal of Common Market Studies*, vol. 32, no. 2, 1994, pp. 149–70.
Fitzpatrick, Barry, Gregory, Jeanne and Szyszczak, Erika, *Sex Equality Litigation in the Member States of the EC*, CEC, V/407/94, 1994.
Flax, Jane, 'Postmodernism and Gender Relations in Feminist Theory', *Signs: Journal of Women in Culture and Society*, vol. 12, no. 4, 1987, pp. 621–43.
Fraser, Arvonne S., *The UN Decade for Women – Documents and Dialogue*, Westview, Boulder, Colorado, 1987.
Fredman, Sandra, 'European Community Discrimination Law: A Critique', *Industrial Law Journal*, vol. 21, no. 2, 1992, pp. 119–35.
Gelb, Joyce and Palley, Marian Lief, *Women and Public Policies*, Princeton University Press, Princeton, 1987.
Grant, Charles, *Delors – Inside the House that Jacques Built*, Nicholas Brealey, London, 1994.
Greenwood, Justin, Grote, Jurgen R. and Ronit, Karsten, eds, *Organized Interests and the European Community*, Sage, London, 1992.
Haas, Ernst B., *The Uniting of Europe*, Stanford University Press, Stanford, 1958.
Hall-Smith, Vanessa et al., *Women's Rights and the EEC – a Guide for Women in the UK*, Rights of Women Europe, London, 1983.
Haug, Frigga, 'The Women's Movement in West Germany', *New Left Review*, no. 155, 1986, pp. 50–74.
Haug, Frigga, 'Lessons from the Women's Movement in Europe', *Feminist Review*, no. 31, spring, 1989, pp. 107–16.
Haug, Frigga, 'The Quota Demand and Feminist Politics', *New Left Review*, no. 209, 1995, pp. 136-45.
Hellman, Judith A., *Journeys among Women – Feminism in Five Italian Cities*, Polity Press, Oxford, 1987.
Hoffmann, Stanley, 'Obstinate or Obsolete: the fate of the nation state and the case of Western Europe', *Daedalus*, vol. 95, 1966, pp. 862–915.
Holloway, John, *Social Policy Harmonisation in the European Community*, Gower, Farnborough 1981.
Holtmaat, Riki, 'The Power of Legal Concepts: the Development of a Feminist Theory of Law', *International Journal of the Sociology of Law*, no. 17, 1989, pp. 481–502.

hooks, bell, *Yearning – Race, Gender, and Cultural Politics*, Turnaround, London, 1991.
Hoskyns, Catherine, 'Women's Equality and the European Community', *Feminist Review*, vol. 20, 1985, pp. 71–88.
Hoskyns, Catherine and Luckhaus, Linda, 'The European Community Directive on Equal Treatment in Social Security', *Policy and Politics*, vol. 17, no. 4, 1989, pp. 321–5.
Hoskyns, Catherine, 'The European Community's Policy on Women in the Context of 1992', *Women's Studies International Forum*, vol. 15, no. 1, 1992, pp. 21–8.
Hoskyns, Catherine, 'Gender Issues in International Relations: the Case of the European Community', *Review of International Studies*, vol. 20, 1994, pp. 225–39.
Hoskyns, Catherine, Orsini-Jones, Marina, 'Immigrant Women in Italy – Perspectives from Brussels and Bologna', *European Jounal of Women's Studies*, vol. 2, 1995, pp. 51–76.
ILO, *Social Aspects of European Economic Integration (Ohlin Report)*, International Labour Office, Geneva, 1956.
Jackson, Pauline Conroy, *The Impact of the Completion of the Internal Market on Women in the European Community*, CEC, V/506/90, 1990.
Jenks, C. Wilfred, *Human Rights and International Labour Standards*, Stevens, 1960.
Katzenstein, Mary and Mueller, Carol, eds, *The Women's Movements of the United States and Western Europe – Consciousness, Political Opportunity and Public Policy*, Temple University Press, Philadelphia, 1987.
Keck, Margaret and Sikkink, Kathryn, 'Transnational Issue Networks in International Politics', unpublished conference paper, April 1994.
King, John, 'Ethnic Minorities and Multilateral European Institutions' in J. Leaman, A. Hargreaves, eds, *Racism, Ethnicity and Politics in Contemporary Europe*, Edward Elgar Press, London, 1995, pp. 179–91.
Klein, Viola, *Women Workers – Working Hours and Services*, OECD, Paris, 1965.
Kok, G.H.S., *Report on the Political, Social and Civic Position of Women in Europe*, Council of Europe, Strasbourg, 1967.
Lacey, Nicola, 'Legislation Against Sex Discrimination – Questions from a Feminist Perspective', *Journal of Law and Society*, vol. 14, no. 4, 1987, pp. 411–21
Lambert, John, *Solidarity and Survival: a Vision for Europe*, Avebury, Aldershot, 1994.
Laubier, Claire, ed., *The Condition of Women in France: 1945 to the Present – a Documentary Anthology*, Routledge, London, 1990.
Laurent, Pierre-Henri, 'Paul-Henri Spaak and the Diplomatic Origins of the Common Market 1955–56', *Political Science Quarterly*, vol. 85, 1970, pp. 373–96.
Lauretis, Teresa de, *Technologies of Gender – Essays on Theory, Film, and Fiction*, Macmillan, Basingstoke, 1989.
Lauretis, Teresa de, 'Upping the Anti (sic) in Feminist Theory', in M. Hirsch, E. F. Keller, eds, *Conflicts in Feminism*, Routledge, New York/London, 1990.
Leibfried, Stephan and Pierson, Paul, 'Prospects for Social Europe', *Politics and Society*, vol. 20, no. 3, 1992, pp.333–66.
Lewis, Jane, ed., *Women and Social Policies in Europe – Work, Family and the State*, Edward Elgar, Aldershot, 1993.
Lint, Roland Van, 'L'égalité des rémunérations entre les travailleurs masculins et les travailleurs féminins pour un même travail', *Cahier du Droit Européen*, vol. 5, 1969, pp. 375–403.
Lizin, Anne-Marie, *Emilienne Brunfaut*, Archives de Wallonie, Charleroi, 1987.
Loenen, Titia, 'Different Perspectives in Different Legal Studies: A Contextual Approach to Feminist Jurisprudence in Europe and the USA', *Feminist Approaches to Law and Cultural Diversity*, European University Institute, Florence, 1993.
Lovenduski, Joni, *Women and European Politics*, Wheatsheaf Books, London, 1986.
Luckhaus, Linda, 'Changing Rules, Enduring Structures – Equal Treatment and Social Security', *Modern Law Review*, vol. 53, no. 5, 1990, pp. 655–68.
Luckhaus, Linda, 'The Role of the "Economic" and the "Social" in Social Security and Community Law', in G. Weick, ed., *National and European Law on the Threshold to the Single Market*, Peter Lang, Frankfurt, 1993.
Luckhaus, Linda, 'Individualisation of Social Security Benefits', in C. McCrudden, ed.,

Equality of Treatment between Men and Women in Social Security, Butterworth, London, 1994, pp. 147–62.
Lumley, Robert, *States of Emergency – Cultures of Revolt in Italy from 1968 to 1978*, Verso, London, 1990.
Macey, David, *The Lives of Michel Foucault*, Hutchinson, London, 1993.
MacKinnon, Catharine A., *Feminism Unmodified – Discourses on Life and Law*, Harvard University Press, Cambridge, Massachusetts 1987.
Majone, Giandomenico, 'The European Community Between Social Policy and Social Regulation', *Journal of Common Market Studies*, vol. 31, no. 2, 1993, pp. 153–70.
Mandel, Ernest, 'International Capitalism and "Supra-Nationality"', *Socialist Register*, 1967, pp. 27–41.
Marjolin, Robert, *Le travail d'une vie – Mémoirs 1911–1986*, Editions Robert Laffont, Paris, 1986.
McCrudden, Christopher, ed., *Women, Employment and European Equality Law*, Eclipse, London, 1987.
Meehan, Elizabeth, *Citizenship and the European Community*, Sage, London, 1993.
Milward, Alan S. *The European Rescue of the Nation State*, Routledge, London, 1992.
Moravcsik, Andrew, 'Negotiating the Single European Act: National Interests and Conventional Statecraft', *International Organisation*, vol. 45, no. 1, 1991, pp. 19–56.
Morokvasic, Mirjana, *Minority and Immigrant Women in Self-Employment and Business*, CEC, V/1871/88, 1988.
Neri, S. and Sperl, H., *Traité instituent la Communauté Economique Européenne*, Cour de Justice des CE, Luxembourg, 1960.
Norris, Pippa, *Politics and Sexual Equality – the Comparative Position of Women in Western Democracies*, Wheatsheaf, Brighton, 1987.
Ostner, Ilona, 'Slow Motion: Women, Work and the Family in Germany', in J. Lewis, ed., *Women and Social Policies in Europe*, Edward Elgar, Aldershot, 1993.
Outshoorn, Joyce, 'Is This What We Wanted? Affirmative Action as Issue Perversion', in E. Meehan and S. Sevenhuijson, eds, *Equality Politics and Gender*, Sage, London, 1989.
Pescatore, Pierre, 'The Context and Significance of Fundamental Rights in the Law of the European Communities', *Human Rights Law Journal*, vol. 2, 1981, pp. 295–308.
Philip, André, 'Social Aspects of European Economic Co-operation', *International Labour Review*, September 1957, pp. 244–56.
Phillips, Anne, 'Political inclusion and political presence. Or, why should it matter who our representatives are?', *European Consortium on Political Research*, Leiden, April 1993.
Phizacklea, Annie, ed., *One Way Ticket – Migration and Female Labour*, Routledge, London, 1983.
Picciotto, Sol, 'The Control of Transnational Capital and the Democratisation of the International State', *Journal of Law and Society*, vol. 15, no. 1, 1988.
Picciotto, Sol, 'The Regulatory Criss-cross – Interaction between Jurisdictions and Global Regulatory Networks', in W. Bratton, et al., eds, *International Regulatory Competition and Coordination*, Oxford University Press, Oxford, forthcoming 1996.
Picq, Françoise, *Les Années-Mouvement Libération des Femmes*, Seuil, Paris, 1993.
Pillinger, Jane, *Feminising the Market – Women's Pay and Employment in the European Community*, Macmillan, Basingstoke, 1992.
Pinder, John, 'Positive Integration and Negative Integration: Some Problems of Economic Union in the EEC', *World Today*, vol. 24, 1968, pp. 88–110.
Plender, Richard, 'Competence, European Community Law and Nationals of Non-Member States', *International and Comparative Law Quarterly*, vol. 39, 1990, pp. 599–610.
Prechal, Sacha and Burrows, Noreen, *Gender Discrimination Law of the European Community*, Dartmouth, Aldershot, 1990.
Prondzynski, Isabelle Von, 'The Social Situation and Employment of Migrant Women in the European Community', *Policy and Politics*, vol. 17, no. 4, 1989, pp. 347–54.
Rex, John and Drury, Beatrice, eds, *Ethnic Mobilisation in a Multicultural Europe*, Avebury, Aldershot, 1994.
Rhodes, Martin, 'Whither Regulation? "Disorganised Capitalism" and the West

European Labour Market', in L. Hancher, M. Moran, eds, *Capitalism, Culture and Economic Regulation*, Clarendon Press, Oxford, 1989.
Rhodes, Martin, '"Subversive Liberalism": Market Integration, Globalisation and the European Welfare State', *European Consortium for Political Research*, Madrid, April 1994.
Rich, Adrienne, *On Lies, Secrets and Silence*, Virago, London, 1980.
Rifflet, Raymond, 'Bilan et evaluation de la politique social communautaire', in J. Vandamme, ed., *Pour une nouvelle politique sociale en Europe*, Economica, Paris, 1984.
Rosenthal, Glenda Goldstone, *The Men Behind the Decisions*, Lexington Books, London 1975.
Roudy, Yvette, *A cause d'elles*, Albin Michel, Paris, 1985.
Rowbotham, Sheila, Segal, Lynne and Wainwright, Hilary, *Beyond the Fragments – Feminism and the Making of Socialism*, Merlin Press, London, 1979.
Rowbotham, Sheila, *The Past Is Before Us – Feminism in Action since the 1960s*, Pandora Press, London, 1989.
Rubenstein, Michael, 'The Equal Treatment Directive and UK Law', in C. McCrudden, ed., *Women, Employment and European Equality Law*, Eclipse Publications, London, 1987 pp. 74–102.
Rutherford, Françoise, 'The Proposal for a European Directive on Parental Leave: some reasons why it failed', *Policy and Politics*, vol. 17, no. 4, 1989, pp. 301–10.
Scheiwe, Kirsten, 'EC Law's Unequal Treatment of the Family: the Case Law of the European Court of Justice on Rules Prohibiting Discrimination on Grounds of Sex and Nationality', *Social and Legal Studies*, vol. 3, no. 2, 1994, pp. 243–65.
Scott, Hilda, *Working Your Way to the Bottom – the Feminization of Poverty*, Pandora Press, London 1984.
Shanks, Michael, *European Social Policy Today and Tomorrow*, Pergamon Press, Oxford/New York, 1977.
Shortall, Sally, 'Power Analysis and Farm Wives: an Empirical Study of the Power Relationships Affecting Women on Irish Farms', *Sociologia Ruralis*, vol. XXX11, no. 4, 1992, pp. 431–51.
Simmonds, Kenneth R., 'The concertation of Community migration policy', *Common Market Law Review*, vol. 25, 1988, pp. 177–200.
Sjerps, Ina, 'Indirect Discrimination in Social Security in the Netherlands: Demands of the Dutch Women's Movement', in M. Buckley and M. Anderson, eds, *Women, Equality and Europe*, Macmillan, Basingstoke, 1988, pp. 95–106.
Smart, Carol, *Feminism and the Power of Law*, Routledge, London, 1989.
Smart, Carol, 'Feminist Jurisprudence', in P. Fitzpatrick, ed., *Supplementary Justice*, Pluto, London, 1990.
Smart, Carol, 'The Woman in Legal Discourse', *Social and Legal Studies*, vol. 1, no. 1, 1992, pp. 29–44.
Solomos, John and Wrench, John, eds, *Racism and Migration in Western Europe*, Berg, Oxford, 1993.
Spelman, Elizabeth V., *Inessential Women – Problems of Exclusion in Feminist Thought*, Beacon Books, Boston, 1988.
Spivak, Gayatri Chakravorty, 'French Feminism Revisited: Ethics and Politics', in J. Butler and J. W. Scott, eds, *Feminists Theorize the Political*, Routledge, New York, 1992, pp. 54–85.
Stetson, Dorothy McBride and Mazur, Amy G., eds, *Comparative State Feminism*, Sage, Newbury Park, 1995.
Streeck, Wolfgang, 'From Market-Making to State-Building? Reflections on the Political Economy of European Social Policy', in S. Leibfried and P. Pierson, eds, *European Social Policy – Between Fragmentation and Integration*, The Brookings Institution, Washington DC, 1995.
Streeck, Wolfgang, 'Neo-Voluntarism: A New European Social Policy Regime?', *European Law Journal*, vol. 1, no. 1, 1995, pp. 31–59.
Sullerot, Evelyne, *Histoire et sociologie du travail féminin*, Editions Gonthier, Paris, 1968.
Sullerot, Evelyne, *L'Emploi des femmes et ses problèmes dans les états membres de la Communauté Européenne*, CEC, Brussels, 1970.

Sullerot, Evelyne, *Women, Society and Change*, Weidenfeld, London, 1971.
Swiebel, Joke, 'The Gender of Bureaucracy: Reflections on Policy-Making for Women', *Politics*, vol. 8, no. 1, 1988, pp. 14–19.
Teague, Paul, *The European Community: the Social Dimension*, Kogan Page, London, 1989.
Tribolati, Madeleine, 'Salaires féminins dans les pays du Marché Commun', *Informations Sociales*, September 1958.
Troy, Colette de, The Specific Training Needs of Immigrant Women, CEC, V/1909/86, 1986.
Troy, Colette de, Migrant Women and Employment, CEC, V/928/87, 1987.
Truong, Thanh-Dam, Rosario, Virginia del, 'Captive Outsiders: Trafficked Sex Workers and Mail-Order Brides in the European Union', in J. Wiersma, ed., *Insiders and Outsiders: on the Making of Europe II*, Pharos, Kampen, 1994.
Vallance, Elizabeth and Davies, Elizabeth, *Women of Europe – Women MEPs and Equality Policy*, Cambridge University Press, Cambridge, 1986.
Van Gerven, Walter, 'Contribution de l'arrêt Defrenne au développement du droit communautaire', *Cahiers de Droit Européen*, 1977, pp. 131–43.
Vogel-Polsky, Eliane, 'L'Article 119 du traité de Rome – peut-il être considéré comme self-executing?', *Journal des Tribunaux*, Brussels, 15 April 1967.
Vries, Petra de, 'Feminism in the Netherlands', *Women's Studies International Forum*, vol. 4, no. 4, 1981, pp. 389–407.
Wolton, Dominique, *La dernière utopie – Naissance de l'Europe démocratique*, Flammarion, Paris, 1993.
Wandor, Michelene, *Once a Feminist – Stories of a Generation*, Virago, London, 1990.
Watson, Philippa, 'Social Security and the European Communities', in G. Whyte, ed., *Sex Equality, Community Rights and Irish Social Welfare Law*, Trinity College, Dublin, 1988, pp. 60–77.
Watson, Sophie, ed., *Playing the State: Australian Feminist Interventions*, Verso, London, 1990.
Weiler, Joseph, 'The Community System: the Dual Character of Supranationalism', *Yearbook of European Law*, vol. 1, 1981.
Weiler, Joseph, 'The Transformation of Europe', *Yale Law Journal*, vol. 100, 1991, pp. 2403–83.
Whyte, Gerry, ed., *Sex Equality, Community Rights and Irish Social Welfare Law*, Trinity College, Dublin, 1988.
Wieviorka, Michel, ed., *Racisme et xénophobie en Europe – une comparaison internationale*, Editions La Découverte, Paris, 1994.
Wilson, Elizabeth, *Only Half Way to Paradise – Women in Postwar Britain: 1945–1968*, Tavistock, London, 1980.
Young, Iris Marion, *Justice and the Politics of Difference*, Princeton University Press, Princeton, 1990.

Index